Call in Pinkerton's

Allan Pinkerton, founder of Pinkerton's
National Detective Agency.

PA

Call in Pinkerton's

American Detectives at Work for Canada

David Ricardo Williams

DUNDURN PRESS
TORONTO · OXFORD

Editor: Barry Jowett
Design: Scott Reid
Printer: Webcom

Canadian Cataloguing in Publication Data

Williams, David Ricardo
    Call in Pinkerton's

Includes bibliographical references and index.
ISBN 1-55002-306-3

1. Pinkerton's National Detective Agency — History.   2. Private investigators — Canada — History.   I. Title.

HV8099.C3W54 1998   363.28'9'06071   C98-930781-6

1 2 3 4 5 BJ 02 01 00 99 98

THE CANADA COUNCIL | LE CONSEIL DES ARTS
FOR THE ARTS | DU CANADA
SINCE 1957 | DEPUIS 1957

We acknowledge the support of the **Canada Council for the Arts** for our publishing program. We also acknowledge the support of the **Ontario Arts Council** and the **Book Publishing Industry Development Program** of the **Department of Canadian Heritage.**

Dundurn Press
8 Market Street
Suite 200
Toronto, Ontario, Canada
M5E 1M6

Dundurn Press
73 Lime Walk
Headington, Oxford
England
OX3 7AD

Dundurn Press
2250 Military Road
Tonawanda, NY
U.S.A. 14150

Table of Contents

"There is a detective on our trail."

"Why, man, you're crazy.... Isn't the place full of police and detectives, and what harm do they ever do us?"

"No, no; it's no man of the district. As you say, we know them, and it is little that they can do. But you've heard of Pinkerton's?"

"I've read of some folk of that name."

"Well, you can take it from me that you've no show when they are on your trail. It's not a take-it-or-miss-it Government concern. It's a dead earnest business proposition that's out for results, and keeps out till, by hook or by crook, it gets them. If a Pinkerton man is deep in this business we are all destroyed."

From *Valley of Fear*, by Sir Arthur Conan Doyle

To my wife, Laura, for her support and help.

List of Illustrations

Sources:
British Columbia Archives and Records Service (BCARS)
National Archives of Canada (NAC)
Pinkerton Archives, Encino, California (PA)

Acknowledgements

In the preparation of this work, I have received much valuable assistance. First, I must mention Pinkerton's, Inc. itself and its officials: Tom Wathen, the Chairman; Gerard Brown, formerly Executive Vice-President; and Jeannie Kihm, who was Marketing Manager during my visit to the Pinkerton's Archives in Van Nuys, where I met and interviewed all three. (The company has since moved its headquarters to Encino.) It is heartening to a researcher to find a corporation as conscious of its history as Pinkerton's and, of course, there is much to be conscious about. Pinkerton's has an extensive collection of historical records relating to investigations in the nineteenth and early twentieth centuries to which I was given unlimited access, as well as a desk at which to examine them. Tom Wathen was most generous of his time in talking to me about Pinkerton's, past and present, and has a continuing interest in this writing project.

I am grateful to Robert Fraser, senior editor, *Dictionary of Canadian Biography*, for his suggestions about the Hamilton Street Railway Strike of 1906; to the late Mr. Justice David McDonald of Alberta for his suggestions about Sir John A. Macdonald and the Fenians; to my friend and fellow author Peter Murray for first drawing my attention to the investigation of the Manitoba election scandals of the 1890s; to Lee Gibson of Winnipeg who was also helpful concerning those scandals; to Jim Midwinter of Ottawa for drawing my attention to *The Valley of Fear*, the Sherlock Holmes novel by Sir Arthur Conan Doyle which is based on a famous Pinkerton's episode, the "Molly Maguires"; and to Professor Peter Russell for background information on the threatened invasion of the Yukon.

As is my habit, I solicited, through the good offices of newspapers, information from the general public, to which I had a most enthusiastic response from many people. I cannot mention them all, but I must thank Professor Michael Hadley of the University of Victoria for drawing my attention to the espionage conducted by

Pinkerton's on behalf of Canada during the First World War; to Mary Ann Murphy of the Legislative Library in Victoria, who drew my attention to Pinkerton's materials amongst her library's holdings; to Peggy Imredy for drawing my attention to her ancestor James Dye, an Assistant Superintendent of Pinkerton's, in connection with the Bill Miner train robberies; to Kenneth Dye, the grandson of James Dye, for the loan of his grandfather's scrapbook; to Dr. Kenneth Williams and Lloyd Greene for their recollections of Pinkerton's industrial espionage in the hiring halls for loggers in Vancouver in the 1930s.

To Paul St. Amour, head of Pinkerton's Canadian operations, I express my gratitude for his co-operation in making available archival records in the Montreal office and also to Harold Pountney of that office for his friendly assistance. My friend Professor Dale Gibson, now of the University of Alberta at Edmonton, has been researching Canada-U.S.A. extradition cases, in some of which Pinkerton's figured. This research has resulted in our paths crossing, to the advantage, I think, of both, but certainly of me. Colleagues of mine in the Faculty of Law at the University of Victoria have been helpful and supportive, particularly Professor John McLaren who steered me to the Arnprior, Ontario, prostitution investigation. My friend, Warren K. Taylor, a retired judge of the Superior Court of California, was helpful in elucidating the mysteries of American criminal law and its administration.

And, finally, I record my gratitude to my secretaries at the Faculty of Law, University of Victoria, Freda Kardish and Sheila Talbot, for their unfailing assistance, good humour, and tolerance.

Preface

Pinkerton's National Detective Agency was founded in Chicago, probably in 1850. Other detective agencies in the United States were later established, chief among them the Burns International Agency and the Thiel Agency, but Pinkerton's was pre-eminent.

The very name "Pinkerton" has become a household word. It has crept into the dictionaries: a "Pinkerton" is defined as a "detective."[1] So widely known was the agency that it figured in the humourist Stephen Leacock's hilarious story, "My Financial Career." An intending bank depositor, who from his conspiratorial air was believed by an unsuspecting bank manager to be a Pinkerton man come to investigate a serious theft, turned out to be so timid that no sooner had he deposited his paltry sum than he withdrew it. The agency's motto, chosen by the founder, Allan Pinkerton, "The eye that never sleeps," became the "eye," and later still became the catch phrase "private eye."[2] Pinkerton's, Inc., the successor company to the agency,

The Thrill That Comes Once in a Lifetime   By Webster

THE BOY WHO TOOK A MAIL COURSE IN SLEUTHING FINDS HIMSELF ACTUALLY STANDING IN FRONT OF THE SHRINE

uses to this very day an eye as its logo. The name is also worth money in the marketplace. When the successor company acquired the assets of Pinkerton's for $95 million in 1988, the value of the name — "goodwill" as the accountants phrase it — was fixed at $55 million.

In the course of research for my various other published works, I have frequently run across references to Pinkerton's and its activities in Canada, which persuaded me to write about the agency and its work for Canadians. Much has been written about Pinkerton's and its role in criminal investigations, labour disputes, and industrial espionage in the United States, but this is the first account of its business in this country on instructions from Canadian government departments, Canadian politicians, and police forces. I have included occasional references to work done by Pinkerton's for private clients but only when such investigations were approved, implicitly or explicitly, by a public authority, such as an attorney general. I might have been inclined to expand the work to include a survey of private investigations but the research materials are simply not available. Materials relating to Pinkerton's work for Canadian public bodies are found in government records in public archives, but in cases when a family or private corporation hired the agency the records are not available or, if still in the hands of the agency itself, are confidential and may not be examined. The book is not intended as a history of policing in Canada during the six decades dealt with, from the 1860s onward (though there will be some references to law enforcement issues and methods), but as an account of an American detective agency that played a significant part in law enforcement in Canada during that period.

The reader will observe that Pinkerton's did more detective work in British Columbia for the local police than in other parts of Canada. This is due mainly to the later development of British Columbia; by the time B.C. entered Confederation in 1871, the Maritimes, Quebec, and Ontario had reasonably competent systems of crime investigation. As an example, Ontario detectives worked on the case of Patrick James Whelan, convicted of murdering D'Arcy McGee in 1868, and were assisted by a detective from the Montreal police force.

What this account is chiefly concerned with, therefore, is the remarkable circumstance of an American detective agency usually employing American detectives from its offices in the United States, though in perhaps two or three instances employing detectives from its Toronto and Montreal branches in helping to solve Canadian crimes and conduct espionage for Canadians. In one extraordinary instance of espionage, a Pinkerton man from the United States was employed by Canada to infiltrate the ranks of fellow Americans suspected of plotting the invasion of the Yukon in 1901. One might say it was "free trade" in police work.

The period covered by this account is roughly sixty years, from 1866 onward. So far as I can discover, no Canadian government official or local police force engaged Pinkerton's in the investigation of crime after the 1920s, when the Ontario government employed it in the notorious Smith-Jarvis scandal (described in chapter 10), but the agency was active in British Columbia in the 1930s in industrial espionage for private clients.

It is fitting that Pinkerton's role ended with its retainer by Ontario politicians in 1924 because its entrance onto the Canadian scene was at the instance of Canadian politicians some sixty years earlier. John A. (not yet "Sir John A.") Macdonald, advised by the remarkable Gilbert M. McMicken, truly one of the great Canadians of the nineteenth century, repelled the raids of the Fenians operating from American soil with the aid of Pinkerton detectives in the United States. During most of the years between 1866 and 1924, Pinkerton's role was essentially investigative, both in the United States and Canada. In the United States, it filled a void: Pinkerton's was disciplined, incorruptible (though not infallible), and formed, in effect, a national police force. Because of the fragmented administration of justice, state by state, with few national standards, Pinkerton's thrived in detective work. This changed with the advent of the Bureau of Investigation in 1924 (oddly, the same year as the Jarvis-Smith trial). The new bureau, though limited to jurisdiction over federal but not state criminal cases, soon set a standard of honest law enforcement emulated by individual states. In Canada, since 1867, there were always national standards of law enforcement, though there was no codification of them until the advent of the Canadian Criminal Code in 1893. The problem in Canada was not the lack of uniform definition of criminal behaviour, but the difficulty of enforcing those standards in a population scattered thinly across a vast country several thousand miles wide. Local police forces were often handicapped by lack of trained detectives on their own force, and were compelled to seek assistance from private agencies. Pinkerton's was not the only agency to carry out investigative work in Canada; there were a number of private detective firms in the country ready and willing to do work during the period covered by this book, but they were seldom consulted on matters of importance. Rather, Canadian officials, like Lieutenant-Colonel A.P. Sherwood of the Dominion Police, chose to rely on much more experienced American agencies if outside assistance was required. Of those agencies, two were paramount: Pinkerton's and Thiel. The latter was founded by a former Pinkerton man, but though his agency was from time to time consulted, it was Pinkerton's which was the private agency of choice in the era embraced by this book. As suggested in the text, this had much to do with the personal relationship between Canadian law enforcement officials and William and Robert Pinkerton. Lieutenant-Colonel A.P. Sherwood's close friendship with the two Pinkerton brothers, and the equally warm relationship between F.S. Hussey, superintendent of the British Columbia Police, with the Pinkerton agents on the west coast, (particularly P.K. Ahern in Seattle) are illustrative.

Though Pinkerton's did not successfully conclude every matter referred to it (nor did other agencies, or in-house detectives), it did bring integrity and dependability to the task. Gradually, however, there was slippage from crime detection to crime prevention, from capturing criminals to mounting security guards to repel them. This shift coincided with the development in Canada of more sophisticated methods of crime detection which effectively sounded the death knell of American detective agencies acting for Canadian lawmen. But the "knell" still reverberates: Pinkerton's has become a household name (though in some households it is still hated), and a by-word for law enforcement and for stern action against lawlessness.

Lieutenant-Colonel A.P. Sherwood, head of the Dominion Police, who frequently consulted Pinkerton's.
NAC C44904

One

A Brief History of the Agency

To understand the confidence placed by Canadian officials in Pinkerton's National Detective Agency during the roughly sixty years encompassed by this book, one must recall its history.[1] Clients not only in Canada but throughout North America — and in the United Kingdom and Europe — held the agency in high regard, indeed in awe. The fact that it was founded by a Scot born in 1819 in the Gorbals district of Glasgow unquestionably created esteem among law enforcement officials outside the United States. Allan Pinkerton, the founder, never lost his Presbyterian "Scottishness": dour, incorruptible, stubborn, unwilling to brook criticism — not even from his children as they grew up — and a strict teetotaller, although when working undercover he could, to keep up a disguise, drink whisky as heartily as any of his companions. These traits characterized him during the thirty-five years he ruled the agency until his death in 1884.

Pinkerton grew up in squalor. His father, who had held various menial jobs, most latterly as jail guard (perhaps a presage of his son's devotion to law and order), died when the boy was eight years old. Allan's mother, a spinner in a weaving mill, could not support the family and Allan was forced to work in a factory for a pittance. At the age of 12, he apprenticed in a cooperage and, showing promise, quickly mastered the trade of making barrels, at which he made his living until his abrupt departure for North America in 1842.

He had become actively involved with the Chartists, the populist reform movement which sought electoral reforms, principally universal suffrage. Pinkerton was present at the bloody riot in 1839 when troops fired on demonstrating Chartists following the rejection by the House of Commons of any concessions to the movement. Thereafter Allan became even more zealous in its cause. (Many writers have remarked on the irony that in Scotland Pinkerton laboured hard to advance the interests of the working class yet, later, in the United States, he was utterly opposed to the organization of unions among the working class — opposition reflected in the willingness of the agency to assist employers in anti-union activities, which led to much criticism and vilification.) Early in 1842, learning of an outstanding warrant for his arrest, Pinkerton went into hiding. Without fanfare, he married Joan, a young woman he had been courting, and a month later they were smuggled aboard a vessel bound for North America, which they reached after a stormy and dangerous passage. The vessel foundered on the shores of Nova Scotia with the loss of all the passengers' possessions. Left virtually penniless, the young couple managed to make their way to Montreal where Pinkerton soon found work as a cooper. After a few months, the Pinkertons decided to move to the Chicago area where to the end of their days they made their home. Neither saw the United Kingdom again; neither saw Montreal again. It may not be wholly a coincidence that late in 1899 Pinkerton's first Canadian office was opened in that city.[2]

At first, Allan and Joan lived in Chicago itself, then a city of 12,000 inhabitants, but a year later they moved fifty miles northeast to Dundee, an enclave of Scottish emigrants, into which milieu Pinkerton and his wife settled comfortably — and happily. Again he took up the cooperage trade, but this time he did more than subsist, he prospered as an entrepreneur by dint of hard work. At Dundee, Pinkerton formed his life-long habit of retiring to bed at 8:30 p.m. and rising at 4:30 a.m.; it was the old nursery rhyme vindicated: "early to bed and early to rise makes a man healthy, wealthy, and wise."

In 1847 Pinkerton became a detective through sheer chance — perhaps "fluke" would be the better word. Near his cooperage flowed a river, not far from the edge of which was an island where Pinkerton cut clear-grained saplings for barrel staves. One day he noticed the remains of a campfire. Puzzled, since as far as he knew no one except himself ever visited the island, he kept watch for several days but saw nothing. He decided to mount a night watch, hiding in a thicket. He observed the dim shapes of several men going ashore and a fire lit soon after. The following morning he reported the suspicious circumstances to the local sheriff who, with Pinkerton, organized a small posse which raided the island that night to arrest the men, who proved to be counterfeiters, caught red-handed in possession of spurious money.

This episode understandably attracted much local notoriety, all complimentary to Pinkerton who, it was said, had a nose for sniffing out crime. Not long afterwards a store owner in Dundee was bilked by a well-dressed stranger who had paid for merchandise with bogus currency and, recalling Pinkerton's exploit, the proprietor asked him to help in catching the perpetrator whom he believed to be still in the area. Pinkerton at first disclaimed any inherent talent for crime detection but, when urged by the merchant, agreed to do what he could. Adopting a pose as a hayseed willing to purchase counterfeit money at a discount of $25 of genuine funds for $100 of spurious bills, Pinkerton entrapped the man, who was arrested. This episode, of course, added to Pinkerton's reputation and he was hired as a deputy sheriff for the local county. But his reputation soon went beyond the pastoral community of Dundee to Chicago, which by 1848 had grown to a city of some 16,000 persons. Pinkerton in that year decided to leave Dundee upon being offered the post of deputy sheriff and the following year he was appointed the first detective for the Chicago police force. After serving in that post for a year, he resigned to become a special agent of the United States Post Office hired to crack a number of unsolved mail thefts. It was apparently in the same year, 1850, that Pinkerton decided to start his own detective agency and he must have taken tentative steps towards doing so. Some historians of the agency question the accuracy of the date[3] but the agency itself had no doubt on the subject, for its letterhead proclaimed it "established in 1850." As lawyers say, that is the best evidence and it should be accepted. The reason for any doubt may lie in the fact that at first Pinkerton's involvement with his own agency was part-time only since he continued with the post office for a year or two more. By 1853, however, he devoted all his time to the agency.[4]

As with the date of the agency's establishment, so is there some uncertainty about its name. Pinkerton at first seems to have called it the Northwest Police Agency and sometimes "Pinkerton & Co.," but after 1858 he decided to stick with his own name and in that year it became "Pinkerton's National Police Agency." (It is uncertain just when the name was altered to "Pinkerton's National Detective Agency" but likely it was late in 1867.[5]) The change to "Pinkerton's National Police Agency" followed his successful and widely publicized investigation of thefts from the Adams Express Company which, along with American Express Company, was the largest shipper of valuable goods in the United States. Owners wishing to ship currency, securities, and jewellery consigned them to express companies which owned express cars hauled by individual railways. Pinkerton's work for express companies was a logical outcome of his earlier business association with the railroads themselves. In the mid-1850s he had contracted with many railroads to provide guards for their rolling stock. These connections proved extremely remunerative and, perhaps more important, expanded the agency's reputation beyond the Chicago and mid-west region.

In 1858, $40,000 was embezzled from the Adams Express Company, a very large sum of money at the time. At the suggestion of its representative in New York City, Adams forwarded to Pinkerton a thick dossier with full details about the embezzlements and the Adams employees who might have had some knowledge of, and hence fall under suspicion for, the theft. Pinkerton, on reading the material, concluded that the manager of one of Adams' major offices was probably the culprit and should be placed under surveillance. Accordingly, Pinkerton organized an undercover investigative team, including a female detective, which ultimately led to the arrest and conviction of the man Pinkerton suspected. The successful unmasking of an employee apparently of the highest integrity who had been placed in a position of great trust by a large express company was an enormous feather in Pinkerton's cap. Although since its inception in 1850 his agency had prospered year by year, largely through investigations of counterfeiting and other forms of fraud, it was the railway and express company relationships which cemented his reputation. It was at this time that Pinkerton was first styled the "Eye," a term which came into common usage to symbolize the uncanny ability to be on the watch at all times, night or day, to apprehend a criminal.

Thus by 1860 when the American Civil War loomed menacingly, the agency and Pinkerton himself were well poised to play an important role. Pinkerton had always been a fervent abolitionist who as early as the 1840s had been a member of the "underground railway," which helped fleeing slaves escape into Canada. In 1859 he sheltered the famous John Brown and a group of slaves. Brown, who was on the run from a charge of murder, had come to Pinkerton's home in Chicago, which he maintained as a safe house for runaway slaves. Pinkerton collected money from like-minded associates and with it organized a successful escape of Brown and his party into Canada.

Not surprisingly, Pinkerton was a devoted supporter of Abraham Lincoln, whom he had met while Lincoln was a lawyer for one of the railroads which the Pinkerton agency guarded. Pinkerton's former business association with Lincoln, coupled with his personal admiration led, early in 1861, to a well-known incident, still the subject of controversy; because it has contributed so much to the ethos of the Pinkerton agency, it is worth recounting. What actually occurred is clear enough. It had been publicly announced that after visiting Harrisburg, Pennsylvania, Lincoln, recently elected president but not yet sworn in, would return to Washington via Philadelphia, stopping en route in Baltimore, which was considered by Unionists as a hotbed of secessionists. He was advised by Pinkerton that a plot had been hatched to assassinate him while travelling through the streets of Baltimore from one railway terminal to another to make his connection to Washington. To foil alleged conspirators, Pinkerton arranged a special train from Harrisburg to Philadelphia, where on arrival Lincoln, in disguise as a woman, was surreptitiously taken by carriage to the terminal from which the direct train to Washington departed. Lincoln, accompanied by Pinkerton and a female Pinkerton operative posing as a companion of the other "lady" as well as by Ward Lamon, a friend of Lincoln, boarded a sleeping car as an apparently ordinary passenger. Though the train stopped at Baltimore, Lincoln did not disembark and the onward journey to Washington was uneventful. Pinkerton placed operatives along the entire route who by pre-arranged signals kept him advised of the train's progress, ensuring that no other trains came onto the track. He also arranged for the railway telegraph lines to be cut to prevent the possibility of messages being sent by conspirators.

The controversy arises from doubts whether a plot actually existed. Lincoln himself was reportedly embarrassed by charges of cowardice and Pinkerton has been accused of staging an elaborate publicity stunt. Pinkerton himself was at first reticent to discuss his part in the journey because it had been agreed by those involved that the so-called Baltimore plot would remain secret. However, in 1867, publication of a book by a historian of the Civil War, Benson J.

Lossing, resulted in the plot becoming public knowledge. Lossing wrote that the chief of police of New York City at the time, John Kennedy, had been the real saviour of Lincoln, and not Pinkerton, who was understandably infuriated. Pinkerton wrote everyone connected with the affair, including Ward Lamon, to whom he pointed out that although Kennedy had been on the train to Washington he had had absolutely nothing to do with the clandestine journey and was not even aware that Lincoln was a fellow passenger. Pinkerton asked Lamon for a full statement corroborating Pinkerton's role which, Pinkerton said, he would use "for publication in the press of the United States."[6] Lamon did not respond. Pinkerton wrote a second time; still no reply.[7] Five years later, Lamon levelled a diatribe, accusing Pinkerton of having invented the plot for his own purposes, but in 1895 Lamon, in a book of reminiscences about Lincoln, published a recantation although Pinkerton, sadly, had not lived to read it.

One need not go over the many arguments put forward on the one hand by Pinkerton's supporters and on the other by his detractors. The real question is whether there were reasonable grounds for believing a plot had been formed and to an impartial observer it seems inconceivable that given Pinkerton's probity, he would risk sullying his reputation by mounting an elaborate fraudulent scheme for self-aggrandizement. (Also, others had warned Lincoln that to show himself in Baltimore would be dangerous.) This view is given irrefutable weight by the actions of Lincoln himself. Just days after the outbreak of the Civil War, Pinkerton wrote Lincoln offering to organize a secret service to infiltrate Confederate ranks and gather intelligence by espionage. Lincoln accepted and sanctioned Pinkerton's appointment as head of the secret service of the Union army. One of those recommending Pinkerton to the president was General George B. McLellan, who before the war had been a vice-president of the very railroad for which Lincoln had been a lawyer. McLellan and Pinkerton were not only business associates but good friends. McLellan ultimately became Commander of the Army of the Potomac with Pinkerton as head of espionage. (Amongst Pinkerton's operatives, incidentally, were two women and G.H. Thiel, who later left the Pinkerton agency to found a rival firm.)

Pinkerton's background in undercover surveillance stood him in good stead as a spy master but when, apparently by osmosis, as it were, he gradually assumed the role of military analyst for McLellan, gathering information about troop strengths and movements, he was far less successful, in fact a hindrance. On two historic occasions, the battle for Richmond, and the battle at Antietam, McLellan broke off his army's engagement of the Confederate forces, relying on Pinkerton's gross overestimate of their strength. McLellan's failure, acting on poor advice, to take more decisive action which might have ensured an earlier end of the Civil War, led to his dismissal in 1862 from field command of the Union army and with him went Pinkerton, the intelligence expert. But Pinkerton, the detective, and his agency remained in the employ of the Union until the end of the Civil War, investigating frauds and larceny committed against government property with the result that the reputation of the agency as a detective bureau was unimpaired, indeed enhanced. The post-Civil War period proved profitable for the agency with the burgeoning business of railroads, telegraph, and express companies; as transportation proliferated, so did the opportunities for crime. It was the violent robbery in Indiana of an Adams Express car in 1868 by the Reno gang, some of whom fled to Canada to be tracked there personally by Allan Pinkerton, that first brought the agency to public prominence in Canada.[8]

Though this was the first occasion on which Pinkerton took up a matter inside Canada it was not the first occasion on which he had represented a Canadian interest. It seems that John A. Macdonald, when attorney general of Upper Canada, contacted the agency at its New York office in 1866 as the result of the Fenian raids that year.[9]

Pinkerton had hitherto conducted all his business from his Chicago office but after the Civil War he opened offices in New York and Philadelphia. In another significant development, his two sons, Robert and William, who had served with him during the Civil War, joined the agency — Robert at the New York office and William in Chicago. In the late 1860s and early 1870s, during Allan Pinkerton's convalescence from a stroke which nearly killed him, the two sons ran the agency. But by the time of the Molly Maguire investigation which began in 1873, the father was back in charge. The infiltration of the Molly Maguires by a Pinkerton agent (and the subsequent trials) is one of the most notable episodes in the history of the agency.

"Molly Maguires" was the name given to a clandestine group founded in Ireland at the time of the potato famine to fight absentee landowners. Many Irish émigrés fleeing starvation sought work in the coal mines of Pennsylvania and some, who were "Mollies," formed local cells known as "bodies" to battle the mine owners in efforts to improve working conditions. One of the largest owners was the

Reading Railroad, whose president had had business dealings with
Allan Pinkerton. Legitimate struggles to achieve better working
conditions in coal mines — many of which had deplorable safety
standards — were one thing, but murder and lesser forms of violence
in pursuit of laudable objectives quite another. In 1871, an industry-
wide strike in the Pennsylvania coal mines began, accompanied by
homicides and mayhem in various communities. Alarmed by violent
episodes which by 1872 were frequent, and by attacks on and
intimidation of mine managers, the mine owners were convinced that
the violence was not random, but a deliberate campaign of the
Mollies. The Reading Line president asked Pinkerton for advice in
curbing the attacks and it was decided to infiltrate the Molly Maguires
— if a suitable and willing agent could be found. James McParland, a
29-year-old Irish Roman Catholic who worked for Pinkerton, agreed
to take on the task, beginning in 1873. For nearly three years he
worked undercover, gradually gaining the confidence of Molly
Maguire leaders by a combination of bluster and bravado, eventually
gaining admittance to the inner councils of the society which, like
other secret organizations, had its own cabalistic apparatus. After
learning his cover was blown, and his assassination planned, he
managed to escape to his Pinkerton contacts. His experiences were
extraordinary. Exhibiting courage and ingenuity, talking his way out of
dangerous situations when suspected of being an informer, sending
reports to Pinkerton at great risk, and arranging rendezvous at even
greater risk, he gathered evidence which, combined with his
testimony, eventually resulted in the execution of nineteen Mollies
convicted of murder. Some of those murdered were themselves
Mollies, including the wife of one of them, a killing which became a
turning point for many who had up to that time remained loyal or
sympathetic to the organization. McParland's true identity was not
revealed until he testified; fearing assassination, he was accompanied
into the courtroom by two bodyguards — Pinkerton men, of course.
No attempt on his life was ever made and he became an important
figure in the Pinkerton agency until his death nearly forty years later.

The role of the agency in this remarkable affair has been — and
still is — ambiguous. On the one hand, the agency has been praised
for bringing to justice a group of murderous criminals masquerading as
friends of the working man; on the other hand it has been condemned
for siding with the mine bosses who made life miserable for their
employees. Whatever view one takes, the Molly Maguires and
Pinkerton's are inseparably linked with the history of the labour

movement, but in the eyes of the agency's principal clients, bankers, express company officials, and railroads, the verdict was clear, and Pinkerton gained even more kudos in the business community. Conducting the Molly Maguire operation seems to have sapped the strength of Allan Pinkerton, for following its conclusion his two sons increasingly ran the business of the agency; never again did Allan Pinkerton personally supervise a major investigation.[10]

The transition of Pinkerton's from its initial role of a detective agency solving crimes to a private police force attempting to prevent them by providing security guards is a striking phenomenon; after all, as the adage has it, prevention is better than a cure. It was, however, a fairly rapid process so that by the 1890s the agency had become synonymous not only with detecting criminals but preventing crimes against its major corporate clients. One cannot tell, at this distance, the proportion of its overall work that one might call conventional police work — bringing criminals to justice — and what now we would describe as security. The two concepts — detection of crime and its prevention — have always gone hand in glove. (As of today, the prevention component of Pinkerton's business is roughly 95%, the remaining 5% being surveillance and detection in the traditional manner.[11])

In 1884 Allan Pinkerton, who had become a very wealthy man, died in his large house on his splendid estate "The Larches." He bequeathed the agency business to Robert and William who, three years later, opened two more offices, in Boston and Denver. Still further expansion occurred and by the turn of the century Pinkerton's had offices in most major cities of the United States. More and more the two brothers were forced to shed their roles as investigators to become administrators. William Pinkerton in particular, who had an innate talent for criminal investigation, regretted the shift and never completely divorced himself from personal attention to major investigations.

W.A. Pinkerton, master detective and the driving force of the agency after his father Allan's death.

PA

The agency reached its zenith in police work both as regards its reputation and profitability between 1890 and 1910; thereafter the momentum towards security work gathered an irresistible force. It is not a coincidence that in that era Pinkerton's was consulted more frequently by Canadian officials than at any other time. In that period, to take a notable example, banks were the chief targets of swindlers, forgers, and thieves, and Pinkerton's, acting for the American Bankers Association, achieved an outstanding success rate in capturing them and restoring stolen funds. Many members of the Association displayed signs on their premises that they were guarded by Pinkerton's, and the ever-watchful "Eye" had a significant deterrent effect, as was evident from comparing the number of crimes committed against, and monies recovered from, non-members.

The methods which Pinkerton's employed in sleuthing will be described in the succeeding chapter; suffice it to say at this stage that Allan and William Pinkerton both had that indefinable ability — call it intuition — to recognize in the commission of a particular crime the handiwork of a particular criminal. Today, of course, the categories of crime are so numerous and the population so much larger that one can hardly expect a single police officer or detective to have an all-encompassing knowledge of well-known criminals, as did the Pinkertons. Crimes committed towards the end of the last century, and in the early years of this, were not sophisticated in any technological sense — there were few scientific aids to their detection — and much depended on the accumulated experience of detectives like William Pinkerton and, to a lesser extent, his brother Robert. Perhaps the most striking example of the personal touch was the recovery by William Pinkerton of the Gainsborough portrait of the *Duchess of Devonshire*, stolen in London in 1876. The unravelling of the twenty-five-year-old mystery of its sensational theft is arguably the most celebrated episode in the history of the agency. It is a story about a master criminal, a master detective — and a masterpiece.

At the time of the picture's disappearance William Pinkerton happened to be in London to co-operate with Scotland Yard officials in their investigation of crimes committed in England by American expatriate thieves. Agnew & Company, a top-drawer art dealer — then and now — had purchased the famous painting at a Christie's auction and exhibited it in a gallery on the second floor of its premises in Mayfair. A thief broke into the gallery at night through an outside window, cut the canvas out of the frame, leaving a triangular segment at one corner, presumably to enable positive identification of the picture should the thief bargain with Agnew — or an insurance company — for its safe return. Pinkerton told Superintendent John Shore, of Scotland Yard — the two men would have many dealings — that he suspected the audacious theft could be the handiwork of only one man, Adam Worth, whom he knew to be in London, but was puzzled that Worth would have taken a painting when his forte was the theft of cash, and large amounts of it. Worth's criminal career by 1876 had brought him considerable wealth, allowing him to live in England as a man of apparently honest means in a fine house near Piccadilly Circus, unscathed by police investigators. Pinkerton had encountered — if that is the word for it — Worth in the United States on the occasion of one of only two convictions for which he was imprisoned. Their next meeting was in London a few months after the *Duchess* theft. Pinkerton and Superintendent Shore dropped into the Criterion Bar, near Piccadilly circus, for a late afternoon drink. Pinkerton spotted Worth who lived just a stone's throw away and who frequented the fashionable establishment and, waving at him, invited Worth to join Shore and himself, which he did. Pinkerton introduced the thief to Shore. Worth, who was not to see Pinkerton again for twenty-five years, sized him up as, though he was a policeman, a person even a professional criminal could respect, but he did not take to Shore. The vignette is astonishing: the superintendent of Scotland Yard's criminal investigation division; William Pinkerton who was then establishing his international reputation as a detective; and an American criminal who was at the top of his profession; all having drinks at the Criterion Bar. The civilized encounter between the hunter and the hunted is a scene which today could not be repeated; it was an age of innocence, if one can use that term in talking of criminal activity. Scoundrel though he was, Adam Worth in his long career never used violence, and if in contemplating a job he thought violence might ensue, he abandoned it. Pinkerton knew that, and respected Worth for it.

Over the next twenty-five years Worth carried out a succession of crimes, white-collar crimes we would now call them, in England, France, and Turkey, which gained him the reputation of the most successful criminal of the late nineteenth century. William Pinkerton spoke of him and others of his kind as "silk hat" or "silk glove" men; for their part Pinkerton was the "big Eye." Worth's exploits drew grudging admiration both from Scotland Yard and Pinkerton, but high living exhausted his ill-gotten gains and, late in 1899, William Pinkerton learned from one of his contacts in the shadowy underworld that Worth, in ill health, had returned to the United States bringing with him the *Duchess of Devonshire*, which, precisely because of its fame, he had been unable to turn to a profit. Worth remembered the meeting with Pinkerton and Superintendent Shore in the Criterion Bar in 1876 and thought to turn that social gathering to his advantage by making a deal — the exchange of the painting for immunity from prosecution. Worth believed that Pinkerton, as an honourable man, would be willing to make such an arrangement with another honourable man, as Worth in his twisted mind saw himself. He met Pinkerton, and first talked of the still-outstanding reward for the return of the painting, hinting that if he turned over the portrait to Pinkerton's the agency could collect the reward. Pinkerton told Worth bluntly that his agency did not accept rewards and that all he could do was inform Scotland Yard, and Agnew, that the painting was still intact (except for the triangular segment) and that if the painting was delivered otherwise undamaged he would recommend against any prosecution. Worth agreed, and so did Scotland Yard. Pinkerton contacted Agnew in London and in March 1901 a member of the Agnew family met with Pinkerton in Chicago at a hotel suite Pinkerton had engaged where, minutes later, a messenger from Worth delivered the *Duchess*. It was a magic moment. Agnew later sold the painting to J. Pierpont Morgan for $225,000. Worth died soon after, penniless. His son wrote William Pinkerton to tell him of his father's penury; Pinkerton sent the boy $700 out of his own pocket and later hired him to work for the agency, though in what capacity is unknown.[12]

William Pinkerton travelled frequently to England to consult with Scotland Yard. One of his major collaborations concerned three American forgers, well known to Pinkerton, who had swindled the equivalent of nearly $1 million from the Bank of England; Pinkerton's eventually arrested them. He also visited France, Belgium, and Turkey to confer with police officials about the activities of American criminals in those countries. On one occasion he testified at a trial at the Old Bailey, in London, at which two Americans had pleaded guilty to armed robbery. Scotland Yard, believing each thug had used an alias and suspecting each might have been convicted in the United States, asked for Pinkerton's assistance. In court, he gave the true identification of the pair who were well known to him, and details of their criminal records. He became a well-known figure personally among police officials and it was the agency's reputation that in 1882 prompted the British government headed by W.E. Gladstone to make overtures to Pinkerton's for assistance in apprehending those responsible for the Phoenix Park murders in Dublin that year. One of the victims was a younger son of the Duke of Devonshire, and a nephew of Gladstone, as well as, incidentally, a descendant of the Duchess in the painting. Though Allan Pinkerton spelled out to Gladstone the precise terms on which Pinkerton's would agree to act, nothing came of it.

By the turn of the century Pinkerton's was regarded in international police circles as the premier law enforcement body in the United States. Sharing and exchanging information about crime with foreign police bureaus, and acting as a clearing house for news of international criminals, Pinkerton's had become the Interpol of its time. William Pinkerton himself was a familiar colleague equal in status to the senior officials of Scotland Yard and the French Sureté. He was a frequent participant in conferences of the International Association of Chiefs of Police and often addressed that body. Such was his reputation that, at Winston Churchill's invitation, he went to London in 1911 to work with Scotland Yard during the coronation of George V to prevent possible attacks by anarchists. In the first decade of this century, the agency had much to do with infiltrating the ranks of the Mafia, and one operative, Frank Dimaio, Italian by birth, carried out undercover work equally as dangerous as that by James McParland thirty years earlier. (Pinkerton's also assisted the British Columbia Provincial Police in this period with its investigation of Mafia activity among Italian immigrants in southeastern British Columbia, as will be described in chapter 4.)

Robert Pinkerton's death in 1907 provoked numerous editorials and comments around the world; it was the "end of an era" reaction. But it was not quite the end of an era — though a heavy blow nonetheless — because William was still vigorous. Even so, Robert's death was a watershed because it foreshadowed, as events proved, the weakening of the grasp of the Pinkerton family on the day-to-day business of the agency, although William did his best to keep a hands-on approach from his cluttered office in Chicago. Curiously, the agency had virtually no wartime role in espionage or other investigations on behalf of the United States government; in fact, it did more espionage for the French government and, of greater importance, even more for the Canadian government.

William Pinkerton, after Robert's death, became the elder statesman of the agency. On his many trips to England (besides being a detective he was an anglophile), he led an agreeable social life often in company with his Scotland Yard colleagues who entertained him at banquets at the Savoy — surely the ultimate accolade. In 1922 at the age of 76 he travelled to London on what had become, except for the war, an annual visit. Scotland Yard booked the ballroom at the Savoy for a gala dinner in his honour at which the American Ambassador to Great Britain extolled the virtues and talents of his fellow countryman. It was William Pinkerton's last visit to the United Kingdom; a year later, in a hotel room in Los Angeles, he died of a heart attack. His death was indeed the end of an era but it marked the beginning of another, for in 1924 J. Edgar Hoover was appointed to head the Bureau of Investigation which, in 1935, became the Federal Bureau of Investigation — the FBI. Pinkerton's historic role as a national detective agency ended with William Pinkerton's death, but the value of its contribution to law enforcement in the United States — and in Canada — is undiminished.

Two

Modus Operandi

The adoption by Allan Pinkerton of "National" in the name of his agency reflected the fact that in his time and for many years afterwards no nation-wide law enforcement body existed in the United States. In the early years of the agency, law enforcement was haphazard, weak, and often corrupt. Municipal police forces lacked authority to go beyond municipal boundaries to make arrests, and state police forces, if they existed, were similarly restricted and also inefficiently organized. It was precisely because Pinkerton's could operate across municipal and state borders (though its operatives had no special powers of arrest) that Pinkerton's was able to flourish. The fragmented administration of the criminal law was another circumstance working in Pinkerton's favour. In the United States, individual states define criminal conduct; each state has its own catalogue or code of crimes, and its own rules of procedure to deal with them. Criminal behaviour in one state may not, however, be quite the same as in another, nor are the procedures uniform. Moreover, an accused criminal fleeing from one state to another might have to be extradited since each state is sovereign. Overlying crimes defined by the states are those spelled out by the federal government within its constitutional jurisdiction; sometimes these are concurrent with state laws. In Canada, the position was and is markedly different. The Ottawa government enjoys exclusive jurisdiction to define criminal conduct and procedures for dealing with it, applicable to all provinces. The criminal law in Canada, therefore, is uniform, though it rests with provincial administrations to decide whether to launch a prosecution in a given case. A person accused of crime who flees to another province need only be arrested and not extradited. Pinkerton operatives investigating crimes in Canada had an easier time of it than in the United States, not being hedged about by jurisdictional barriers.

Inevitably the integrity and consistency of local and state law enforcement in the United States improved; citizens became less inclined to consult a private police force about infringements of the law and instead began to rely on public agencies. This transition, or evolution — whatever term one uses — was well advanced by the date of Robert Pinkerton's death, and the process a year later was accelerated, for in 1908 the Bureau of Investigation was established as the investigative arm of the federal Department of Justice. It is true that the Bureau could only investigate crimes which fell within federal jurisdiction, but those categories continually expanded. Private agencies like Pinkerton's (and, of course, there were others, Burns and Thiel chief among them) found that their investigative retainers dwindled. This circumstance was another factor influencing the trend towards security work rather than detective work. That an opportunity existed for providing detective services when Allan Pinkerton started has been amply demonstrated by the history of his agency, but its success could not have been achieved without its founder's utter — some might say fanatical — determination that it should be run on strict lines from which the slightest deviation would not be tolerated. Pinkerton believed a detective should be a professional, deserving as much respect as members of other professions such as doctors and lawyers. As he himself wrote:

> The profession of the detective is, at once, an honourable and highly useful one. For practical benefits few professions excell [sic] it. He is an officer of justice, he must himself be pure and above reproach.[1]

Leaving specifics aside for the moment, there were several hallmarks which distinguished the agency. It was independent, and free of the political influence that bedevilled administration of the law by members of local police forces in the last century. Bribery was virtually unknown; one searches through existing records for any evidence of corruption and rarely finds it. Dissipation was anathema: agents were fired on the spot for excessive drinking, although G.H. Bangs, for many years the general manager in New York City, survived Allan Pinkerton's extreme displeasure when Bangs had been observed, drunk, on a street at nine o'clock in the morning. Agency business, and that of clients, was confidential. Today, a claim of confidentiality is often an invitation to disclosure. In Allan Pinkerton's time, "confidential" actually meant "confidential"; clients had no reason to doubt it.

There was another aspect of Allan Pinkerton's management which is worth noting in the light of current attitudes: Pinkerton from the outset employed women. His instructions to his staff, published in 1867, commenced: "The attention of the General Superintendent, Superintendents, male and female detectives, is called to the following general principles," which he then enunciated. He firmly believed that the employment of women was imperative; without their feminine wiles, intelligently used, some crimes might not otherwise be solved.[2] In this policy, Pinkerton was in the vanguard: not until 1913 was a policewoman employed by a Canadian police force, in Toronto.[3] The most widely known female operative of the Pinkerton agency was an indomitable woman, Kate Warne. Pinkerton first employed Warne in the investigation of the Adams Express Company embezzlements in 1858 when she insinuated herself into the confidence of the wife of the principal suspect, thereby acquiring valuable evidence leading to his conviction. It was she who posed as the companion of the "female" Lincoln on his journey from Harrisburg to Washington. During the Civil War she carried out various assignments for Pinkerton behind Confederate lines. Gossip had it that she was Pinkerton's mistress; it seems unlikely, but certainly he grieved at her untimely death and directed that she be buried in the family plot in Graceland Cemetery in Chicago. It has been said that, after Pinkerton's death, his sons discouraged the use of female operatives, due to their father's warm "friendship," at the very least, with Kate Warne; if so, W.A. Pinkerton at least changed his mind, for in 1915 the first female police officer in San Francisco was appointed on his recommendation.[4]

As the number of agency offices grew, so did the problem of effective administration. Eventually certain major offices were designated as headquarters for a region, thus New York for the eastern region (which included Montreal), Philadelphia and St. Louis for the south, Chicago for the mid-west, and Denver for the west and the Pacific coast. Robert at New York and William at Chicago were still the "principals" in overall charge with Chicago remaining the de facto headquarters of the whole agency during William's lifetime. Morris Friedman, a former clerk in Pinkerton's, writing in 1907, has left the most complete description of the administrative system within the various offices. The methods remained unchanged during William's lifetime.[5] There were four departments: the executive, the clerical, the operating, and the criminal. There was in each office a superintendent and an assistant superintendent, but the larger offices would have as well general superintendents, division managers (James McParland of Molly Maguire fame was one of these), assistant general managers, the general manager, and, at the pinnacle, the principals. In the late afternoon of each day the assistant superintendent (or assistant superintendents if more than one) met with the superintendent to mull over the daily reports of the operatives and to issue instructions if the investigation was a continuing one. The reports would be typed and forwarded, in respect of each case, to the general superintendent for further scrutiny and additional instructions if necessary. All reports on a given case with expense accounts reached the assistant manager and, by chain of command, reached the general manager and ultimately the principals themselves, of whom William in particular made a point of reviewing the material relating to all significant investigations and sometimes the inconsequential ones as well. The clerical department comprised stenographers (Friedman had been one of these), bookkeepers, janitors, and office boys — all under the control of a chief clerk.

It was the operating and criminal departments which were the mainstay of the agency's detective business. Pinkerton's did not employ "detectives" but "operatives" and the rules and regulations applicable to them were meticulous. Friedman, no friend of Pinkerton's, held a grudging admiration for the methods of recruitment of operatives and their deployment on jobs:

> The government of this department [operating] and the military discipline which prevails therein at all times as well as the secret manner of recruiting the force, are illustrious of a thoroughness and attention to detail on the part of the agency which can scarcely be paralleled in any other business institution.[6]

The agency employed operatives in three categories: the special, the general, and the secret, the latter, according to Friedman, being a euphemism for "labour spy." The "special" operative was ad hoc, hired for a particular engagement as distinct from the "general" who was permanently employed on an endless variety of investigations — the professional detective in fact; each agency office kept on staff at least several of the "generals." All were hired through innocuous advertisements placed in newspapers. Friedman gives a typical example: "Wanted — a bright experienced salesman to handle good line — salary and commission. Excellent opportunities for right man to connect with first-class house. State age, experience and references." A Pinkerton man interviewed all applicants and if any struck him as having a potential for sleuthing he would inquire delicately whether the applicant would be interested in becoming a detective and, if so, whether he would like to work for Pinkerton's. If he agreed, he would be given a few "special" assignments to test his mettle and on demonstrating ability he might be taken on as a "general" operative. Whether an operative was a special, a general, or a secret, anonymity was a prerequisite. The client did not know the real name of the operative who was identified by initials or, more commonly, by a number, for example operative #37. In either case, his true identity was known only by the assistant superintendents and their superiors, and not by any of the clerical staff, and if one operative in the course of an investigation encountered another whom he knew, there was to be no sign of recognition.

Each agency office maintained a number of post boxes taken out under assumed names and an operative mailed reports to one of the fictional persons. The operative, when arriving at a city or town to conduct an investigation, rented a mail box also under an assumed name, sending the box number and fictitious name to the agency which forwarded instructions accordingly. The envelopes were addressed by hand so as not to attract attention — this before the days when typewriters were common — and the reports themselves were to be written in ink or, if ink was not obtainable, in indelible pencil. The rationale for secrecy was stated by Allan Pinkerton himself when writing of the qualifications of an effective operative: "The greatest essential is to prevent his identity from becoming known, even among his associates of respectable character, and when he fails to do this; when the nature of his calling is discovered and made known, his usefulness to the profession is at an end, and failure, certain and inevitable, is the result."[7] In other words, a Pinkerton operative must be faceless even among "respectable" neighbours. Thus, should an operative be asked in idle conversation about his occupation, he was expected to reply in conformity with the advertisement which led to his hiring; thus he was, inter alia, a "clerk" or a "salesman." Any lapse from such a pretence resulted in immediate dismissal.

As early as 1867 there were elaborate regulations, formulated by Allan Pinkerton, governing the work of all classes of operatives. These regulations were required to be read, marked, and inwardly digested.[8] The paramount requirement was that an operative's character be "above reproach" since "only those of strict moral principles and good habits will be permitted to enter the service." It followed from this that the operative could have no criminal record or seamy past, nor was he to condone commission of a crime by another person. Operatives need not be teetotallers, but at least must be abstemious, although they could consume liquor in any amount if the detection of a suspect "cannot otherwise be attained." They could not set foot in a saloon or tavern unless "shadowing." Operatives were required to be on call day or night, seven days a week, without complaint. In line with agency policy forbidding acceptance of rewards, operatives signed a waiver to any reward or bonus that might be offered, relying on a salary as their only compensation. The client paid the agency a per diem agreed on in advance. During the period covered by this book, the amount varied from six dollars daily to eight dollars, although in cases of extreme delicacy or difficulty the per diem might rise; out-of-pocket expenses were, of course, additional. In preparing their reports, operatives were to provide information in the minutest detail. Descriptions of individuals must include every physical characteristic; conversations must be repeated verbatim, or as close thereto as possible; locations of buildings and houses, particularly in remote areas, must be so accurate that a stranger could locate the place without difficulty; clothes and jewellery must be precisely noted, and times of departure and arrival must be scrupulously recorded. The agency imposed strict limits on expenditures incurred by operatives; the principle was frugality. When travelling by rail, an operative was forbidden the pleasure of a cigar or a drink in the smoking car unless such an indulgence was absolutely necessary to the investigation, nor could he take a meal in the dining car, unless specifically authorized by a superintendent. An operative could, however, tip the sleeping car porter but, at least to the turn of the century, not more than fifteen cents. Operatives were obliged to stay at medium-priced hotels or boarding houses, but if their assignment was for less than a week they had to pay their own laundry bills. If an operative obtained a job as part of his work on undercover surveillance he could not keep his wages, nor could the agency; they were credited to the client's account. If the operative was unable to secure a job to maintain his cover, the agency would do its best to have the client arrange one, quietly.

All agencies and operatives working from them were governed by identical general instructions in what was known as a general order book. In it were highly detailed rules and regulations governing investigations of the myriad categories of crime. As well, anatomical charts were supplied which, though not up to the standards of Gray's Anatomy, were nonetheless comprehensive and clearly presented. There were specific instructions to reflect local conditions. Thus, in Toronto, operatives were reminded that their reports must be written on both sides of the paper and, lest there be any misunderstanding, were told to write "down the one side and turning the paper over and then [write] down the other side." To make their life more difficult, "operatives will not be furnished with notebooks of any kind or description and must carry their notes upon small slips of paper, upon which nothing will show to whom they belong or where they are from, and these must be attached to each report immediately that the work to which they refer has been completed." All operatives at work in Toronto on Sundays were required to telephone either the superintendent or assistant superintendent at their residences between the hours of eleven o'clock in the morning and twelve noon, the object, of course, being to ensure that the operatives really were working and not having a day of rest. And in compliance with the general rule of frugality, all operatives, when riding on streetcars, were limited to the regular seven-cent fare, and if it was essential that they ride at night on a streetcar when the regular fare was ten cents, the higher rate would be allowed, providing the reasons for incurring it were sufficiently explained in the operatives' report. Although with time the subject matters of investigation and expenses obviously change, the system has not, and to this very day agencies and operatives are similarly governed.[9]

In 1909 Pinkerton's was hired by the British Columbia Provincial Police to investigate a suspicious fatality near Cranbrook, B.C. An operative from Spokane travelled to the area and, in the guise of a lumberjack, secured work in order to keep under observation another lumberjack, one Jack Early, believed to be involved in the death. The operative worked in the woods for thirty-five days. Portions of one of his reports typify the tens of thousands filed by Pinkerton operatives over the decades:

#11. Reports
I talked to Early at different times during the day, but he had not much to say. He said he thought he would return to the camp at times and again said he thought he would go on the CPR tie drive. He is well acquainted with everybody in town, including a few of the businessmen. I do not know where he gets all his money but think he borrows it from Harry Mather, proprietor of the Winsor Hotel. He keeps intoxicated all day, but does not take more than four or five successive drinks, when he will call for a cigar and generally takes a walk alone or with some friend. He is not quarrelsome and does not talk very loud but laughs a good deal. This afternoon he purchased a bucket of beer and took it to the blacksmith shop where he spends a great deal of his time.

During the evening Sam Akin came in from the camp and in company with John Early, Jack Smith, who works on the CPR drive, and myself, Jack Corrigan, Constable Joe Walsh and several other men who live in town were in the Winsor Hotel Bar drinking, but I did not learn anything of interest from the conversation and discontinued for the day at midnight.

The operative had spent a long day and, in the course of duty, finished by drinking in a bar with, among others, the local police constable who was there, off duty. Allan Pinkerton would never have tolerated such behaviour by one of his "constables."[10]

At an agency office, operatives worked in a "detective room." The directions for the use of these quarters are worth reproducing as they exemplify the punctilious nature of all Pinkerton regulations:

The room designated by the detective force in waiting orders, and writing reports, will be vacated by at the latest 10:00 p.m. after which it will not be occupied except when special services shall make it necessary for the detective to be or remain therein. Loud and boisterous talking and laughing, or disorderly conduct nor card playing, nor the use of profane or improper language, nor discussion on religious or political matters, nor any intoxicating beverages will be permitted in the room and the use of tobacco will only be tolerated so long as the rooms are not soiled by those using it. They must tidy up the room after using it putting the newspapers into the wastepaper basket and putting away wearing apparel and shoes and so on into the closets provided. Naturally all forms of gambling is [sic] prohibited nor must an operative associate under any circumstances with a former operative or introduce operatives to ex-employees.[11]

When one reflects on the history of the agency and the autocratic methods — by modern standards — of controlling its employees it is noteworthy that only two accounts critical of the agency's methods have survived. One, already mentioned, is that of Morris Friedman; the other is that by Charles Siringo, the self-styled "Cowboy Detective" who was a Pinkerton operative both in the United States and Canada but who had, like Friedman, a falling out with the agency.[12] One assumes that the numerous, anonymous, and unremembered operatives were content with their lot and, to paraphrase the poet writing of mercenary soldiers, took their pay and died. The fact is that the criteria for the engagement of operatives laid down by Allan Pinkerton and the rigorous control of their conduct provoked little criticism: indeed, clients found comfort in knowing there was such strict oversight of operatives, and that their interests would be confidentially protected.

The fourth major department in the organization, the criminal, was the raison d'etre for the entire organization. It is not too much to say that the development in the last century and the first decade of this of techniques to solve crime — the science of forensics — and their growing sophistication is the history of Pinkerton's itself. Police forces in the United States, Canada, and Europe constantly consulted Pinkerton's, which became a clearing house, a vast repository of intelligence about criminals and their activities, which the agency had garnered. In hindsight, the forensic methods pioneered by Pinkerton's seem self-evident. One would think that nothing could be more obvious, as an aid to identification, than noting the physical characteristics of an accused criminal and comparing them to others recorded on an earlier occasion, yet Pinkerton's brought this seemingly simple process to a high art. Even if the observed characteristics of a person under suspicion did not match those of a known criminal they would be useful in future comparisons. And, of course, it was for the purpose of proving in a courtroom the accurate identification of an accused criminal that Pinkerton directed his operatives to be absolutely precise. If a Pinkerton investigation resulted in the arrest of a suspect, the operative insisted that the suspect be stripped and that every scar, every tattoo, every wart, every mole, every twisted toe, every physical abnormality, be recorded.

An excellent example of the painstaking attention to detail is found in Pinkerton's classic description of the American bandit, Bill Miner, who at gunpoint held up trains in the United States and Canada in the last century and in the early years of this and whose exploits are described in chapter 6. After his arrest and conviction in Canada for armed robbery of a train in 1906, he was imprisoned in the British Columbia penitentiary at New Westminster, B.C., from which he escaped not long after. His flight caused a considerable political commotion, many believing it had been engineered by persons in authority. Pinkerton's sent to the B.C. Police, at their request, a description of Miner which the agency had maintained in its dossier for many years:

William A. Miner, alias William Morgan, alias William Anderson; Canadian [sic], occupation shoemaker, weight 138 lbs. Miner's distinguishing marks are on his forearm and were made by a tattooing needle and Indian Ink when he was a youngster; carries a tattoo at the base of thumb of left hand; also a heart pierced with a dagger; a ballet girl is tattooed on his right forearm and also a star; both wrist bones are large; has a mole in center of chest; mole under left breast and another on his right shoulder; another star tattooed on outside of calf of left leg; a discoloration on left buttock; a scar on his left shin; a scar on his right knee. A mole on his left shoulder blade. Two small scars on his neck. His face is pitted and he wears both upper and lower false teeth.[13]

From visual observation of physical characteristics it was but a short step technologically to the next stage, head and shoulder photographs — the mug shot. Allan Pinkerton's zeal to capture criminals coincided with rapid improvements in photography, and, quickly appreciating the value of photographs in identifying criminals, he began to assemble what eventually became a photographic library of criminals — a rogues' gallery, the earliest of its kind and for many years the most comprehensive. (In Canada the Toronto Police Force was the first to collect mug shots.)[14] Police forces across the continent contacted Pinkerton's, typically sending a photograph of an unknown suspect and requesting positive identification. As an example, in 1908, the British Columbia Provincial Police sent to Pinkerton's a photograph, taken in a morgue, of the fully clothed body of a man killed in a shoot-out after a train robbery. Because the hold-up occurred at the very spot where Bill Miner had held up a train two years earlier, the police theorized that the dead man was connected with Miner and his gang. Pinkerton's gave the photograph wide circulation and eventually identified the dead man who, as it turned out, had no link with Miner.[15]

In 1883, in France, Alphonse Bertillon demonstrated that the size of certain bony structures of the human body remain virtually constant in adulthood, and that systematic measurements of those structures would make it possible to distinguish one person from another. He chose five measurements as the foundation of his system; the length of the head and its breadth, the length of the middle finger and of the left foot, and the length of the forearm from the elbow to the end of the middle finger. The utility of "Bertillonage," as the method came to be known, in the identification of criminals was quickly appreciated, and in 1889 was first used in the United States by the Chicago police department; Pinkerton's soon adopted it. A typical Pinkerton circular of the time incorporated a mug shot, the Bertillonage measurements and a physical description of the subject. The man who introduced Bertillonage to the United States, George Porteous, remained enthusiastic about the value of the system even when it was becoming evident fingerprints were a superior means of identification and likely to make Bertillonage obsolete. Porteous was fond of displaying photographs of the same person taken many years apart from which no visible resemblance could be detected, a failing which, he argued, could be overcome only by the Bertillonage system. And indeed the system, at least in the United States, remained in common use until the early 1920s, partly because many criminals had not yet been fingerprinted and could be identified only by their physical measurements.[16]

In Canada, Bertillonage enjoys a long life, at least in theory. Parliament legislated its use in 1898, empowering police officers to compel, by force if necessary, a suspect under arrest for an indictable offence to submit to "measurements, processes and operations practised under the system for the identification of criminals commonly known as the Bertillonage Signaletic System." The same legislation empowered policemen to force suspects to submit to any other tests sanctioned by "the Governor-in-Council having the like object in view." By virtue of this provision, taking fingerprints has also been authorized and no longer are Bertillonage measurements taken, though the enabling legislation is still in force.[17] The use of fingerprints as a method of identification dates from ancient times when monarchs verified their decrees by a thumbprint — the royal sign manual. The Chinese employed fingerprints for hundreds of years to identify persons and, more recently, Chinese merchants authenticated receipts for goods sold by a thumbprint — a commercial sign manual. Not until 1823, however, was there an attempt to classify impressions by a systematic method. The pioneer of the use of fingerprints classified according to a rigorous system was Sir E.R. Henry who in 1897, as the head of the Bengal Police in India, introduced the system in order to identify native soldiers serving with Indian army regiments. After becoming chief commissioner of the Metropolitan Police in London in 1903 — the head of Scotland Yard — he introduced the system which came into general use by the Yard and wrote a textbook on the subject which became the standard reference work throughout the world.

William Pinkerton, because of his long, familiar association with Scotland Yard, soon became aware of the potential of the system and appreciated that the technique was superior to Bertillonage. He and two others were appointed in 1903 by the National Association of Chiefs of Police to evaluate fingerprinting as an identification tool, and after he and his colleagues went to England in 1905 to study at first hand the fingerprinting system, he became an ardent advocate for its use in preference to Bertillonage. But application of the method in the United States was bedevilled by the fragmented administration of the criminal law. No one agency could decree (as in Canada) that the system should have universal application and, accordingly, its adoption depended on a series of favourable court decisions, state by state. A difficulty faced by the courts but eventually overcome was that compulsion of an accused person to be fingerprinted might amount to a trespass and hence constitute an invasion of constitutional rights. Not until 1911 was there a judicial decision of a higher court in the United States (in Illinois) holding that fingerprint evidence was of overwhelming probative value in a murder case. One of the expert witnesses called by the prosecution to testify to the infallibility of the new method of identification was a Canadian, Edward Foster of the Dominion Police, a protégé of its commissioner,

Lieutenant-Colonel A.P. Sherwood who, personally convinced of the method's utility, had authorized Foster to develop his expertise. But widespread adoption of the method in the United States was slow and, as recently as 1922, a decision by the United States Federal Court to admit fingerprint evidence was hailed as a breakthrough.[18] Nothing more clearly illustrates the advantages of a unified administration of criminal law, which is the case in Canada, as contrasted with the American system, than the use of fingerprint evidence. As already observed, in Canada the federal government has sole jurisdiction over definition of crimes and procedural matters connected with them. Late in the 1890s, L.W. Herchmer, commissioner of the North West Mounted Police (later the RCMP) understood by the turn of the century the utility of fingerprints,[19] but it was Lieutenant-Colonel A.P. Sherwood of the Dominion Police (later to merge with the NWMP) who was responsible for introducing the system into general use in Canada. He set up the Canadian Criminal Identification Bureau, which became in effect a central registry for fingerprints taken in all parts of the country after the compulsory taking of fingerprints from an arrested suspect was authorized in 1908.[20]

W.A. Pinkerton lived to learn of the 1922 decision, which must have pleased him, because since 1905 he had been trumpeting the virtues of fingerprints, principally at meetings in the United States of the International Association of Chiefs of Police. In a speech on the subject in 1918, he predicted that nothing would surpass the efficacy of fingerprints as a means of identification, much as George Porteous predicted permanent use of Bertillonage. Both were wrong, as it turned out, but Pinkerton was always in the vanguard of those urging new methods of scientific crime detection. In his last speech to the International Association of Chiefs of Police in 1921 (he died in 1923) he predicted, correctly, that the science of microscopy, still in its infancy, would become an increasingly important forensic tool. Microscopic examination of poisons, chemicals, scrapings from under fingernails, hairs, the comparison of fibres and materials, and the detection of semen and sperm in sexual cases — all these are now commonplace. If Pinkerton were alive today and were introduced to the DNA method of genetic identification, he would enthusiastically advocate its adoption.[21] In the area of crime prevention, Pinkerton's was very much in the forefront at the turn of the century. It was the first to develop a practical burglar alarm which, on a break-in, rang a warning bell in a Pinkerton office, summoning Pinkerton men to the scene. The agency pioneered the use of a horse-drawn armoured wagon, the pre-cursor of the modern armoured car, to transport cash safely from one point to another.

In 1893, a group of police officers from across the United States met in St. Louis to form the National Association of Chiefs of Police; William Pinkerton and his brother were elected honorary members. William, in his capacity as an ex-officio member of the association, was instrumental in forming a bureau to compile identification records of criminals nation-wide. He was an active member of that body until his death. In 1924 the collection was turned over to the Bureau of Investigation — perhaps because the energetic J. Edgar Hoover had been appointed to head it. By the early 1900s the status of Pinkerton's as a bulwark against crime was well recognized by law enforcement officials of American states and major cities. This may seem surprising when one considers that Pinkerton's were entrepreneurs; Allan Pinkerton had founded the agency to make money, although law and order, philosophically, were close to his heart. Not only was William Pinkerton a notable figure among law enforcement officials in the United States, he was in the eyes of law enforcement officials outside the United States the embodiment of law and order. Though not a member, in the strict sense, of the International Association of Police Chiefs, he was always invited to its sessions.

Much has been written about private police forces, amongst which Pinkerton's is pre-eminent. Sociologists, criminologists, and lawyers debate the efficacy of private detective agencies before local police forces became efficient — and incorruptible. Allan Pinkerton in the 1850s laid down guidelines for effective administration of law — guidelines inspired by his personal morality. He combined his puritanical standard of conduct with entrepreneurial skill — and prospered. In doing so he moulded the future workings of the agency which acknowledged its obligation to him — the Eye shall never sleep.

Three
Early Days

In 1866 Allan Pinkerton opened a New York office, the first outside
Chicago, placing his son, Robert, in charge, using the name "National
Police Agency." (Not until two years later did he include his own
name.) The opening coincided with increased activity by the Fenian
Brotherhood in the eastern United States and its plans to invade parts
of Canada, and led to Pinkerton's first engagement by a Canadian
government authority. The Fenians were Irish expatriates dedicated to
the cause of Irish independence and, by a process of twisted reasoning,
believed that by invading Canada, Great Britain could be forced to
grant independence to Ireland. To that end, the Fenians mustered
thousands of volunteers in the United States eagerly professing
willingness to die in the cause and amassed large amounts of money to
finance the anticipated warfare. These plans did not go unnoticed by
John A. Macdonald (he was not to become "Sir John" until
Confederation a year later) who at the time was attorney general and
minister of militia affairs for Upper Canada. In devising measures to
thwart, or at least to minimize the effects of, any invasion, he relied
for intelligence on his spymaster, Gilbert McMicken — a remarkable
and competent man, and a stipendiary magistrate at Windsor who
built up a network of spies and informers in the United States — to

keep the Fenians under surveillance and, where possible, to infiltrate the ranks of their leaders. As well, he consulted the New York Pinkerton office.[1]

Gilbert McMicken, spymaster for John A. Macdonald and frequent collaborator with Pinkerton's.

NAC C10446

What McMicken engaged Pinkerton's to do is unclear, but undoubtedly it would have involved spying on individual Fenian leaders and tracking deployment of the Fenian forces along the Canadian border. Armed with the military intelligence gathered from his various sources, McMicken was able to predict with great accuracy locations of the raids which in fact occurred in 1866, enabling Canadian defensive measures to be taken. In April of that year an attempted invasion of Campobello Island in New Brunswick proved merely a minor skirmish, but in June the Fenians launched a more ambitious incursion at Fort Erie, in Upper Canada. Estimates of the number of invaders ran as high as 1800 but the lower estimate of 600–800 seems more probable. Nine Canadian militiamen were killed and dozens wounded before the Fenians withdrew.[2] A week later a third group crossed the frontier at Missiquoi Bay in Quebec, remaining on Canadian soil for forty-eight hours before retreating.

In retrospect, these adventures seem pretty small potatoes but at the time they understandably created much excitement, not so much about what had happened but about what might happen. And fears were heightened even more by the assassination of D'Arcy McGee early in 1868. Though at the trial of Patrick James Whelan for his murder, a positive link to Fenianism was not established, there seems little doubt that Whelan, who had been a Fenian member, was at the very least inspired by the movement which viewed McGee as a traitor to the cause of Irish nationalism. McMicken corresponded with Allan Pinkerton in the aftermath of the murder in attempts to identify Fenian culprits, and other correspondence indicates that Pinkerton was paying agents on McMicken's behalf.[3]

McMicken maintained his vigilance, so much so that he had accurate foreknowledge of the two raids the Fenians mounted in 1870 into Quebec from Vermont with a small force of two hundred men (shades of the thousands of volunteers!). These fruitless attacks marked the end of the Fenian threat in eastern Canada. One of those serving with the Canadian forces was Prince Arthur, the third and favourite son of Queen Victoria, who was then attached to a battalion of the Rifle Brigade in Montreal which was called out for service to repel the raids. Later, he and his entourage toured Canada and McMicken, mindful of possible reprisals against Arthur by Fenians, took charge of security arrangements. On learning that some Fenians had been keeping the prince under surveillance, McMicken got hold of Pinkerton's for advice about how to guard him but no threats were ever made. This occasion seems to have been the first engagement of Pinkerton's by a Canadian authority for security rather than crime detection; one will recall that William Pinkerton was asked to London by Scotland Yard for security advice at the coronation of Prince Arthur's nephew, King George V, in 1911. In that same year Arthur became governor general of Canada as the Duke of Connaught. (Throughout that time of Fenian activity McMicken was also dealing with Pinkerton's on other unrelated matters, mostly with the Chicago office.) There was one last attempt by Fenians at invasion, in Manitoba, in 1871. In that year McMicken was ordered to Winnipeg as the federal representative in the new province, but before leaving he learned from his network of a planned raid from Pembina in North Dakota. Prompt interception of the Fenian force by American soldiers aborted the affair.

When Gilbert McMicken was much preoccupied with the Fenian threats and the aftermath of the D'Arcy McGee murder early in 1868, there occurred the celebrated affair of the Frank Reno gang. A violent train robbery in Indiana by the gang, the flight to Canada of two of the perpetrators, their tracking down by Allan Pinkerton, the complex legal struggle to have them extradited, the co-operation between McMicken and Pinkerton and his agents, the attempt on Pinkerton's life, the eventual extradition of the bandits and their lynching before trial — all form one of the most fascinating episodes in the Pinkerton story in Canada.

On May 22, 1868, at Marshfield, Indiana, ten armed men overpowered the crew of a train which had stopped to take on water. The bandits pistol-whipped the fireman, knocking him out, and clubbed the engineer into unconsciousness, seriously injuring him. They uncoupled the engine tender and express car from the main section of the train and in doing so fired at the conductor, though not wounding him. (Those gun shots formed the legal basis for the extradition proceedings taken later.) The thugs forced open the door of the Adams Express car and, as the car moved slowly down the tracks, they beat up the express car clerk and flung him out of the car onto the ground. They then pried open the safes and stole $96,000 in cash and securities. This was a major crime — an armed train robbery was still novel and highly newsworthy. The Adams Express Company was a client of Pinkerton's and within hours Allan Pinkerton himself was en route to the robbery scene. It was established almost immediately that the bandits were members of a gang of notorious desperadoes, led by Frank Reno and two of his brothers, which had been responsible for a series of violent robberies in Indiana and elsewhere in the American mid-west. Through intimidation of witnesses and law enforcement officials and escapes from jail on the odd occasion when they were arrested, the Reno gang seemed immune from prosecution with the result that vigilante committees were formed to combat their lawlessness.

Allan Pinkerton and a number of his operatives assisted the local enforcement officials in tracking down the ten bandits and succeeded in arresting some of them. While three were being taken to jail, a vigilante force overpowered the guards and hanged the bandits on the spot. Three others, also associates of the Renos, were summarily hanged; thus six lynchings had occurred while Frank Reno and a confederate, Charlie Anderson, were fugitives. There developed a contest between the vigilante force and the law enforcement officials to see who could capture the remaining Reno gang members first. Two Reno brothers were found and placed under heavy guard in what was believed to be a secure jail in New Albany, Indiana, to await trial, but

Frank Reno and Anderson fled across the border to Windsor, Ontario, where they had friends and acquaintances prepared to do everything possible to keep them out of the clutches of the Pinkerton men. Allan Pinkerton, in addition to his role as the chief detective of the Adams Express Company, was also appointed as the official representative — or emissary — of the United States government in the proceedings to extradite Reno and Anderson. He had also been given the same authority in respect of two other American bandits, Charlie Thompson and Ike Morton, who had likewise fled to Windsor and found themselves in the same jail as Reno and Anderson. Extradition proceedings in respect of Morton and Thompson were held more or less at the same time as that of Reno and Anderson, but were much less troublesome. In both proceedings, however, McMicken and Allan Pinkerton played central roles. The Canadian authorities were eager to see the Americans extradited, but Reno and Anderson, who had money and willing accomplices, fought extradition tooth and nail, fearing, rightly as it proved, that if they were returned to Indiana they would be lynched.

Extradition of criminals, that is, the mechanism by which a fugitive offender can be returned to the country where the crime allegedly occurred, was and is a very tricky business. Sovereign states sign a treaty setting out the terms on which criminals will be arrested and held for extradition. Prior to Confederation extradition between Canada and the United States was at first governed by the Webster-Ashburton Treaty of 1842, the provisions of which were incorporated into the Fugitive Offender's Act of Upper Canada in 1849, and, ultimately, after Confederation, into federal legislation. It is the essence of an extraditable offence that the crime charged be one particularized in the treaty (or legislation) and that the nature and definition of the crime be similar in both the requesting and receiving jurisdictions. In Reno's case, both robbery and assault with intent to commit murder — or attempted murder for short — were extraditable. For some reason the Americans decided to proceed at first on the robbery charge but after a Canadian magistrate rejected it as a ground for extradition the United States government relied on the charge of attempted murder.

In 1868, Canada, though nominally sovereign, did not have diplomatic representatives in foreign countries and the negotiations on its behalf in the Reno and Anderson case were conducted by Sir Edward Thornton, the British ambassador in Washington. Both governments, Canada and Great Britain, sought assurances from the

United States authorities in Washington that if Reno and Anderson were returned they would be protected from lynching — which everyone had good reason to fear — and would be given a fair trial which would have to take place in Indiana under Indiana law. Those assurances were given and the Canadian government, in effect, consented to the extradition.[4] Briefly, the system worked as follows. The United States Department of State authorized extradition on a particular charge and designated named persons to take custody of the offenders in Canada. Once the United States government issued the formal documents leading to extradition, a lawyer would be appointed in Canada to represent it who would cause the fugitive to be arrested on a special warrant and the fugitive would then personally appear before a judge acting as an extradition commissioner, whose function it was to decide if extradition should be ordered. Until a decision was reached in the case of Reno and Anderson they would remain in custody.

Allan Pinkerton and L.C. Weir, who was an official of the Adams Express Company, were designated, and Pinkerton supervised in Canada the day-to-day progress of the extradition applications and court hearings. That Pinkerton, head of a private detective agency, should be so selected is a vivid illustration of the status he personally, and his agency, enjoyed. (Many years later legislation prohibited federal authorities in the United States from hiring private agencies.) If the Canadian courts ordered extradition the Canadian government would then decide whether to observe the court order (for there was an element of discretion). However, through all this, Reno and Anderson, as was their right, fought extradition at every stage and, but for the ready co-operation of McMicken and other Canadian officials, may well have remained in Canada.

It is not known precisely when Reno and Anderson arrived in Windsor but they were under surveillance by Pinkerton men for at least a month prior to their arrest. On August 6, 1868, the Department of State formally requested the Canadian government to issue a warrant for the arrest of the two thugs and they were taken into custody by Pinkerton men and local police officers on August 13th and incarcerated in the Sandwich Jail in Windsor.[5] Both Reno and Anderson had kept much of the money they had stolen in their various crime sprees and hired prominent lawyers to defend them. They were initially arraigned before a police magistrate at Windsor on a charge of robbery of the express car. The magistrate capriciously discharged the two men. They were immediately re-arrested on a warrant issued by Gilbert McMicken on a charge of attempted murder and once again taken into custody.[6] Speculation in Windsor that the magistrate had somehow been suborned or bribed (a view held, incidentally, by William Pinkerton who was there at the time) was fuelled by later reports that McMicken's son had been offered a substantial bribe by one of Reno's henchmen if he could influence his father in Reno's favour. Following dismissal of the first warrant for their extradition, Reno and Anderson, astonishingly, swore out a warrant for the arrest of Allan Pinkerton on a charge of perjury based on Pinkerton's sworn statements concerning the robbery. Pinkerton was actually taken into custody but released on bail of $400. He was soon freed, the charge against him being dismissed out of hand.[7]

An extradition hearing on the charge of attempted murder ensued before McMicken. He heard evidence from witnesses as to the circumstances of the robbery and the identification of Reno and Anderson as participants. As to the shots fired at the conductor, none had hit him but one passed through his coat. The lawyer for the two accused persuaded McMicken to hear defence evidence, which consisted mainly of alibi testimony. Seventeen men testified they had seen Anderson in Windsor on either May twenty-first or May twenty-second (the latter being the date of the robbery). Of those seventeen, one was a police constable and another, astoundingly, was the chief of police of the city. Not quite so many gave similar evidence for Reno — only six. They included mere tradesmen and not police officers. Since it took sixteen hours to go by train from Detroit to the place of the robbery it was impossible, so it was argued, for Reno and Anderson to have been present during the commission of the crime. When recalling these events many years later, William Pinkerton, who had helped his father in the affair, said that Reno and Anderson had spent a lot of money, firstly, in hiring corrupt detectives to find suitable candidates for perjured testimony and, secondly, in paying the necessary bribes. At that time, Windsor was a well-known hangout and refuge for criminals evading American law-men so that Reno and Anderson would not have had much trouble finding persons or friends willing to perjure themselves. In any case, McMicken ruled that he was not obliged by law to take into account the defence evidence and was required to rule only on the adequacy of the prosecution testimony. He decided there was a *prima facie* case of guilt and ordered the pair to be extradited. Their lawyers then applied to the Chief Justice of the Court of Common Pleas for a writ of *habeas corpus* to challenge McMicken's ruling, and the matter was argued in Toronto in September.

In addition to arguing that defence evidence ought to have been taken into account, the lawyer for Reno and Anderson came up with an ingenious contention: because the shot went through the conductor's coat, one could not infer that the shot was intended to do him serious harm. As the lawyer put it with the hair-splitting ingenuity sometimes displayed by the legal profession:

> The only logical inference which can be drawn from ... the firing of the shot ... and the passing of the ball through the coat is that the agent — the person who fired the shot intended it should pass through the coat, because he in the absence of proof to the contrary must be taken to have intended the direct and immediate consequence of his act.
>
> Syllogistically stated the argument stands thus: ... The direct and immediate consequence of the act of the person who fired the shot in question was that the ball [bullet] should so pass; and as a necessary corollary he did not intend to kill and murder.[8]

The judge adjourned the case for a few days to think about his decision, which he handed down on October 6. He ordered the two men extradited. All that remained to be done was to secure the formal ratification by the Governor-General-in-Council (the Cabinet), but the lawyer for Reno and Anderson did not give up the fight. He compiled a lengthy submission to the Cabinet recapitulating all the arguments he had made before the chief justice who, in ordering extradition, had observed that defence evidence — the alibis, etc. — could not be considered by the courts but could be submitted to the Cabinet in the hope that the Governor-General-in-Council would exercise his discretion and refuse extradition. That submission went to the Cabinet on October 15. It is not known whether the lawyer was aware of the assurances given by the United States to Canada of safe conduct for the prisoners if they were extradited, but Reno and Anderson knew well enough what fate was likely in store for them should they be returned to the United States, and attempted an escape from jail the very day their lawyer made his submission to the Cabinet. They had discovered in their cell a defective paving stone which they lifted to reveal a tunnel which had been made by another prisoner two years earlier in an attempt to escape. Reno and Anderson started tunnelling under the prison wall but were detected by one of the guards.[9]

And then, a day or two later, while word was awaited of the Cabinet decision, an attempt was made on Allan Pinkerton's life. He had received threats of violence during his protracted stay at Windsor and soon after the arrest of Reno and Anderson had asked the United States government to give him protection from their friends who were threatening to kill him. The United States complied with his request but one cannot tell for how long Pinkerton was guarded. On October 18 he and Gilbert McMicken were riding in a buggy on their way back from a visit to the Sandwich Jail. Another buggy with two men in it drew abreast of them. McMicken noticed one of the men reach into his pocket for what appeared to be a revolver and shouted at Pinkerton, "Look out, Major, he is going to shoot you!" ("Major" had been Pinkerton's rank during the Civil War.) McMicken and Pinkerton then drove away rapidly. An hour or two later, Pinkerton encountered the same man who uttered further threats and made the same menacing gesture. Later that same day Pinkerton took the ferry from Windsor to Detroit. Just as the ferry was about to dock at Detroit, he was jostled and, turning around, looked straight into the barrel of a revolver pointed at him by the man who had earlier threatened him. Pinkerton instantly grabbed the weapon, managing to get his finger onto the trigger guard to prevent a shot being fired, and the would-be assailant was wrestled to the ground by a bystander.[10] According to a Toronto newspaper, Pinkerton, when interviewed soon afterwards, said the man was a complete stranger and he could give no reason for the attempted assassination.[11] That may have been a first impression, however, for material in the Pinkerton archive makes it clear that the assailant was a notorious American criminal who had been hired for the job by friends of Reno, and William Pinkerton himself believed partisans of Reno had been responsible; the assailant escaped from jail in Detroit and was personally recaptured by William Pinkerton.[12]

News of the attempted shooting caused a sensation and there was no doubt in the minds of the public that it was connected with the Reno-Anderson affair, a view reinforced by the events of the next few days. On October 24 word arrived from Ottawa confirming the extradition and the prisoners were formally delivered into the custody of Allan Pinkerton and L.C. Weir, who immediately made plans for their transportation to the United States. It will be recalled that though Washington had jurisdiction over extradition, the state of Indiana had jurisdiction over the anticipated trial and it was to that state that the prisoners had to be returned. The arrangements for

return were made in the greatest secrecy. Pinkerton chartered a steam
tug to convey the prisoners to Cleveland, so as to minimize travel by
train (which would be more vulnerable to attacks by Reno partisans),
thence to Cincinnati by special train and from there by riverboat to
Floyd County, Indiana, where the trial was scheduled. The prisoners
were put aboard the tug guarded by officers of the Dominion Police
and a detachment of special guards from the United States. To fool
observers, the tug steamed upstream from Windsor into Lake St.
Clair as if making for Michigan City in Indiana, but upon a series of
pre-arranged signals, it turned around and, steaming down the
American side of the channel in darkness, headed for Cleveland.[13]
The tug met another vessel upward bound and, apparently through
faulty navigation, the other vessel rammed the tug squarely
amidships, cutting it in half; it sank in less than a minute.
Miraculously, all sixteen people aboard were pulled safely from the
water, including, of course, Pinkerton and his men. Reno and
Anderson, in heavy manacles, were rescued from drowning only with
the greatest difficulty and by good luck. They eventually arrived at
Cleveland as planned, and were taken to the jail at New Albany,
close to the trial venue, there to be greeted by the other two Reno
brothers already in custody.[14] Both Allan Pinkerton and his son
William saw nothing sinister in the marine collision but one would
have had difficulty in persuading a law-abiding citizen of Windsor
that the sinking was a coincidence.

The jail at New Albany, though hardly a fortress, was reasonably
well secured and guarded by the sheriff and his deputies who were
continually on the alert in view of the threats made by vigilantes. All
was quiet until December. On the seventh of that month the
engineer who had been seriously hurt during the robbery died of his
wounds, adding to the fears of reprisal. A week later, at midnight, a
train pulled stealthily into the station at New Albany and from it
descended seventy-five men, each carrying a firearm and a heavy
club. All wore flannel masks. They moved off to the jail, which was
not far away; the train awaited their return. The jail was surrounded
by men placed at intervals. Half a dozen vigilantes seized a prison
guard, tying him up, and then forced their way into the living
quarters of the sheriff who had been awakened by the noise. He
refused to hand over the keys to the cells and physically resisted
attempts to take them. He was shot, though not fatally, and the man
taking the keys opened the jail and gained access to the cells. Besides
the three Reno brothers and Anderson, there were ten other convicts

in cells who, fearful for their own lives, watched as the vigilante committee went about its business, and some later gave chilling accounts of the lynchings. Simeon Reno was pulled from his cell and, on resisting, was clubbed into unconsciousness. His hands were pinioned behind his back and a stout rope with a hangman's knot, brought for the purpose, was placed around his neck. The rope was tied around a rafter from which he was hung to his death. Charlie Anderson was next. His pleas for time to pray were ignored. He was lowered from a rafter in the same fashion as Simeon but the rope broke, and he dropped to the floor. He was strung up again, this time successfully. Frank Reno was hanged without incident; he said nothing and did not struggle. The last to die was his brother William. He pleaded for mercy, shouting that he was innocent, and called on "the Lord" to look after his father and sister. Of the four he struggled the hardest but was eventually subdued and, like the others, left to strangle at the end of a rope suspended from a rafter. The vigilantes, once satisfied that all were dead, returned to the station to catch their train, first telling a bystander to summon medical help for the sheriff, who was not seriously wounded. No effort was made to apprehend the lynch mob even though the identities of many of its members were well known; no one was ever charged.[15]

The lynchings were a considerable embarrassment to the United States government, which saw its pledge of protection and fair trial broken by the failure of Indiana state officials to ensure the pledge was carried out. The Canadian and British governments felt betrayed by the failure and made heated protests to Washington. The British ambassador, Sir Edward Thornton, in a letter to the state department, referred to the lynchings as "unjustifiable and painful" (that is, distressing to the authorities, not "painful" to those lynched). There was speculation that the Canadian government, supported by the British, would abrogate the extradition provisions with the United States. To mollify both governments the United States administration rushed a bill through Congress which specifically provided federal protection for extradited fugitives.[16]

McMicken and Allan Pinkerton were thrown together a good deal during the extradition proceedings and became fast friends, so much so that one of McMicken's sons later became a Pinkerton operative in Chicago. (Pinkerton's as yet had no office in Canada.) Pinkerton's and McMicken's involvement with the Renos didn't end with the lynching. Frank Reno was survived by his wife (and also by his mother and sister) who had stayed in Windsor during her husband's incarceration. A personable woman, she didn't look like the wife of a hard-bitten criminal. Though not directly implicated in his crimes, she was believed to have held his ill-gotten gains and to have disbursed them as required in Windsor in efforts to secure his release. By April 1869, Allan Pinkerton had not recovered the bonds stolen from the Adams Express Company car and was convinced Mrs. Reno had them in her possession. On the seventh of that month he wrote McMicken to ask that she be "shadowed" if she was in Windsor so that if it was discovered she in fact had the bonds in her possession they could be seized. He told McMicken, "I will talk the matter over very fully with William [his son] so that he may talk with you and I know you will give him the best advice in your power. He will be instructed to act upon it, and I only desire to bring my views on this matter [that is, the recovery of the bonds] as I unfortunately was prevented from doing so when you were here. I am under many obligations [to you]."

When Pinkerton said "when you were here" he was writing from Chicago and McMicken's own diary entry of April 3, made in Chicago, refers to a visit he made to that city with his son Hamilton (who became the Pinkerton operative) and to instructions given to Hamilton "to look after Mrs. Reno,"[17] that is, presumably, in an attempt to find the bonds by keeping her under surveillance. The bonds were never recovered but Allan Pinkerton reported to Gilbert McMicken on April 22, 1869 that he learned that they had been sold in New York. As a sort of windup to the whole affair, Pinkerton went to Windsor to visit his friend before his own return to Chicago. The Reno case was over.[18]

The first recorded investigation by Pinkerton detectives of a crime committed in eastern Canada occurred in 1897 following a bank robbery at Napanee, Ontario; it is also an early example of co-operation between Pinkerton's and local police forces.[19] On arriving for work at the Napanee branch of the Dominion Bank on August 27, the staff found the vault open and the cash missing, $32,000 in all. In those days, long before the Bank of Canada, individual banks issued their own bank notes which were legal tender. The largest number of notes stolen had been issued by the Dominion Bank, $22,000, with smaller amounts by other banks, all of which had a real interest in recovering the stolen currency.

It seemed obvious that the theft had been an inside job, for both the outer and inner vault doors were undamaged, having been opened by someone knowing the combinations. Local police investigated, as well as police in Toronto; the Dominion Bank hired Pinkerton's, who worked in conjunction with them. Suspicion fell upon a teller at the branch but no immediate arrests were made. Some of the stolen notes were fresh, not having been circulated, and the number recorded. A year or so later, some of these began circulating in Montreal and Pinkerton's, this time in conjunction with the Montreal police, began to track down the source. Their investigations led to charges being laid against the suspected teller, named Ponton; Parre, a professsional criminal born in Canada but a resident of the United States, mostly in jails, and a third man, another long-time criminal.After the robbery Parre had returned to the United States, to New Hampshire where, following surveillance by Pinkerton's, he was arrested and extradited to Canada. He escaped from custody and fled to Campbellton, New Brunswick. Re-arrested, he confessed to the crime and, in doing so, implicated Ponton. Parre was imprisoned in Kingston, dying soon after. Ponton was lucky, facing three trials and being acquitted every time.

Pinkerton's was in the thick of the investigation working with Silas Carpenter, at the time the chief of detectives in Montreal, and with bank officials, in tracking the currency, and supplying information about Parre and his confederate from their files. A story about the case in a Montreal newspaper quoted Carpenter's tribute to the agency: "I simply aided these gentlemen [the Pinkerton men] as a public officer and I did what I could but the Pinkerton detectives and the police ... deserve a great deal of praise for the work they have done."

Fenian activity re-emerged at the end of the century. There was an off-shoot of the Fenian movement known as Clan-Na-Gael, three members of which were arrested for the dynamiting on April 21, 1900 of lock 24 on the Welland Canal at Thorold, Ontario, near Niagara Falls. There had been fears even in McMicken's time about possible "outrages" against the canal and he had engaged men specifically to keep eye on it following the 1866 Fenian raids.[20] But in 1900 there was no specific security as such, though there was a lock-keeper who resided in a cottage at each gate. The three suspects, John Nolan, John Walsh, and a man who gave his name as Dullman but whose real name was believed to be Rowan, were known to the Irish police, and were suspected of complicity in dynamitings in the Dublin area. They had sailed from Ireland to Philadelphia in November of 1899. Dullman was the brains behind the canal explosion; the other two carried it out by placing dynamite against the lock gates. The damage was extensive but did not cause a catastrophic release of water. The two men, who had been in Thorold for over a week before setting off the charges, had been observed by many townspeople and several citizens got a good look at them as they placed the dynamite — carried in valises — against the gates. The two were arrested within an hour of the explosion and Dullman soon after that. On their first appearance in court, a local newspaper gave a description typical of the journalism of the day, free of any constraints of libel or slander:

> The whole group is picturesque, and appear to be about the toughest looking specimens of humanity imaginable. Dullman, who, according to the crown theory is the chief conspirator looks like the manager of a medicine wagon or a "sapho burlesque". He is fat, pockmarked, yellow, with prematurely white hair. He is glib of tongue, moreover, and said to be well informed on many themes. The police have had to give him whiskey since his arrest, because he was on the verge of D.T.'s. The other prisoners, Walsh and Nolan, are typical degenerates. Neither knows how to spell his own name which accounts for the numerous variations. Walsh stands about 5'10" and is smooth shaven with big rabbit teeth; his mouth is always open, and he has a hairless and vacant face. He would be called a gossoon in his native land. Little Nolan, the third prisoner, is what biologists call a low-browed plug-ugly. He has a good natured face, tolerant of any kind of crime. He is the type of man that cleans spittoons because he has not enough enterprize to be a burglar. Dullman is the "slick" man of the trio. The other two are degenerate outcasts who would with encouragement confess. When arraigned before the magistrate they were both shaky in the knees, whereas Dullman had his nerve with him, though feeling badly in need of a drink.

The three men were tried, convicted, and sentenced to life imprisonment.[21]

On one of them had been found a number of letters and names and addresses of people in the United States. Lieutenant-Colonel Sherwood, head of the Dominion Police Force, had photographs taken of the suspects and sent them to Pinkerton's in New York requesting assistance in verifying the identity of the accused and asking Pinkerton's to investigate every person whose name had been found. Regrettably, copies of the subsequent correspondence on the subject between Sherwood and Robert Pinkerton in New York and his brother William in Chicago are indecipherable due to fading, so that one cannot tell precisely what it was Pinkerton's did, nor the outcome.[22] Later, Sherwood, learning from the British consul in Chicago of an alleged plan to free the convicted men by blowing open a wall of the penitentiary at Kingston, warned the warden, who took extra precautions.

Though the Welland Canal explosion seems to have been the last act of violence by Fenians or the associated Clan-Na-Gael, there was a Fenian scare on the west coast barely a month after the canal episode. It was a curious and shadowy business, investigated by Pinkerton's, which ultimately led nowhere or, rather, proved no actual threat of violence existed. Early in May 1900, Frederick S. Hussey,

Superintendent F.S. Hussey of the British Columbia Police, in his office c. 1910.

BCARS G-9549

superintendent of the British Columbia Provincial Police, had gone to San Francisco for treatment of a serious condition of his only eye. While there, he learned of a report from Victoria published in a San Francisco newspaper that extra security guards and police forces had been posted at the big naval dockyard in Esquimalt (near Victoria) as the result of rumours that sympathizers of the Boers in South Africa were planning to damage the installation. Because the naval facilities at Esquimalt were part of the Royal Navy establishment, the matter was referred to the British consul general who in turn, learning of the superintendent's presence in the city, consulted Hussey. The two men, knowing of the serious explosion on the Welland Canal, believed that if a threat of violence at Esquimalt was genuine, it was more likely to have been inspired by Fenian activity rather than by Boers, or, possibly, by the two groups in conjunction. The consul general claimed to have information indicating an Irish connection. The source of his information was a female undercover detective (not from Pinkerton's), and in view of her previous connections with "Irish secret society" Hussey and the consul general were dubious about the reliability of the information passed on by her. There were rumours also that the Parliament Buildings in Victoria, not the dockyard, were the intended target.

Word of this reached the deputy attorney general in Victoria, and he telegraphed Pinkerton's superintendent James Nevins in Portland to have him look into the matter. Nevins contacted the assistant superintendent in San Francisco who called on Hussey and discussed with him at considerable length how an investigation should proceed to determine whether a Clan-Na-Gael plot really existed, and accordingly Pinkerton's shadowed a man in Victoria believed to be a Fenian. But it had all been talk. There was no attack on any building. Hussey returned to Victoria, cured medically, and satisfied professionally.[23]

Four

British Columbia Police and Murder

In the first two chapters reference was made to the long and fruitful collaboration between William Pinkerton and Scotland Yard. In Canada, there was also a long and fruitful association between the Pinkerton agency and two important police forces: the Dominion Police, headquartered in Ottawa (also briefly referred to earlier and the subject of a later chapter) and the British Columbia Provincial Police (referred to from now on simply as "B.C. Police") headquartered in Victoria. Measured by the volume of cases, Pinkerton's work for the B.C. Police was greater but not necessarily of more importance than that for the Dominion Police.

During the years we have been describing so far, British Columbia in the eyes of eastern Canadians was a wilderness, a sort of outer darkness populated by strange and uncivilized persons. A fiefdom of the Hudson's Bay Company until 1858, the new colony of British Columbia created that year gained legal status, but policing arrangements were very much ad hoc. The colonial government in New Westminster appointed law enforcement officials as need was perceived; when the colony of British Columbia merged in 1866 with the colony of Vancouver Island to form a single colony with the capital at Victoria, law enforcement improved, but not even in 1871, when the unified colony entered Confederation as the Province of British Columbia, was there an organized provincial police force. Such a force did not appear until 1889 when the province established the B.C. Police. The intention was to provide policing and law enforcement outside municipal and city boundaries. In that year only a few cities, Victoria, Vancouver, and New Westminster among them, maintained their own police forces; the B.C. Police looked after the rest. As the province grew, communities wanted their own local forces, and the role of the B.C. Police gradually became confined to the rural areas of the province. The force at its outset and for many years afterwards was comprised largely of veterans of the various colonial wars fought in the British Empire. They had sworn loyalty to the Queen and, upon enlistment in the B.C. Police, transferred their monarchical allegiance to British Columbia by upholding the Queen's law.

In the period we are concerned with, the force was never very numerous, rising at one time to a strength of just over 130 but generally running around one hundred officers. Even so, the force was far larger than all the municipal police forces combined and remained so during most of the time we are concerned with.[1] These officers, though small in number, were scattered around the province, often in one-man detachments, and to the general public represented law and order. Not only that, they were effectively government agents in the smaller communities, discharging a wide variety of tasks besides policing: they were registrars of marriages, births, and deaths; they issued business and trade licences and any other licences required by law — mining and water, for example. As a consequence, an officer was pretty much restricted to his rural post and ventured farther afield only in emergencies or to compile voters' lists or to take census figures. Indeed, during the tenure of one attorney general, officers were specifically prohibited from leaving their posts to go on patrol, however desirable it might be to "show the flag" as it were. This directive caused consternation among members of the force and was observed more in the breach than otherwise.[2]

There was, however, one task local police officers did not discharge: the investigation of serious crimes involving undercover work. Who did that? The answer was given by the superintendent of the force, Frederick S. Hussey, in his annual report for 1906:

Secret Service. There are no special men employed by the government for secret service duty [that is, undercover investigation]. When such officials are needed, the Pinkerton

Detective Service Company [*sic*] are usually employed and they furnish suitable men for the work required.[3]

Even though Pinkerton's was the detective agency of choice, other agencies were occasionally engaged. There were a few small agencies in Vancouver and Seattle who pestered the B.C. Police for business, without luck, but the Thiel agency was the only other one who did detective work of any consequence for the B.C Police. The agency, founded by Gus Thiel, a former Pinkerton superintendent, had by the turn of the century grown into a large and successful operation with offices across the United States and several in Canada (though not in Vancouver), and was a great rival of Pinkerton's. Until 1903 the Portland office was in the charge of W. St. M. Barnes, who may have been an Englishman who had lived in B.C., for he was a friend of Hussey. In any case, he visited Victoria often in attempts to drum up business and was sometimes successful. In 1900, his agency investigated a post-office theft at Quatsino, on Vancouver Island;[4] in 1901 another post-office robbery in Grand Forks, and in the following year a case of arson in Ashcroft, B.C.[5] Observing that not one of these investigations led to a prosecution, let alone a successful one, and observing the very large accounts that were rendered, it is impossible not to conclude that Barnes — or Thiel — was gouging, looking at the B.C. Police as a cash cow. Barnes, to judge from his frequent correspondence, was a slick salesman: "Leave our operatives on a few days yet" he would say and a favourable result would undoubtedly be achieved; when it was not, it was because the solution was at hand and only a few days of further work by the operative would be all that was required. It was often difficult to resist these blandishments, as the Ashcroft case well illustrates. He was let go by Thiel perhaps because of his over-zealousness; after he left, he went into business on his own but was not hired by the B.C. Police.[6] Pinkerton's were never pushing, like Barnes; they took the business as it was offered to them but there were undoubtedly occasions when they could not supply operatives on short notice, thus affording an opportunity for Thiel.

There was a great deal of political favouritism involved in the appointment of police officers because, although the force was administered by an impartial superintendent, the attorneys general had considerable influence on appointments; they could look after their friends. Notwithstanding this — indeed patronage in every aspect of government service was far more rampant than nowadays — the force as a whole consisted of dedicated, loyal men; not brilliant men, perhaps not even clever, but solid. Collectively they were for the most part a fine body of men, and the superintendents who headed the force were also admirable. In 1891, Hussey was appointed superintendent and remained so until his untimely death in 1911. He was succeeded by Colin Campbell. These two men headed the force during the twenty-odd years of its connection with Pinkerton's, but of the two it was Hussey who served longest and developed a close rapport with Pinkerton's. An English expatriate like many of his men, Hussey was first a police officer, then a government agent, and then superintendent of the force, a position which made him an important figure in the apparatus of government. A good shot, and a fine rider with a "good seat" (although he died of a fall from a horse), he was incorruptible, hardworking, and a stout defender of the members of his force. A few days after his death, William Pinkerton and his nephew, Allan (grandson of the founder), wrote to the B.C. Police to express sorrow at his death, expressing admiration for his character and speaking of him as one who "will be regretfully mourned by us as a friend and business associate."[7] And certainly the association between one police force and the other (even though Pinkerton's was a private force) was so close that one cannot describe the letter as mere ritual.

Most of Hussey's dealings with Pinkerton's were through the Seattle office headed by Philip K. Ahern, whose tenure was longer than Hussey's; the two men became very close. Quite apart from correspondence and consultations relating to particular crimes which Pinkerton investigated for the B.C. Police, there was from 1895 onward, the first year in which the B.C. Police employed Pinkerton's, constant contact between the two on a wide variety of topics. What was the best design for secure prison cells in a small detachment office, and what did Pinkerton's recommend? What were the United States regulations for the safe storage of gunpowder and dynamite? Pinkerton's reponded to both of these requests.

On one occasion Pinkerton's asked Hussey for a copy of the rules and regulations of the NWMP. Hussey, who knew Lieutenant-Colonel A.P. Sherwood of the Dominion Police and realized he would have ready access to the rules, asked Sherwood to forward him the information; as will be seen, Sherwood also enjoyed a harmonious relationship with Pinkerton's. Ahern and Hussey frequently exchanged information about known criminals and their activities on both sides of the border. Hussey would be asked to have his men keep an eye on unsavoury characters who had crossed into Canada, and Pinkerton's vice versa. Often as a personal favour each man would keep tabs on some acquaintance of one or the other, or a friend or associate of an acquaintance of one or the other — young women who had gone astray, for example, or errant young men. Frequently Ahern or Hussey would detail men to meet ships when docking at Seattle or Victoria or to keep an eye on vessels sailing for distant parts in an attempt to find wanted men, or to check hotels in Victoria, Vancouver, or Seattle for them. In more innocent matters, Hussey and Ahern would meet steamers to welcome travellers known to one of them and make sure suitable accommodations could be found. And for a projected trip to San Francisco for his ailing wife and himself Hussey asked Pinkerton's if they could secure a rail pass for her (but not for himself); not even Pinkerton's could manage that. And once when visiting Seattle, Hussey found himself short of cash; Ahern gladly helped him out by lending him some. Perhaps one should not dwell too much on the close personal relationship between the head of the B.C. Police and the Seattle superintendent of a large private police force and, to a lesser extent, of the superintendents of the Spokane, Portland, San Francisco, and Los Angeles offices, but it forms the backdrop against which Pinkerton's investigated many actual and suspected crimes in British Columbia.

The agency carried out six murder investigations in British Columbia on instructions from Hussey: three on Vancouver Island, one in Victoria, two near Nanaimo, and three in the Kootenay region in the southeast of the province. Four were unremarkable, if any murder case can be thought of as routine, but the other two were very much out of the ordinary. The Chenoweth investigation by Pinkerton's in Rossland in 1900 led to a trial unique in the annals of Canadian crime and probably unique in the annals of any country which has adopted the English system of criminal law. The other case, also in the Kootenay, in 1910, involved the Black Hand or Mafia.

In 1900 Rossland was the centre of intense mining activity. Standing at the base of Red Mountain where several gold mines were located, the town had attracted thousands of new citizens lured by the prospect of good jobs not only in the mines but in other business activities which had been spawned by the mining craze. Railroads were built into the city, banks established branch offices, professional men, doctors, dentists, and lawyers hung out their shingles, small businesses like jewellers and haberdashers thrived, several hotels looked after the needs of travellers, and housing construction spurted. The commercial activity attracted several hundred Chinese who, denied jobs in the mines by law, worked industriously as small shopkeepers, laundrymen, café owners, and servants. The Chinese Benevolent Association from Vancouver had representatives in Rossland to try to protect their fellow Chinese from blatant discrimination — and hostility. British Columbians of the day generally looked on Chinese with a combination of fear (lest the white men lose jobs to them), distrust (that in some way they might be unclean with unknown contagions), and contempt (based on a belief that Chinese were a lower order of humanity). There were three newspapers published in Rossland at the time, all editorially hostile to the Chinese race. One, the *Industrial World* — aimed specifically at miners, and generally at organized labour — was more virulent than the other journals.[8] One of the Chinese who came to Rossland was a nineteen-year-old, Mah Lin, who had only recently arrived in Canada and come to Rossland to seek employment as a cook. A newly arrived family was the Chenoweth household consisting of Mrs. Mary Chenoweth, a single mother as we would say nowadays, and her three sons, two of whom worked in the mines; the third, Ernest, was an eight-year-old school boy. Mrs. Chenoweth worked as a cook in one of the local hotels. To make life easier for herself and her two hardworking sons, she hired Mah Lin. He came to the house early in the morning to cook breakfast for the family and make sandwich lunches for the two older boys; after cleaning up he went away to his own quarters and returned in the afternoon to prepare supper for the family.

On the late afternoon of May 23, 1900, a neighbour called at the Chenoweth house intending to have a friendly visit.[9] There apparently being no one home, she peered through the kitchen window and saw Mah Lin, hands clenched, lying in a pool of blood near the kitchen stove. With admirable presence of mind, she went into the house, removed a bubbling saucepan of potatoes from the stove, and went for help. The doctors found Mah Lin had been shot in the head by a single bullet which had severed the carotid artery; death must have been instantaneous. Who could have shot him? Neither the visiting neighbour or any other person had heard shots, nor seen any strangers loitering in the neighbourhood. Mah Lin had cooked breakfast that morning and so must have been murdered in the afternoon; the doctors believed he had been shot an hour or so before the discovery of his body. But there was no doubt in the minds of the publishers of the Rossland papers: Mah Lin, for some reason known only to those Chinese who had come from the mysterious east, had aroused the wrath of one of the Tongs — the Chinese secret societies — who had settled a score with him. As the *Rossland Miner* newspaper put it, "the Mongolian [one of the opprobrious terms used to denote the Chinese] has only to thank the all-too frequent crimes undoubtedly committed by this class on the coast and elsewhere for the very natural suspicion which arises." In the same issue, the newspaper dismissed local speculation that young Ernest had shot Mah Lin, as just that — sheer speculation. How could an eight-year-old be responsible?

But the speculation had some grounding. Ernest was the only member of the family to have been home in the afternoon; the schools had been let out early to allow the children to prepare for the Queen's birthday holiday the following day — May 24. There was a rifle in the Chenoweth house that Ernest, in company with his brothers, had occasionally used for target practice. The rifle was found in the house after the killing, in the place where it was normally kept, and showed unmistakable signs of having recently been fired. It turned out that Ernest, after coming home from school, had been seen by a neighbour around the Chenoweth house but, as he himself told the police, he had soon after gone to play with school friends in the nearby railway yards. Called as a witness at the inquest, Ernest, because of his age, could give only unsworn testimony. He said that on coming home from school he had found Mah Lin at work in the kitchen peeling potatoes and putting them in a pot on the stove (the very pot the neighbour had found). After staying in the house for a short while, Ernest went to join his friends. He was asked about the rifle. Yes, he had fired it occasionally when with his brothers and agreed it had a hair trigger but he knew how to be careful and stated proudly he was strong enough to fire it from his shoulder like older people. His coolness was impressive.

Two months went by and there was still no solution to the mystery, although the newspaper accusations against the Chinese community continued unabated. Finally, the Chinese Benevolent Association stepped in. It had hired lawyers to attend the inquest but now it was prepared to go further and hire Pinkerton's. It had tacit support from the B.C. Police officers, both at Rossland and the adjacent community of Trail. John Ingram at Rossland, the senior policeman in the area, was sceptical of Chinese involvement in the crime and had his own ideas of the real killer. The association, resenting accusations that a member of the Chinese community was the killer, met with Ingram and asked him to arrange an investigation by an outsider, that is, by

someone other than members of the local police force. Nothing came
of it. The association then went further. A representative met with
the government agent at Rossland requesting him to tell
Superintendent Hussey in Victoria that it wanted Pinkerton's to
investigate the murder and that the association would pay the cost.
When contacted, Hussey mulled over the unusual proposal and
eventually agreed. He travelled surreptitiously to Seattle to see Ahern
(it was not unusual for Hussey to travel incognito to Seattle to consult
Pinkerton's on investigations) who accepted the assignment. Ahern
would go personally to Rossland, not as an undercover operative, but
as a publicly announced investigator; he arrived in less than twenty-
four hours. He spent his first day interviewing members of the B.C.
Police, examining the Chenoweth house (which had become
notorious), looking at the railway yards where young Ernest said he
had played, and talking to the doctors who had performed the autopsy
on the unfortunate Mah Lin. Ahern discarded any notion that a
Chinese Tong had wreaked revenge and, like Chief Constable Ingram,
became convinced that, unbelievable as it may have seemed, eight-
year-old Ernest was the culprit.

The following day he spent with Ernest. Ahern, accompanied by a
constable, went to the hotel where Mrs. Chenoweth worked and, with
her permission, took the boy to a basement room for interrogation.[10]
There the boy changed his story from that which he gave at the
inquest. While at home, he said, he heard a shot and, going into the
kitchen, saw Mah Lin fall to the floor, bleeding profusely. This
prompted Ahern to take him to the house where the boy repeated his
story, adding that if any ordinary boy had shot Mah Lin he would
have run away leaving the rifle on the floor but that if he, that is,
Ernest, had shot him he would have been smart enough to have put
the rifle back where it belonged (as, indeed, had been the case).
Ahern, convinced he was on the right track, took the boy to the
railway yards and lastly to the police office where he showed Ernest
the weapon and the bullet which the doctors had removed from Mah
Lin's head during the autopsy. The sight of these was evidently too
much for Ernest who then gave a full confession to Ahern. Also
present were the constable and the coroner, who made notes; the
confession therefore is largely a paraphrase of what Ernest said, not his
exact words. Still, Ernest's aplomb in his description of the homicide
is astonishing:

I was watching the chickens for Mrs. Wright a little after four o'clock on May the 23rd. I remember it was the day before the Queen's birthday. I saw Mah Lin, the Chinaman, employed by my mother as cook, enter the kitchen by the back door. I went in by the same door shortly afterwards and he, Lin, was slicing potatoes. I said to Mah Lin, "I kill-em you," meaning I kill you. I left the kitchen and passed to the front room and into the bedroom and got over the bed which was in the Southwest corner of the room and took a 32 calibre Remington rifle, which belonged to my brother Roy, which was standing in the corner of the room at the back of the bed, and left the bedroom and passed into the frontroom. Before going into the front room, and while I was on the bed, I raised the trigger and snapped it, then I went towards the Chinaman, Mah Lin, and said as I raised the gun and aimed at him, "Now here you go John." ["John" was a name used contemptuously by North Americans to denote Chinese.] I then pressed the trigger. I was standing near the door of the kitchen. He smiled as I said "Here you go." He had a dish of beans in his hands. I pulled the trigger and he fell towards me, his head toward the front room door. He kicked around and blood was running from his mouth and nose. He did not speak but made a gurgling sound. Then I put the gun back where I found it, and then I went to the kitchen and said, "Did I kill you, John, did I kill you?" I then ran out the back kitchen door and went down towards the depot and I met Johnny Perry then at the depot. I then went down Lincoln Street and met my mother and Mrs. King coming up from town. I did not tell her that I killed Mah Lin, but I killed him and didn't want to tell her for fear she would whip me. I told my mother about it before the inquest in Court. She told me not to say anything about it. She was the only person I told of having killed him. [If Ernest told the truth, he made a perjurer of his mother who testified under oath at the inquest that her son knew "nothing of the matter."] I put the gun back in the corner again after I shot him. I was standing in the dining room when I shot him.

Q. Was you much scared when you killed him?

A. No, not much, was glad one Chinaman was out of the way. I was afraid of the Chinaman for fear they would kill me, that was the reason I didn't tell the truth at the investigation. He smiled when I pointed the gun at him, but the smile left his face mighty quick when I shot him.

In his confession Ernest offered a motive: fear of the Chinese. The statement reflected the anti-Chinese views of the community and also those of his brothers, both miners, and more particularly, it reflected Ernest's fears engendered by the recent reports carried in the Rossland papers and discussed in the Chenoweth household, of atrocities committed in China during the Boxer rebellion.[11]

On the strength of the confession the police formally arrested Ernest on a charge of murder, and hastily convened a preliminary hearing as a necessary step leading to a trial. The prosecution faced two formidable hurdles before Ernest could be found guilty. The circumstances under which the confession was taken, an interrogation of an eight-year-old for over four hours without any member of his family being present, made its legal admissibility questionable. And the prosecution made a tactical error in allowing Ahern to return to Seattle without testifying at the preliminary hearing in an attempt to bolster the confession. (Nor was he called as a witness at the trial.) Because of the boy's age, the old English common-law rule applied (the case occurred before enactment of the Young Offender's Act or similar legislation). Although any juvenile over seven and below fourteen could be convicted of any crime and, in the case of murder, pay the ultimate penalty, it was necessary for the prosecution to prove that the boy, in shooting Mah Lin, had a guilty knowledge he was doing wrong or, to put it another way, that he had a substantial understanding of the consequences of his action.

Nonetheless, the prosecution pressed on. The boy was sent up for the trial which took place in Nelson, B.C. in October. No one in Canada so young had ever been through a full dress trial before judge and jury, nor has anyone of that age since been tried. The boy was so small that, seated in the high-sided prisoner's dock, he was invisible to everyone in the courtroom except the judge, who sat on a raised dais. At the trial Ernest's confession was rejected, and though he had made incriminatory statements to other witnesses, the jury acquitted him without leaving the jury box.[12] Pinkerton's had solved the case, no doubt about that, but no one at the time thought Ernest would be held legally responsible and, in fact, many citizens felt he had performed a public service.

There was a tragic aftermath which was also referred to
Pinkerton's. The chief constable at Rossland during the Chenoweth
investigation, John Ingram, left the force. In 1905 he was blown up in
an explosion at a mine site where dynamite was stored. The accident
— if such it was — occurred at a time when there had been other
explosions at mine sites in the United States which had been
investigated by Pinkerton's. Suspicion fell on a mine union, the
Western Federation of Miners, which had a local in Rossland. Ingram
had taken a prominent role against the union during strikes in
Rossland. His brother, a member of Parliament in Ottawa, fearing foul
play, contacted Lieutenant-Colonel Sherwood of the Dominion
Police who in turn wrote Allan Pinkerton, a grandson of the founder
who had joined his father, Robert, in the New York office, and, in
fact, went to New York to see him. Pinkerton's went to some trouble
over the affair, without sending bills for their time; James McParland,
manager of its western division and highly knowledgeable about mine
unions (he was the same man who played the undercover role in the
Molly Maguire affairs described in chapter 1) doubted that any
criminal conduct had led to Ingram's death. This advice allayed any
worries about union involvement in the death held by Canadian
officials, among them Mackenzie King, then in the federal
Department of Labour, to whom a copy of McParland's report was
sent. The explosion was truly accidental.[13]

The second notable murder in British Columbia investigated by
Pinkerton's occurred in Revelstoke in 1910 as the culmination of a
series of trials of Black Hand members. Pinkerton's had conducted a
great many undercover operations into Black Hand or Mafia crimes
— the two names are interchangeable — and it was only natural
that the B.C. Police should turn to the agency for assistance. The
notorious Mafia, or Black Hand, the Honoured Society, had its
origins in Sicily. Italian immigrants had established cells in the
southern United States by the 1870s, and the movement spread
northward from there.[14] Though it was tightly organized, and though
its members looked upon themselves as brothers, there was very
little benevolence displayed to outsiders for it was a criminal
organization. Extortion through threats of violence was common
and often led to murders of informers, witnesses, and unco-operative
victims. This behaviour characterized the activities of the Black
Hand in the Kootenay region of British Columbia after the turn of
the century where the developing mines and railways of the region

attracted many Italian labourers — among them criminal elements
which had come into Canada from nearby Spokane.

View of Fernie, B.C., c. 1907, where the "Black Hand" flourished.
BCARS F-03030

The troubles began at Fernie, a coal-mining town in southeast
B.C., not far from the Alberta border. The town had a large
population of Italians, many of whom were miners or railroad
employees. In the spring of 1908, twelve men, all of Italian origin and
all believed to be members of the Black Hand, were arrested on
charges of extortion from and intimidation of prominent members of
the Italian community.[15] During their preliminary hearings it came out
that some of the accused had assaulted one of the prosecution
witnesses in an attempt to silence his testimony. Five of the accused,
jailed while awaiting trial, escaped through a coal chute and though
they were recaptured a few days later the two events, the assault and
the escape, caused alarm throughout all segments of Fernie, but
particularly among the law-abiding elements of the Italian
community. In July of 1908, a group of them drew up a petition to the
attorney general deploring the lawlessness of the Black Hand but soon
realized that the whole community, not just the Italians, was alarmed,
so the petition was changed from being one from "Italians" only to
being from "residents."

To The Honourable,
The Attorney General,
Victoria, B.C.

The Petition of the under-signed residents at and near Fernie,
B.C.

1. That it is our desire to follow and obey all laws of the
Dominion of Canada and to aid in the suppression of all
Societies and organizations which have for their object the
setting aside of law and order.

2. That there is a society among the Italians known as the
Black Hand, which has branches throughout the world.

3. The said Black Hand Society has for its object, extortion of
money; the wounding of persons who do not yield to its
requests, and, in many cases, it commits murder.

4. That there is no society that we know of that is so
desperately criminal as that of the Black Hand.

5. That we believe that a branch of this society was recently
organized in the City of Fernie by agents of the said Society
coming here from the United States for that purpose.

6. That if the said society be not suppressed, crimes may be
committed by it, including the crime of murder, and not only
persons of the Italian race, but persons of other races, may
suffer financially and in person from its operations.

7. That the Black Hand Society is one which does not
hesitate to commit crime, including the crime of murder, and
so well are its criminal deeds known among the Italians, that
a message from it to an Italian against whom it may have
aimed its attack, very often compels that person to flee from
his domicile, in order that he may save his life.

8. We do not wish to exaggerate, nor are we in the least doing
so, when we direct your attention to the fact that we have in
our midst in Fernie and thereabouts, a most dangerous

criminal element which, unless it be at once suppressed by very firm measures, will, in all probability, cause a great many crimes to be committed.

WE THEREFORE respectfully request you to take all steps, including the sending here of detectives, to suppress and wipe out this society of criminals, and we shall as in duty bound, ever pray.

This remarkable document which asked for detectives to be sent (a request eventually granted by hiring Pinkerton's) was signed by 332 citizens, mostly men but some women, a large proportion of the wage-earning population of Fernie and representative of a broad cross-section of the community. There were, not surprisingly, more miners than anyone else but one finds bank managers and other bank employees, a bartender, a mine inspector, two union officials of the United Mine Workers of America, storekeepers, a medical doctor, pharmacists, the agent of the Singer Sewing Machine Co., teamsters and harness-men, a railway superintendent, and, perhaps most impressive, the local brewing company. The attorney general took no immediate action on this plea, but in the meantime nine of the twelve accused were tried, convicted, and sentenced.[16]

Almost exactly a year later there occurred two cases, another in Fernie and one in Revelstoke, also in the Kootenay region of British Columbia, which led to renewed alarm. At Fernie in June 1909, Joseph Raniera stood trial on a charge of attempted extortion of another Italian, Louis Carosella, by writing threatening letters signed "Mano Nera" — i.e. Black Hand. The principal evidence against Raniera consisted of a piece of torn letter paper found in his possession which matched a torn letter which Carosella had received. Raniera was convicted and sentenced to fourteen years imprisonment. Before the trial, Carosella had received an unsigned letter threatening him with death if he testified and, following the trial, someone shot at him through the window of his house, wounding him; he, well-armed, returned the fire. As a result of this case, Hussey began seriously to think about calling in Pinkerton's. He urged the attorney general to engage Pinkerton's to supply an Italian detective "to get at the source of the supposed work of the Black Hand Society at Fernie," but the attorney general did not immediately act on the advice.[17]

The other case, in Revelstoke, occurred almost at the same time as the Raniera trial in Fernie, and led to murder. Two men, Vincenzo Romero and Frank Schildo — both Italian — were accused of the attempted murder of one Frank Orsetti by cutting his throat. All three were railway employees. The case received a great deal of local publicity, so much so that the lawyers for the accused tried, unsuccessfully, to have the trial moved away from Revelstoke. The two men were convicted and sentenced to ten years.[18] One of the prosecution witnesses, Mike Julian, had gone to the United States after the arrest of the accused. Hussey engaged Pinkerton's to find him, which they did after a great deal of trouble, and Julian very reluctantly, after payment of his lost wages and expenses, testified at the trial, returning to the United States immediately afterwards. The victim of the assault, Frank Orsetti, was the son-in-law of one Frank Julian, who made it his business to track down the two suspects in the crime. He located the two men in Calgary, informing the police of their whereabouts. Julian had also helped the police in their investigation of other Black Hand trials, and following the conviction of Romero and Schildo was in real fear of his life, telling friends at Revelstoke he fully expected the Black Hand would "get him." He went to Victoria to lie low. In February 1910 he spotted in Victoria three men from Revelstoke who he was convinced were Black Hand members come to "get him." Alarmed, he went to a sergeant of the city police who later described Julian as "much agitated." The sergeant told him to see Superintendent Hussey. Apparently Julian did not, and left Victoria soon afterwards. At some point he returned to Revelstoke where on the twenty-first of September, 1910, while showing a property owned by him to three men who ostensibly were interested in buying it, Julian was brutally murdered by a blow from an axe so forcible that he was nearly decapitated. When his body was discovered, police noticed black marks on his face which chemical analysis showed had been etched by some corrosive acid.[19]

No one was arrested in spite of a reward of $500 offered by the Revelstoke City Council and $1,000 by the provincial government, although the three supposed purchasers were suspect. The extortion trials and now a murder, all connected with the Black Hand, forced the B.C. government into action, particularly since the local police could get no information whatsoever from the Italian community, members of which, terrified, feared the same fate suffered by Julian.[20] The attorney general gave the necessary instructions to Hussey who wrote Ahern. The latter assured Hussey that Pinkerton's had a number of operatives who had worked undercover in Black Hand cases and one of these would be assigned to the Revelstoke case. One Pinkerton man who would undoubtedly have been consulted was Frank Dimaio whose undercover Black Hand exploits had become legendary. Pinkerton's sent out a man from Buffalo. Hussey travelled to Seattle to interview him and was satisfied with the choice. The operative went up to Revelstoke and found employment as a labourer. Unfortunately, while carrying a heavy load, he fell and was badly hurt; after a ten day convalescence in hospital in Revelstoke he was obliged to return to Buffalo; the government paid all his expenses. Pinkerton's sent out a replacement and this time the attorney general himself, W.J. Bowser, went to Seattle to scrutinize the operative and, finding him satisfactory, authorized his employment which began early in December 1910. After a month or so, he was replaced by still another Italian operative who remained undercover in Revelstoke until April 1911.[21] The prime suspect in the murder left the area and was never charged — nor was anyone else — so the murder remained unsolved. There were two other attempts at extortion by mail threats in the region. The first, at Grand Forks in 1909, was taken seriously enough that Pinkerton's conducted a brief investigation out of its Spokane office; the other was at Greenwood, not far away. In each case, the "Black Hand" letter was proved to be bogus, sent, no doubt, by a "copy-cat" would-be extortionist.[22]

Pinkerton's role in all this had one salutary effect: after the Julian murder there were no further Black Hand crimes. Quite probably, the word had spread that Pinkerton's had been called in, and would be involved in any investigation of future crimes.

Five

British Columbia Investigations

One cannot recite every investigation carried out by Pinkerton's for the B.C. Police over a period of years. They were all performed by American detectives; that is to say, operatives assigned from the various Pinkerton offices in the United States. Sometimes the Pinkerton men did not operate independently but in tandem with B.C. Police officers. Such an instance — amusing in retrospect but not thought humorous at the time — occurred in 1911.[1] One Carrigan, a soldier stationed at an army barracks at Esquimalt (outside Victoria) had disappeared and was listed as a deserter. He was to have been an important witness in an upcoming trial for burglary of a friend — a fellow soldier — and at first it was believed he had vanished to avoid the unpleasantness of having to testify against his friend. When efforts by local officials to find Carrigan failed, Superintendent Hussey telegraphed Ahern at his residence, trying to maintain secrecy, for an operative to be sent up. Ahern replied in kind by wiring Hussey that he would "send package forward to you tomorrow." Operative 29S showed up in Victoria the next day (this was the same operative who was to work undercover for five months in the Nanaimo coal strike of 1913). At first working undercover, the operative, posing as a businessman interested in buying one of the local pubs, spent several days in bars and pubs ostensibly to inspect them, trying to glean information about Carrigan. Oddly, the police had been unable to get an accurate description of the man from the army depot, so the operative would not be able to identify Carrigan even if he was in the area, which, as it turned out, he was not; nor was it possible to learn of the whereabouts of Carrigan's family, believed to be living in the United States, from whom a description might have been obtained.

The operative reported his progress — or, rather, the lack of it — to Hussey who was in hospital suffering from injuries sustained after being thrown from his horse. (Hussey would succumb to these injuries two months later.) Hussey told him that a friend of Carrigan's, one Bryan, also scheduled to appear as a witness, was being held in custody at the provincial jail in Victoria while awaiting trial on unrelated charges. Hussey referred the operative, who had now dropped his cover, to the jail warden, who in turn had Bryan brought out of the cells for an interview in the hope he would be able to give an accurate description of Carrigan and offer some clue as to his whereabouts. Bryan did give the operative a minute description of Carrigan's physical appearance and told him Carrigan had deserted not because of loyalty to a friend, but because he feared detection for various burglaries he had committed. However, he said he had no idea where Carrigan was, but would be prepared to identify him if he saw him; he was returned to the cells.

Overnight Bryan began thinking he might be onto a good thing, knowing the anxiety of the police to find the deserter. The next day he contacted the warden who took him by a "hack" to Hussey's hospital bed. With the operative present, Bryan told the superintendent that he could now locate Carrigan in Vancouver and was willing to go there for the purpose. Arrangements were quickly made for his temporary release from prison and Bryan, freshly shaven and outfitted in new civilian clothes purchased for him, was accompanied by the operative and a B.C. Police constable on the overnight boat to Vancouver. Bryan slept in a comfortable state room. Just before embarking, Bryan, feigning reluctance, professed to be nervous about what his friends might think of him if they learned he was to inform on Carrigan whereupon, as the operative reported, he and the constable "kept him saturated enough so that he keeps up his nerve without getting an excess of liquor, and thus lose his usefulness."

Arriving in Vancouver Bryan led 29S and the constable on a merry song and dance. In reality, he hadn't the slightest idea where Carrigan was but saw a chance for a night on the town or as many nights as he could manage. Wine, women, and song were the order of the day — and night — and Bryan succeeded in spinning out his good luck and skill as a con man for a week. On that first night in Vancouver, he revealed his true colours to the unsuspecting operative: "Bryan requires an exceeding amount of liquor and smokes besides which he made a request that he be allowed to visit a sporting house and this I granted, letting Dunwoody [the provincial constable] take charge of him there. The cost to me is added into incidentals." He does not hint at whether Dunwoody tasted the delights of the establishment. During the week, on their excursions, either the operative or Dunwoody accompanied Bryan or, when Bryan complained that Dunwoody's appearance was too much that of a police officer inhibiting people from speaking freely to him, kept him under surveillance without his being aware of it. On one occasion they let him off the leash so that, he claimed, he could make contact with two men whom he recognized as deserters who might know of Carrigan. But it was necessary, he said, to have some more money which he could spend in a bar entertaining the two in an attempt to elicit information. Later that same day, when in company with the operative, Bryan indicated a passerby who he said was a deserter from Victoria. The operative confronted the man who admitted that he was indeed a deserter whereupon the operative offered him a deal: tell us where Carrigan is and we will not turn you in. The man could not, and was arrested.

The three then visited hotels, rooming houses, pool rooms, and factories as Bryan's whim dictated, in every section of the city and in Eburne (then a separate town in what is now the Marpole District of Vancouver). As the operative recorded, "We drift continually about from one to another of the loafing places of idle men and of whom there are vast crowds everywhere." On their final day in Vancouver, the operative, becoming suspicious, accused Bryan of duplicity, a charge which he stoutly denied. The operative records he was "completely disarmed by the apparent frankness and boldness of Bryan's story and work," and, giving him some money, allowed Bryan his "freedom" for the day. By the end of that day, however, after reflecting on the week's activities, the operative concluded: "I am positive that he is a fantastic liar not trying to do any direct harm, but weak and in his anxiety to assist Mr. Hussey he has concocted the story throughout ... of Carrigan's presence in Vancouver," and that he "has led us on a fool's errand." The operative even at that stage was charitably inclined to put Bryan's conduct down to weakness, but in his final report he grasped the true situation: "I was now convinced that the whole story told by Bryan from the first is concocted in his own brain."

The operative and Dunwoody with the captured deserter and Bryan, also again in custody, returned to Victoria. Hussey took the affair in good part, agreeing that nothing more could be done, whereupon 29S returned to Seattle, no doubt feeling rather foolish, a sadder and wiser man. Bryan went back to his stark cell in jail where he could dream of sporting houses and savour a week of debauchery at the expense of the police — and Pinkerton's.

An arson case in Nelson, B.C. in 1912 affords another example of the working arrangements between Pinkerton's and the B.C. Police, though it had a more satisfactory outcome than the Carrigan affair. In the previous year and early in 1912 a series of deliberately set fires alarmed the community. The local police chief was unable to find evidence implicating the man suspected, a John Bradshaw. The B.C. Police, worried that injury or death might result from future fires, took the case very seriously and late in March telegraphed Ahern in Seattle to come immediately to Vancouver to discuss an investigation. Ahern did so, meeting the attorney general, W.J. Bowser, and B.C. Police superintendent Colin Campbell, who had succeeded Hussey

Premier Richard McBride (on left) and his attorney general W.J. Bowser c. 1910. McBride frequently consulted Pinkerton's.

BCARS H-2678

the year before. Later the same day he met again with Bowser and Campbell, this time joined by the premier, Sir Richard McBride. The four men decided to launch a twin-pronged operation putting one operative undercover to gain the confidence of Bradshaw in the hope of getting incriminating statements from him, and another operative to work in the open. The two operatives came to Vancouver the next day and, as was customary, met the superintendent for scrutiny and went to Nelson to go to work. The investigation was complicated by the fact that Nelson had its own police force, albeit a small one, and strictly speaking the B.C. Police — or Pinkerton's on their behalf — had no jurisdiction. The series of arsons was so worrisome, however, that the premier authorized the B.C. Police to step in and, in fact, besides the Pinkerton men, the B.C. Police assigned one of their constables to work on the case also. The undercover man posed as a drifter and ne'er-do-well. During one of the evenings he spent with Bradshaw the Pinkerton operative suggested a visit to the "sporting houses," but Bradshaw expressed revulsion and would not spend three dollars in going to one. No doubt the operative viewed the proposed visit as being in the line of duty, and Bradshaw's attitude led him to think he might be a "moral pervert." Bradshaw did confide in him by describing the method of setting the fires. The other operative worked with the police, who gathered physical evidence which, combined with the incriminating statements, was thought sufficient to get a conviction and Bradshaw was charged. A preliminary hearing was held. Along with many other witnesses, the Pinkerton undercover operative testified, but to the anger of the B.C. Police the presiding magistrate refused to commit Bradshaw for trial, holding that the evidence against him was insufficient to warrant a trial. From a letter written just after the decision, the B.C. Police constable at Nelson told Campbell that the "efforts" of the B.C. Police and Pinkerton's were "not appreciated by the police of the City of Nelson" nor by the police commissioners and that the Nelson police had done "everything in their power to assist the defence." Thus it seems resentment by the local police of the visiting officers was also shared by the magistrate. The two Pinkerton men returned to the States.

Three months later other fires were set and once again Bradshaw was put under surveillance and subsequently arrested. This time it was decided to place a Pinkerton operative in the cells with him. The previous Pinkerton man had learned that Bradshaw was a member of the International Workers of the World (the "Wobblies") and a rabid advocate of violence against industrial plants. When instructing

Ahern to engage an operative, Campbell said it was imperative that
the operative also be an IWW member so he could talk to Bradshaw
on his own terms. This was done. Campbell made arrangements with
the B.C. Police constable and the warden of the provincial jail at
Nelson for the operative's arrest on a trumped up charge; there he
was lodged in the cells, where Bradshaw told him of all the fires he
had set — including the one for which he had just been arrested. A
different magistrate sent Bradshaw up for trial and he was convicted.
The operative testified at the trial (as well as at the preliminary
hearing). This is the only instance the author can discover in which
an operative took the stand at a trial in Canada. Pinkerton's didn't
like their operatives testifying, but with undercover work it was
sometimes inevitable.[2]

Pinkerton's charged a set fee of six dollars per diem plus expenses,
though not all the fee went to the operative; the agency retained a
fixed amount. The operatives were well paid by the standards of the
time — more than a constable of the B.C. Police, for example.
Sometimes this disparity and the feeling of B.C. Police constables that
they were perceived as being not quite up to the mark in conducting a
criminal investigation led to jealousy of the Pinkerton man, and
resentment. Such was the case during an investigation in 1906. A
house near New Westminster was badly damaged by an explosion.
The owner, who had been in the house at the time, claimed any one
of several people might have had a grudge against him and could have
been responsible and, accordingly, the investigation turned into one
for attempted murder. Hussey telegraphed Ahern for an operative to
be sent, though not to work undercover. The operative interviewed
many people and generally conducted a thorough investigation. He
and the local chief constable did not hit it off. Eventually the
Pinkerton man concluded the owner had himself caused the
explosion, for some twisted reason, and so reported. The constable
complained that that was exactly the same conclusion that he himself
had reached, though he had not passed on his opinion until the
Pinkerton man had expressed his. The constable said that the
Pinkerton man's employment had been a waste of money. Hussey
made no comment.[3]

Two of the many theft cases were embarrassing. The very first case of
any kind investigated for the B.C. Police by Pinkerton's was that of a
clerk in the office of the Registrar of Land Titles at New Westminster,
who in 1895 absconded with approximately $1,000 in cash. He fled to

St. Paul, Minnesota, where Pinkerton's, investigating, learned he had gone to Spokane where in fact he was arrested by two Spokane police officers and returned to Canada for trial. After the Spokane officers collected the reward for his arrest, Pinkerton's took pains to point out to Hussey that it was against agency policy to accept rewards and it was unfortunate that the B.C. Police had had to pay up.[4]

Five years later, a far more embarrassing embezzlement occurred: Hussey's own administrative sergeant, W.R. Atkins, ran off with $1,200 in public funds. The episode, though treated with extreme seriousness has, in retrospect, its amusing aspects. Atkins, a well-educated and personable Englishman, had been appointed to his position in 1897 with recommendations from Senator C.F. Cornwall, formerly lieutenant-governor of British Columbia, and Walter Langley, mayor of Calgary. Though his work with the B.C. Police was satisfactory he must have hankered for broader pastures, for he applied to Pinkerton's two years later for a position in its Portland office.[5] The superintendent there asked Hussey about Atkins since he had given Hussey's name as a reference. For whatever reason, Atkins did not get the job. On June 13, 1900, Atkins failed to show up for work. Not until several days later was it realized he had disappeared, and it was still later when funds were found missing. Atkins had gone to Seattle where, on the sixteenth, he called on Ahern at Pinkerton's, with whom he was, of course, well acquainted through dealings with the agency. He told Ahern he was in Seattle in connection with a B.C. Police matter but regrettably was a bit short of money as unexpectedly he had to remain at a hotel overnight, and could Ahern lend him twenty-five dollars to tide him over? Of course. Atkins gave a receipt. Next morning he called again on Ahern to say he was obliged to return to Victoria and required further funds. Could Ahern let him have another twenty dollars? Certainly, and another receipt was given. But Atkins did not go to Victoria; instead he completely disappeared. It was soon realized that he had absconded from Victoria and had conned Ahern into lending him money; the British Columbia government repaid it.

The ensuing search was relentless, for the B.C. Police had red faces and so did Pinkerton's: so embarrassed were the B.C. Police that even six months after Atkins' disappearance he was said to have "retired." Over two thousand posters bearing Atkins' photograph were printed in Portland under the imprint of Pinkerton's National Detective Agency on behalf of the B.C. Police offering a reward. Copies were sent to every police force in Canada and to virtually every police force in the United States, from the major cities — such as Denver, Boise, Philadelphia, St. Paul, and San Francisco — to a host of obscure places, such as Gypsum, Colorado; Laramie, Wyoming; and Miles City, Montana. Since Atkins had at one time worked as a ranch hand and in cattle yards, copies were sent to packing-house companies including — a marvellous name — the Slaughter Livestock Company of Albuquerque, New Mexico. Internationally, circulars went to Calgoorlie and Geelong (Australia), Liverpool, and Southampton. Circulars went to every newspaper of any consequence in Canada and in every state of the union, to steamship offices, including Cunard and Hamburg-American Lines, to every railway company on the continent, among them the Atchison, Topeka and Santa Fe; the Wabash; and Lehigh Valley. William Pinkerton in Chicago, and his brother Robert in New York, made it their personal business to ensure maximum distribution.

But all to no avail. Atkins had dropped out of sight. However, the Bible says, "Behold, your sin will find you out." Somehow, a Pinkerton circular came to the attention of the Natal police in Pietermaritzburg, South Africa. An officer of the force there wrote Hussey in 1901 (the circular, though headed by Pinkerton's name, gave the address of the B.C. Police) to say a billiard marker working in a Durban canteen matched exactly the description of Atkins given on the circular and that the man "would be shadowed." Nothing happened for a year. Then the chief of police at Bloemfontein, also in South Africa, telegraphed Hussey to say that Atkins was being held in custody, and that they were awaiting instructions from the B.C. Police. Hussey replied, "Not proceeding with charge." Atkins was released.

Why did the B.C. Police decide to forgive him? Did he have friends at court? Quite possibly. He also had unbounded nerve. In September 1910, Atkins wrote Hussey from Calgary where he was working as an accountant with the big meat packing firm, P. Burns and Co. Ltd. Atkins told Hussey that his wife was in ill health and only a return to a mild climate and a lower altitude on the coast would improve it. He went on: "I beg to enclose herewith an application to the Honourable the Attorney General to take up residence in Vancouver. The firm [P. Burns and Co. Ltd.] wishes me to join the Vancouver District office staff ... and if I do not go I expect I shall be looking for employment again." The extraordinary effrontery displayed by an embezzler asking, in effect, for immunity was successful: he was not prosecuted. He may have slipped back across the border into British Columbia but certainly not with the blessing of the British Columbia attorney general. Pinkerton's reaction to all this is not recorded.

It is the nature of police work that urgent attention must be given to some crisis or disaster. The foundering of the passenger steamship *Iroquois* was just such an occasion. It capsized and sank within minutes of leaving the dock at Sidney, B.C. en route to Nanaimo through the cluster of islands lying off Vancouver Island in the Gulf of Georgia. The vessel, built in 1900, was well known in the coastal shipping trade and at one time sailed between Seattle and Victoria; indeed, Ahern of Pinkerton's had travelled on her on his occasional visits to Victoria. At the time of its sinking the skipper, Captain A.A. Sears, along with the purser, A.D. Munro, were the owners. Sears was a blustery, abrasive individual who was inclined to cock a snoot at the law. He had three times been convicted of bootlegging liquor off his ship. He had a liquor licence to sell drinks to passengers in transit but he sold liquor by the glass and bottle to crew members and to anyone else who came aboard during stopovers.

S.S. *Iroquois* passing through the narrow channel between north and south Pender Islands c. 1910.

BCARS F-335

The *Iroquois* set off on her last voyage on Easter Monday, April 10, 1911, in a brisk wind and choppy sea. She carried nineteen passengers and a crew of thirteen: the skipper, mate, engineer, purser, cook, and deckhands. She also carried about thirty tons of freight, some of it loosely stowed on deck including such disparate items as horseshoes, sacks of rice, and bales of hay; the weight of the deck cargo contributed further instability to an already top-heavy vessel. One seasoned traveller who had booked passage — a former mariner — took one look at the *Iroquois* pitching at the dock and, considering the weather, refused to board her; he also talked another passenger out of embarking on her.

The *Iroquois* pulled away in the teeth of the wind. Hearing expressions of alarm, Sears yelled to assure the passengers all would be well once the vessel was away from the dock. When she was hardly a mile off, the deck cargo shifted and the *Iroquois*, struck by a heavy wave beam on, healed over and capsized. Those who were not trapped in the saloon or the engine room were thrown into the frigid waters. A few passengers managed to get into a lifeboat which came free of its davits, but its planking was rotten and it soon foundered; all those in it drowned. As the vessel foundered the superstructure broke apart and passengers and crew clung to pieces of it as well as to other bits of flotsam and jetsam. Meanwhile the skipper, the engineer, and three deckhands got into the second lifeboat and headed for shore, making only perfunctory attempts to pick up survivors struggling in the water, and reassuring others clinging to wreckage that the tide would soon carry them safely to land. Once ashore, Sears walked to his nearby home to change his clothes, then called at the police station to report the disaster. The police already knew of the sinking, as did the whole population of Sidney, but it was some little while before the death toll was known. Of the crew, seven survived. Of the passengers, four survived; only one woman was saved. In all, twenty-one drowned and eleven survived. Sears' conduct had hardly been in line with the great traditions of the sea.

The public outcry against him was so great that the B.C. Police feared he might try to decamp before they decided what, if any, charges should be laid against him. They summoned a Pinkerton man to shadow Sears and keep him under constant surveillance until a decision was made. Sears was eventually charged with manslaughter, not because of his callousness towards his drowning passengers and crew, but for gross dereliction of duty in the maintenance of his vessel and setting sail in bad weather when he knew the ship was badly loaded and top-heavy. He was acquitted by a jury after a trial in Nanaimo (held there because of hostile public feeling in Victoria) but lost his mariner's ticket after a hearing in Admiralty Court. The sinking is still recalled as one of the worst marine disasters on the British Columbia coast.[6]

Until fairly recently abortion was a criminal offence or, as it was termed in the Criminal Code, an act (or attempt) to procure a miscarriage, unless of course an abortion was performed to preserve the life of the mother. The crime was a common one. Unmarried, pregnant women had to make a difficult choice: risk social ostracism if they carried the baby to term or risk their lives by having an illegal abortion performed by "abortionists" in less-than-sterile conditions; the woman frequently died of septicaemia or haemorrhage. Occasionally, if the family of the pregnant woman could afford it, a medical doctor could be persuaded to perform the operation safely, but since discovery would result in his professional ruin, a large fee would be required. Often a Canadian woman seeking an abortion would travel to the United States for the procedure and American women would come to Canada. Pinkerton's was involved in investigations of both sorts for the B.C. Police. The cases were grubby but one is worth noticing because of the social standing of the accused, the behaviour on the bench of one of the judges involved in the case, and the fact that the case went to the Privy Council in London (until 1950 the court of last resort for Canada.)[7]

George A. Walkem was a member of a prominent legal, political, and judicial family of British Columbia. He had formed a passionate attachment to a young unmarried woman named Blanche Bond, who was equally smitten by him; she became pregnant. They both agreed she should have an abortion, but where? And by what means? Walkem at first persuaded her to ingest ergot, a fungus preparation that induced uterine contractions which would expel the fetus. She took the drug orally but it was ineffective. They then decided she should go to Seattle to have a surgical abortion. She did, and the pregnancy was aborted safely. Word of all this reached the ears of the Vancouver police and an investigation was undertaken. Pinkerton's was hired by the B.C. Police even though the offence, if there was one, occurred in the city; as had happened in the Bradshaw case, the attorney general of the province decided that the matter should be taken in hand by the provincial authorities. Pinkerton's tracked down the abortionist in the state of Washington — a female doctor who, as it turned out, was well-known for having performed many abortions. No attempt was made to bring her to Canada to appear at the trial. Because none of her patients were known to have died she was in a sense given immunity from prosecution.

In February 1908 Walkem stood trial on two charges, one of counselling an abortion to be performed in the United States and the other of having supplied a drug, namely ergot, to produce a miscarriage. He was convicted. His lawyers appealed to the British Columbia Court of Appeal on the grounds that it was not a criminal offence in Canada for a resident to counsel an offence to be performed in the United States. Even though the evidence was clear that Walkem had supplied ergot in B.C. and therefore had committed an offence within the province, a majority of the judges agreed it was not an offence to counsel what would be a crime in Canada if it was carried out elsewhere and ordered a new trial. This rather erratic ruling may have had something to do with the erratic behaviour of the chief justice, who during an afternoon session of the hearing was clearly intoxicated and passed out on the bench.[8] The conduct of the chief justice, Gordon Hunter, was a public scandal; he had been driven to drink because of a long-festering quarrel with one of his colleagues. He eventually broke his habit and served thereafter with distinction.[9]

The attorney general was so incensed by the decision that he authorized an immediate petition to the Privy Council in London for special leave to appeal, there being no automatic right of appeal. The Privy Council generally refused to hear criminal appeals from Canada and the Walkem case was no exception. It was additionally galling to the attorney general that the Privy Council ordered payment of Walkem's costs of fifty-three pounds, seventeen shillings.[10] The second trial went ahead, however, and Walkem was convicted and sentenced to nine months' imprisonment "without hard labour."

The illegal sale of liquor, or "bootlegging," to use the common phrase, was a frequent occurrence in pre-Great War British Columbia, which is surprising at first glance since it was easy to get a drink in a public tavern. The sale of liquor to Indians, however, was illegal and in the more remote parts of the province, or in the scattered logging and mining camps, the absence of saloons encouraged enterprising individuals, prepared to pay an occasional fine or incur a brief term in jail, into supplying their needs. Thus, public consumption was not tightly regulated (Sundays excepted), but bootlegging was and

Pinkerton's (like other agencies) was often hired to do undercover work to catch bootleggers. One can't help but think the operatives would have relished the task since it compelled them to enjoy drinking sprees in the line of duty. The investigation in 1908 by Pinkerton's of drinking and gambling in the railway and mining towns and camps in the East Kootenay region of British Columbia is a good example of attempts to regulate these activities.

Reports reached Victoria of unbridled gambling and drinking in Golden, a mining town on the Columbia River, and Field, in the Rockies, a railway divisional point about three hours distant from Golden by train. Hussey decided Pinkerton's should investigate.[11] Ahern assigned an operative experienced in tunnel and rock work, which, it was thought, would provide him cover by enabling him to secure a job in railway construction at Field. First though, he went to Golden where investigations centred on several hotels, at one of which he stayed (the Queen's), letting it be known he was looking for a mining or railway job. At another, he observed poker games being played openly and illegally in the bar with the house taking a rakeoff. The next day, a Sunday, the operative with a new-found companion bearing the delightful name of Jack Coffee, who was looking for a drink, talked the hotel proprietor into serving them whisky at 7:45 a.m., before breakfast. Several times later in the day the proprietor also served them drinks but complained he had to be cautious because of meddling by a local clergyman, which had resulted in the Sabbath laws being more strictly enforced. The proprietor, who said he had been serving liquor on Sundays for twenty years, felt hard done by at that turn of events.

The operative, learning that a railway tunnel was under construction at Field, announced he would go there to seek work, which he did, getting a job two days later. The Monarch Hotel at Field seemed to be one of the centres of social life for the "tunnel men and construction labourers" when "in town carousing," and the operative found that the local police officer was an habitué, drinking there heavily morning and evening and becoming "intoxicated" and "boisterous." Any of the construction crew in camp wanting a drink hitch-hiked a ride on a slow-moving freight train to Field, heading for a bar; they lamented the absence of an establishment where "drinking, gambling and women are found together" such as one could find in the United States.

Hussey had speculated liquor was being sold illegally out of the company store at the construction site but the operative saw no certain proof of it. However, liquor was being sold by the bottle at the Monarch, evidently with the connivance of the constable, who was plied with liquor by the hotel proprietor when on the premises and, on one occasion, supplied with four bottles which he took away with him. The constable also winked at the poker games being openly played in the bar with the hotel taking its "regular house rake-off." The operative found that a second hotel, the Strand, also did a brisk business in selling liquor by the bottle to construction workers and decided to give it a close inspection. He found it, if anything, a livelier place than the Monarch. Also among its regular clientele was the constable, who evidently divided his time between the two establishments. The Strand was a rip-roaring sort of place complete with heavy drinking, continuous poker games, professional gamblers, and the occasional prostitute doing business in the rooms (though not circulating in the bar). The operative has left a vivid description of life at the Strand:

> [I]t is of the usual type found at or near construction camps. It is an agency for relieving Railroad employees of their earnings in the least possible time at the least possible expense and trouble. At the Strand, two agencies are used, namely the bar and gambling tables. The bar is operated very much on the same lines as saloons in the states. Seats are provided for rounders and loafers who loiter about waiting for men who come from camps with their earnings.

Because the Strand is only one of two places where paycheques can be cashed, men, he says, go there "and this of course calls for drinks and treating and the rounders gather round and the man is importuned for drinks and money to eat on. In most cases the man becomes intoxicated and spends or gives away his money in the course of an evening. The practice is to permit him to drink as long as he can stand at the bar." Those who didn't spend all their money at the bar fell prey to the gamblers.

The operative, believing he had done and seen all that had been asked of him, returned to Golden the following day, finishing off his stay again at the Queen's Hotel, and also on a Sunday. He was able to purchase a drink for himself at the hotel from a reluctant proprietor. The operative's final observation was that to judge by "the number of thirsty men in town" no liquor was being sold illegally. His reports about the Strand Hotel and the disorderly conduct of the police officer in Field certainly caught Hussey's eye, and undoubtedly action would have been taken against the hotel and the constable dismissed from the force, but Pinkerton's took no part in those measures.

Occasionally Hussey would help out old friends by engaging Pinkerton's for them. Such a one was William Ward Spinks, the judge of the County Court of Yale, a judicial position not quite so elevated as that of a Supreme Court judge but considerably above that of justices of the peace and magistrates.[12] Their friendship went back to the days when Spinks practiced law at Kamloops, B.C., where Hussey, before his appointment as superintendent of the British Columbia Police, was government agent and court registrar. For some years Spinks had lived in rather baronial splendour in a large house at Vernon, British Columbia, employing several Chinese servants, including the cook, and a housekeeper, Mrs. Elizabeth Blackwood, a Scottish lady who served also as Mrs. Spinks's maid.

In the spring of 1908, Spinks and his wife noticed an item of jewellery was missing. He suspected one of the Chinese servants had taken it and, accompanied by his "boss Chinaman" and armed with a warrant he had managed to obtain, searched various premises in Chinatown. He wrote Hussey, telling him what he had done. In August, he and his wife were alarmed to discover a quantity of really valuable jewellery was gone — necklaces, pendants, brooches, rings, and bracelets. This time he suspected the housekeeper, who had left Spinks's employment a little earlier, and immediately wrote Hussey for help: "Put a good man on but I know you of old. If anything can be done you can do it." In the upshot, Hussey went to Seattle to consult Ahern and the two decided a female operative should be sent to Vernon to strike up an acquaintance with Mrs. Blackwood and to gain admission to her house in an attempt to either see the jewellery or have her talk about it. The operative, from Spokane, went to Vernon, reporting to Spinks, but learned nothing. (This seems to be the first, and only, occasion on which Pinkerton's sent a female undercover operative into Canada.) Meanwhile, Pinkerton's had printed and circulated a poster throughout the United States with exact descriptions and drawings, made by Spinks, of the missing jewellery in the hope that an antique dealer or pawnbroker who had bought any of the articles might come forward. No luck.

Spinks then vacated his role as judge and took up that of a detective investigator, working with a male Pinkerton operative who had also been sent up to Vernon. He made elaborate cloak and dagger arrangements to have Mrs. Blackwood shadowed by Pinkerton's when she travelled to Victoria to see her husband, who was working there. In Vernon, the Pinkerton man searched the Blackwood house and, though not finding the valuable missing jewellery, did find a few trinkets including a small silver box, identified as belonging to Mrs. Spinks. The judge, accompanied by the Pinkerton man, interviewed Mrs. Blackwood. Spinks told Hussey he had been careful to administer the "usual warning" — that is, "You need say nothing but anything you do say may be used in evidence," or words to that effect. The lady gave contradictory explanations for her possession of Mrs. Spinks' items. Spinks then, quite improperly even had it been by a police officer, offered her immunity from prosecution if she would "give up the jewellery." She broke down, weeping, but admitted nothing. Later, Spinks and his wife interviewed her again (this time without administering a warning which Spinks realized, as he told Hussey, would probably invalidate any incriminating statements made by her). She claimed Mrs. Spinks had given her the articles. Mrs. Blackwood left Victoria where, soon after her arrival, she was arrested on a warrant taken out by Spinks after laying formal charges, and returned to Vernon. She stood trial early in November 1908 before a Supreme Court jury with Mr. Justice Archer Martin presiding, charged with the theft of the few trivial items but not of the important ones. Both Spinks and his wife testified; Mrs. Blackwood testified in her own defence, giving innocent explanations. The local newspaper described the "bullying attitude" of the Crown prosecutor in his cross-examination of her, which gained her the sympathy of the jury.[13] It was her word against that of the Spinks. It must have been humiliating for the judge and his wife when the jury stayed out only ten minutes before acquitting her.

Throughout this remarkable episode — characterized by his most injudicious behaviour — Spinks bombarded Hussey with letters describing the progress of his (that is, Spinks's) investigation. Hussey must have wished he had never gotten involved in the business; perhaps his only consolation was that Spinks, and not the British Columbia government, had paid Pinkerton's.

Six

Manhunts

Pinkerton's played a prominent role in the search for two fugitives whose exploits have passed into the folklore of the country. The agency was hired a number of times by provincial police authorities to find escaped criminals — and sometimes to find a parent who had run off with children following a matrimonial dispute — but the cases of Bill Miner, the train robber, and Simon Peter Gunanoot, the trapline outlaw and accused murderer, have become legendary.

Bill Miner in the jail yard at Kamloops, B.C., awaiting his trial for train robbery.

PA

Born in 1843, Bill Miner was an American thug. Until 1904, the year he became notorious in Canada, he had established in the western United States an unsavoury reputation as a robber of stagecoaches and trains, and had spent more of his life in jail than out of it. His robberies were always at gunpoint, though you could say this much for him; he never actually shot anybody. In 1901 he had been released from San Quentin prison in California after serving twenty years of a twenty-five-year sentence for train robbery. Two years later he and his confederates bungled a train robbery in Oregon, but Miner managed to evade capture and escaped into Canada. Pinkerton's had been very much involved with Miner and his crimes in the United States, and had assembled a fat dossier of his exploits and jail records. Miner was not a nice man — he was a pistol wielding bandit — yet he could turn on the charm and beguile strangers into believing he was a fine fellow and a law-abiding citizen or, as will be seen, he could beguile prison officials into believing a hardened criminal had reformed. It was in just such a guise that, early in 1904, under the name of George Edwards, an alias which he was to use often, he came to the tiny community of Aspen Grove, a few miles to the north of Princeton, B.C. There he assumed the role of a southern gentleman seeking a rural life and wanting nothing more than to run a few cattle and to lead a Christian life in peace and quiet. In doing so, he became a local fixture, one who patted babies on the head, and took up religion. But he had not forgotten about train robberies.[1]

On the evening of September 10, 1904, the Canadian Pacific Railway Company's transcontinental express, the *Imperial Limited*, was westbound from Toronto. The train slowed down as it approached Mission Junction (now simply "Mission"), a small community about an hour's run from Vancouver, to take on water. The train was made up of engine, tender, express and mail cars, the baggage car, and a number of passenger coaches. In a safe in the express car were two separate shipments of gold dust (valued at about $6,000) destined for assay offices, and approximately $1,000 in cash. But through bad luck, Miner and his gang took much less than they had expected. They had been tipped off that a far larger consignment of gold dust would be on the train, but the shipment was late in arriving at the connecting point in Ashcroft, B.C., and did not make it aboard the westbound train.[2] As the train was pulling away from the water tower masked gunmen who had climbed over the coal tender into the engine cab confronted the engineer and fireman and, at gunpoint, ordered them to take the train down the tracks a couple of miles where it was to stop. The crew obeyed. At the stop the bandits ordered the crew to disconnect the passenger cars. This was done. The bandits ordered the truncated train further down the track a couple of miles before stopping again. While the crew were held at gunpoint, Bill Miner — for he it was — got into the express car and forced the guard to open the safe, taking out the gold and cash. Although virtually everyone writing about Bill Miner says he also stole Australian government bonds valued at $250,000 and another $50,000 in United States bonds, their actual existence, as will be seen, is in question. In any case, there was no doubt about the theft of the gold and cash. The night was foggy and Miner and his two confederates disappeared into the murk.

Canada had just experienced its first train robbery, and it caused a sensation. First on the scene were officials of the railway company, officers of the B.C. Police, followed soon after by Pinkerton men headed by Assistant Superintendent James E. Dye from Seattle, hired jointly by the CPR and the B.C. Police and, still later, by Inspector R.G. Chamberlin of the Dominion Police, from Ottawa, who happened to be in Vancouver at the time of the robbery. Pinkerton's, with its long knowledge of Miner and all his works, led the initial search. Dye, from descriptions of the bandits and their modus operandi, immediately confirmed Miner's identity as the ringleader. He found the tracks of three men leading to a point on the Fraser River where a boat had been reported stolen, picked up the tracks on the opposite shore which led to the remains of a campfire, and ultimately to Linden, Washington, which was about ten miles south of Mission. There the trail petered out, in spite of searches over the next six months to find him. Rewards were posted: $6,000 by the CPR and $2,000 by the B.C. Police. The last to give up on the search were the Dominion Police; by May 1905 A.P. Sherwood stopped looking for him and relied on the rewards to flush him out.[3] It seems that Pinkerton's may have had Miner in its grasp at one stage and then lost him. In writing to G.E. Burns, the man in charge of the Miner investigation for the CPR, Sherwood said mysteriously: "Many thanks for your kindness in sending me the enclosed. It is certainly pretty rough on the Pinkerton people and I am sure 'W.A.' [Pinkerton] must feel very cheap. He has of course done the honourable and straight thing in making a clean breast of the whole matter." At the very least, it seems, Pinkerton's was responsible for some unexplained lapse in the search.[4]

Miner had undoubtedly gone back to the United States, but not for long since soon after the robbery "George A. Edwards" reappeared in Aspen Grove, still kindly in appearance with his flowing hair and grey walrus mustache, still likable, and evidently prosperous, for he had money which he quite freely spent in the area.[5] But his bucolic life was a sham, for it was train robbery that was in his blood. Early in 1906 he hooked up with two fellow thugs from the United States, one a man named Shorty Dunn, and began planning the holdup of another CPR train, this time near Kamloops, B.C. about seventy miles north of Princeton. In a statement he made to the B.C. Police after his conviction and incarceration in the British Columbia Penitentiary, Miner said he had travelled with his companions up to a point about fifteen miles east of Kamloops where they camped for five or six days, scouting the situation and deciding on the most favourable place to stop the train and rob it.[6] On April 30, 1906 at 1:00 a.m. the westbound CPR train, the same scheduled *Imperial Limited* as the one held up at Mission, made a stop at Ducks (now Monte Creek). After getting underway, the engineer was startled to find an older man, masked by a handkerchief and goggles, pointing a revolver at him. The robber, who proved to be Bill Miner, ordered him to stop and disconnect the engine and tender, and first car, which Miner assumed would be the express car, from the rest of the train. This done, the engineer on Miner's orders took the train down the tracks and stopped at a point indicated by Miner for a rendezvous with his two companions. They approached what they thought was the express car only to find it was the baggage car, which for some reason had been coupled ahead of the express car which was, therefore, still attached to the main section of the train two miles distant and too far away to bring back. In angry frustration, Miner and his confederates forced the baggage clerks out of the car and looked for loot. The bungled robbery netted them about fifteen dollars in cash that was lying loose around the baggage car. In his haste Miner missed several packages which held a total of about $40,000 in bank notes. The train went on its way. Miner and his friends returned to their camp, shouldered their packs, and headed south towards Princeton hoping, vainly, they would find some stray horses they could ride. They got as far as Douglas Lake, where a posse of police and trackers found them. Miner insisted he was George Edwards, but one of the mail clerks had been aboard the train in 1904 which Miner robbed, and recognized him when his mask slipped. His description of Miner was verified by Pinkerton's, who, though not directly involved in the search, supplied from its records a detailed physical description.

Justice moved quickly in those days and by June 2 all three, Miner and his two henchmen, had been tried, convicted by a jury, and sentenced. Although the mail clerk could swear that the same man had robbed both trains, he could not identify him as Bill Miner; that evidence was supplied by the warden of San Quentin Prison, who had had Miner in his custody for over twenty years. Miner and Dunn were sentenced to life imprisonment, the third man to twenty-five years. The life sentences resulted from Dunn's firing a shot at the police in resisting arrest, wounding one of the officers. All three were taken immediately to the British Columbia Penitentiary at New Westminster.

Stories abound of the manner in which Miner ingratiated himself with prison authorities to secure favours and favourable treatment; of how he insinuated himself into the confidence of the wife of the acting warden and their daughter to convince them he was really a religious man deserving of punishment and resigned to his fate. The favours allegedly included being allowed to grow his hair full length and not be cut to short regulation length; Miner deviously planned this, so it was said, in order that once he escaped he would not have the shorn head of a convict. He was allowed relative freedom of movement within the penitentiary as a trusty, his intentions being to spy out the land so as to determine the best point of escape. On his incarceration he had predicted his escape, and certainly the antiquated prison encouraged him to think he would succeed. The outer wall was wooden and within it was another, but even flimsier, wooden wall. Miner had noticed that there were sections of the wall not within the field of vision of the guard towers. He escaped, with three others, on August 8, 1907, news of which caused as much of a sensation as the train robberies. Most authors writing of Miner agree that he burrowed under the inner fence and, with a ladder, scaled the outer wall to freedom. Because the penitentiary was a federal prison, it fell under the jurisdiction of the federal police force, the Dominion Police. Writing to the inspector of penitentiaries who was investigating the escape, Lieutenant-Colonel Sherwood said he had reliable information that Miner had escaped through the main gate with the complicity of a guard.[7]

By whatever means, Miner had gone and the penitentiary officials were vastly embarrassed by the escape of so notorious a prisoner; the acting warden was later relieved of his post for laxness of duty but not for corruption or connivance in the escape. He had been warned about Miner's plans to escape some days beforehand but had failed to take any precautions. A massive search was launched and rewards posted. Pinkerton's was contacted yet again for Miner's complete physical description, and photo, which were incorporated into police circulars sent to all parts of North America. Various alleged sightings of Miner on islands in the Fraser River and in locations in the Fraser Valley were reported to the police and, though followed up, revealed no trace of him.[8] It was also reported that Miner had made his way back to the Princeton area whereupon the Dominion Police hired a man who had been with the CPR railway police at the time of the 1904 robbery to conduct a search for him. This man, seeing a fine opportunity to make money, bought a complete outfit, revolver, saddle, and kit which he tried to charge off as an expense of the search. Lieutenant-Colonel Sherwood would have none of it, nor did the man find Miner.[9]

Early in 1910, the B.C. Police received reports that Miner had been sighted living on the Flathead Indian reserve at Kalispell, Montana, a small town tucked into the northwest corner of the state, east of Spokane and close to the Canadian border. The police took the reports seriously and hired Pinkerton's to track him down. An operative was dispatched from Spokane, who reached Kalispell on February 6. On the premise that useful information can invariably be found in saloons, he headed for one, but it was Sunday, and all saloons in the town were closed. (One does not expect to find such puritanism in a frontier community.) The Flathead reserve was a very large one on which lived 2,700 Indians in scattered settlements and camps and on which were seven government town sites. In his first detailed report the operative reported that a number of Indians had set up their teepees near Kalispell but there were a greater number at Polson and Dayton, which were two of the town sites on the reserve. As to the local social scene at Kalispell, he reported, "The French prostitutes have all left here and only parlor houses are operating at the present time." The operative does not say if he made inquiries about Bill Miner at these establishments, but he gained no information elsewhere about him. He turned up what he thought was a promising lead. A man named Lawrence Ryan had been allotted a valuable piece of land the previous summer in a government land-settlement scheme, but had never shown up to claim it, nor had he claimed mail sent to him at a Spokane address; the circumstances were so odd that the operative thought the man may have been Bill Miner, unwilling to reveal himself. The operative spent a great deal of time in attempts to locate Ryan, returning to Spokane and checking out every person living there with the name.

The operative then concentrated on finding any white man living on the Indian reserve which, strictly speaking, was forbidden, and accordingly travelled to a number of Indian encampments. He travelled on horseback to some of the more remote communities, calling on ranches and logging and wood-cutting camps, riding up into the hills and into the gulches, and putting up at flea-bitten hotels. He spoke to virtually everyone he met and visited all the saloons and pool halls, always showing Miner's photograph in the hope someone might recognize him. No one did. He did all this in appalling weather: blizzards, heavy drifting snow, and extreme cold. He visited the construction site of a power dam and scrutinized all the workmen; he attended a Roman Catholic church service, peering at all the parishioners. He literally called on butchers, bakers, and candlestick makers in exhaustive but fruitless attempts to find Miner.

On February 22, the operative ruefully acknowledged he was "decidedly out of luck." As it happened, a few days earlier Hussey reached the same conclusion, and the operative was pulled off the assignment on February 28. No one could have been more conscientious in a hopeless task. Miner simply was not in that line of country and remained a will-o'-the-wisp.[10]

Soon after his escape, speculation and rumours grew that Miner had cut a deal: if he was set free he would reveal the location of the $300,000 worth of bonds supposedly stolen from the CPR express car in 1904. Many of those writing of Miner have paid at least lip service to this theory but his biographers have gone to the greatest lengths in alleging it. They have given instances of meetings between Miner and Dunn with police officials, CPR officials, and Pinkerton men in attempts to retrieve the bonds in return for a seeming escape, which was no real escape but a release. Another author, Frank Anderson, on whom the biographers rely as an authority, says that Pinkerton's spent "nearly six months" visiting the penitentiary in connection with these negotiations. There is no reference in official correspondence at the time or in the Pinkerton archive material to any such visits. At the time of the robbery only the gold and cash were reported missing — no reference to bonds whatsoever. And the only member of the train crew whose comments have been recorded,[11] the trainman, talked of the theft of gold dust and cash only — no bonds. In 1907, before Miner escaped, W.A. Pinkerton gave his recollections of Bill Miner and, in referring to the 1904 robbery, made no mention whatsoever of stolen bonds, referring only to the money and gold.[12] And in 1909 the then-president of the CPR, T.G. Shaughnessy, stated that there were no bonds stolen and therefore there was nothing to deal in.[13] To accept the proposition that bonds were in fact stolen and that Miner had hidden them, one has to assume the CPR deliberately concealed their existence and theft in order to save face and avoid embarrassment. Such behaviour is possible, of course, but it really makes no sense. There is nothing in contemporary accounts to support the view and to accept it makes the president a liar. Also, to accept the proposition that the federal government would release a notorious train robber sentenced to life imprisonment as the result of some deal between the CPR and the prisoner is inherently improbable. It seems that if there were discussions about bonds they were the result of one more tale spun by Miner for his own potential advantage; if there is one thing about Miner on which there is universal agreement it is that he seldom told the truth. Still, the speculation about favoured deals for Miner roused controversy which in 1909 reached the floor of the House of Commons, sparking heated exchanges between Minister of Justice A.B. Aylesworth and Conservative members, in particular the member from New Westminster. The debates led nowhere; the government refused to order any official inquiry into the circumstances of the escape, stating it was satisfied the episode had been dealt with satisfactorily by officials on the spot.[14]

On February 28, 1911, P.K. Ahern telegraphed Superintendent F.S. Hussey that Bill Miner had been arrested at Gainesville, Georgia after a train robbery and that "Hussey should lodge detainer" — in other words, start proceedings to extradite him.[15] However, no formal proceedings were taken. Miner was convicted and sentenced to a lengthy prison term. In June 1912 he escaped with two other convicts. Pinkerton's was engaged by the state authorities to find them, which they did; the three men had stumbled into a swamp, one drowned and Miner became seriously ill after drinking the brackish water. He was returned to prison at Milledgeville, Georgia where he died on September 2, 1913. His funeral expenses and grave headstone were paid for by local citizens, hundreds of whom attended his funeral, which was conducted by an Episcopalian minister.

Miner, after what proved to be his final arrest, reportedly said he wanted to be returned to Canada to serve out his term in New Westminster. In a report on the case, Pinkerton's said an assistant superintendent had seen Miner in jail in Georgia to discuss with him a possible return to Canada and that, on the authority of the CPR, Pinkerton's told the state authorities the railway company would pay all the expenses incurred by the state if Miner was sent back to Canada to serve out his term. The authorities, however, concluded he should first serve out his sentence in Georgia. There was no suggestion by Pinkerton's in its record of these discussions that the CPR wanted to get Miner back to Canada so as to make a deal to recover supposedly stolen bonds.[16]

It is hard to explain the hold which Miner had — and still has — on the public imagination. It is compounded in part by the fact that he was one of the downtrodden, robbing trains owned by railway barons — the Robin Hood syndrome, one might say. As a popular joke in British Columbia had it at the time, "Oh, Bill Miner is not so bad, he only robs the CPR once every two years but the CPR robs us every day." In his robberies, he only threatened violence but never injured anyone. There is no denying he had, particularly when older, an old world charm about him, and people not knowing his past or, often when they did know, were prepared to forgive him. When brought to the courthouse at Kamloops for his trial in 1906, approximately one thousand sympathetic persons turned out to greet him. Even the B.C. Police had a grudging respect for him. Let Superintendent Colin Campbell have the last word on the subject. In writing Pinkerton's on learning Miner had escaped from the Georgia prison he said: "The old man is good stuff and may yet visit his old hunting grounds in British Columbia."[17]

The search for Miner was nothing compared to the time and energy spent by Pinkerton operatives in looking for Simon Peter Gunanoot during the summer and winter of 1909–1910 in the north-central region of British Columbia. It was in fact the longest and most expensive investigation undertaken by Pinkerton's on behalf of any government or police body in Canada. Gunanoot was a wanted man, accused of the murders of two men in Hazelton, B.C., in 1906. He

Simon Peter Gunanoot after his surrender in 1919.

BCARS A-4796

had fled to avoid arrest and when Pinkerton's was hired he had been a fugitive for three years. A member of the Gitksan tribe, Gunanoot was born at Kispiox just north of Hazelton about 1874. He was law abiding, well liked, and respected in the small inland community of Hazelton, and also prosperous. He owned a general store at Kispiox, he was a successful trapper on his own traplines; he farmed his fine property along the banks of the Skeena River, on which he kept a string of pack horses.

Packing was big business at Hazelton in those days. The town was at the head of navigation on the Skeena. After the ice break-up in the spring, paddle-wheel ships steamed up the fast-flowing and hazardous river bringing in supplies. Much of this freight was transshipped by pack train to settlements and communities even more remote than Hazelton. One of the major destinations was the Yukon

Fourth Cabin — Yukon telegraph line. The Pinkerton men called at this cabin during their fruitless search for Simon Peter Gunanoot.
BCARS B-1319

telegraph line which ran from Ashcroft to Dawson city. North of Hazelton there were nine maintenance cabins roughly every twenty miles manned by two men, who depended on the pack trains to bring in sufficient supplies to tide them over the long winters marked by frigid temperatures and heavy snow. There were also unmanned cabins, known as refuge cabins, holding supplies for emergency use by winter travellers. Before the days of the railroad and motor vehicle transport Gunanoot and other pack train operators made a good living at hauling in tons of supplies to their isolated customers, all of whom had to be supplied before winter ice halted navigation on the Skeena. What with trapping and hunting in the mountainous region north and east of Hazelton and with packing, Gunanoot was thoroughly familiar with the vast area, knowing it like the back of his hand — knowledge which served him in good stead during his time on the run.

On an evening in June 1906, Gunanoot, in what proved to be a tragic decision, dropped in to the Two Mile Hotel to see packer friends who had gathered for a night of roistering before setting out next morning on the pack trail to Babine Lake. The pack animals, horses and mules, grazed contentedly on the adjacent meadows while their owners and handlers got drunk in the bar. One of the employed packers, not an owner like Gunanoot, was Alex MacIntosh, a local rowdy who had that very day been released from jail on condition he leave town for a while by joining a pack train. Both he and Gunanoot had known and disliked each other for years. That night each man had far too much to drink. When Gunanoot spotted MacIntosh helping himself to several bottles of liquor while the bartender, who had passed out, lay on the floor, Gunanoot remonstrated with him. MacIntosh drew a knife and slashed Gunanoot's cheek, cutting his own finger badly in the process. Not surprisingly the two started fighting; MacIntosh made insulting remarks about Gunanoot's wife, saying she was nothing better than a prostitute and bragging that he had often slept with her. In the presence of various witnesses, Gunanoot, enraged, vowed to ride home — about five miles distant — to get his gun and return to "kill" or "fix" MacIntosh. Gunanoot then left the bar. An hour or so later MacIntosh decided to ride over to the nearby hospital to have his finger dressed before setting off on the trail. He did not return, nor did Gunanoot. Several hours later MacIntosh's body was found on the hospital trail with a single bullet wound through the back. Still later the body of another packer, Max Leclair, a stranger to both Gunanoot and MacIntosh, was found, also with a bullet through the back, on the trail in the direction of Gunanoot's property. Leclair had not been one of those partying at the hotel.

Gunanoot had in fact returned to his house for his gun, behaving like a wild man according to his wife and a neighbour, riding off yet again, still in a frenzied state, in the direction of the hotel with his brother-in-law, Peter Himadam. It seemed pretty evident to the police that Gunanoot shot MacIntosh, but what reason could there have been to shoot Leclair? Perhaps Leclair was simply unlucky: having shot one man Gunanoot encountered Leclair and, unhinged, shot him, or, more likely, Himadam or Gunanoot shot him to protect themselves in the belief Leclair was a police officer sent to arrest them. (At that period B.C. Police were non-uniformed.) The police summoned a posse of "specials" — men sworn in as constables for a particular purpose — and rode out to Gunanoot's ranch. They found his wife, Sarah, his father, and Sarah's sister, the wife of Peter Himadam who was suspected of complicity in the homicides but who, along with Gunanoot, had eluded the police by hiding in the dense bush. Over the next two days, Gunanoot and Peter covertly made their plans for escape. Gunanoot shot his horses, presumably to prevent their use in any search for him, and all his dogs. He gathered up his family — his wife and three children, his father, and his mother — and Himadam and his wife and the party clandestinely set off on foot up the Skeena River Valley heading for Kisgegas and thence to Bear Lake northeast of Hazelton, a long journey on foot. (Gunanoot had ancestral connections with the area; he was married at Bear Lake and two of his children had been baptized there.) Thus began Simon Peter Gunanoot's long exile.

For two years the police made continuous and intensive efforts to find him by mounting one unsuccessful search party after another. The attempts were bedevilled by Gunanoot's friends, who did their best to warn him of impending danger, by ineptitude on the part of police officers and rivalry among them to gain the glory of a capture, and, more important, by the vastness of the area into which he had fled. The police never really had any idea where Gunanoot might be at any given time and Gunanoot's friends in the region, white and native alike, were not prepared to inform on him; consequently the searches amounted to chasing down rumours. After 1908, the police launched no further search parties hoping the posted rewards would flush Gunanoot out, although they did hire several informants claiming to have knowledge, but who turned out to be opportunistic frauds.

In May 1909, Superintendent F.S. Hussey decided as a last resort to call in Pinkerton's. First he sought authority from the attorney general, W.J. Bowser, who in turn sought authority, readily granted, from the premier, Richard McBride. Once again, Hussey travelled surreptitiously to Seattle to consult P.K. Ahern. The retainer of Pinkerton's was odd. There was no doubt in the minds of the police who the perpetrators of the murders were; the problem did not lie in solving a crime but finding the men responsible. Obviously Pinkerton men could not be sent openly into the hinterland but would have to go under some guise which would conceal their purpose; Hussey and Ahern decided the Pinkerton men should pose as prospectors.

Gunanoot was known as an avid prospector who had staked many claims and it was reasoned that if he heard of prospectors nearby he would approach them out of curiosity or in the hope of being given badly needed supplies. If he did reveal himself, the Pinkerton men would get word of his location back to the police in Victoria on the Yukon telegraph line using a pre-arranged code; officers would then be sent out to make an arrest. As well, the Pinkerton men were to keep their eyes and ears open for potential witnesses, persons who spoke to Gunanoot and Himadam after the murders and to whom they might have made incriminating statements. Ahern assured Hussey that Pinkerton's could supply operatives with practical experience as prospectors and accordingly two Pinkerton men left Seattle for Vancouver on May 19, 1909 (sailing, incidentally, on the SS *Iroquois*).[18] Hussey took with him to Seattle copies of police reports, statements of witnesses, evidence from the inquests, relevant correspondence, and maps — all of which he left for the operatives to study before they embarked. It was not encouraging to find from their first report that they had not read the maps correctly, for they placed Bear Lake "southeast" of Hazelton and not "northeast." The operatives were correct, however, in identifying the lake as the place where Gunanoot was last seen, for quite by chance a party of prospectors had bumped into him there soon after the murders, but not knowing of events had not realized until several weeks later who it was they had met on the shores of the lake.

On arrival in Vancouver they outfitted themselves: broad brimmed hats, thick wool shirts and mackinaw jackets, heavy underwear and trousers, stout high-laced boots, as well as a tent, mosquito netting, picks, shovels, billy-cans, and, most important perhaps, guns and ammunition, for they would have to live off the land as they travelled. They also purchased a reliable map to take the place of the rudimentary sketch which had led them into error. With delayed sailings of vessels from Vancouver and lengthy delays of the vessels travelling upriver on the Skeena, the two operatives did not reach Hazelton until June 4, having amassed, however, from fellow passengers, considerable information about Gunanoot and Himadam and the reputed circumstances of the homicides — all of which they incorporated in meticulous detail into their lengthy reports.

The two operatives spent a full week in Hazelton at a hotel. The town was crowded, relatively speaking, with prospectors and packers either getting ready to leave for interior points or recuperating from long stays in the backwoods. They were obviously adept at steering the conversation towards Gunanoot and Himadam and the details of the crime without compromising their cover. Several points consistently emerged from everyone they spoke to. The two fugitives would never be turned in because they had universal sympathy from community members who felt MacIntosh got all he deserved for his insulting remarks about Gunanoot's wife, though there was less unanimity about Leclair. All those speaking to the operatives said it would take a ruse to capture the two men — perhaps, somebody suggested, policemen disguised as prospectors since there was a lot of prospecting in the area where Gunanoot and Himadam were believed to be. All agreed it was most probable the two fugitives were roaming the regions around Bear Lake, a small lake, and Babine Lake, a very large one. But no one knew for sure and the fugitives might just as well have been somewhere else within what was considered the limits of the search area. This comprised roughly a rectangular chunk of north-central British Columbia bounded on the west by the present-day Stewart-Cassiar Highway to the edges of Spatzizi country (now Spatzizi Wilderness Park) where the headwaters of the Stikine River are found, about 250 miles distant from Hazelton. Thence the line ran eastward to Gunanoot Mountain (as it has been officially known since 1945), a peak in the Skeena mountains from which a line ran southward to Groundhog Mountain — and Groundhog country — where prospecting for anthracite coal was active and where the sources of the Skeena River were; still farther southeast the line ran to Bear Lake and to Babine Lake, the northern end of which is about fifty miles from Hazelton. Within this area are mountain ranges, soaring peaks, deep river valleys, dense bush, and steep terrain, though there is considerable open country around Groundhog Mountain. The region is magnificent, though black flies and mosquitoes plague man and beast in summer and heavy snow and frigid temperatures make winter travel dangerous. Indeed, Gunanoot's father died from the effects of the extreme cold, the temperature in the winter of 1906–1907 falling to a record low of fifty degrees below zero on the Fahrenheit scale. Gunanoot announced the death of his father to all and sundry by blazing the news on a tree in the Kispiox Valley and signing his name.

The operatives not only passed on information about Gunanoot and Himadam — which in retrospect was reasonably accurate — they also reported violations of the liquor and hunting laws by Indians and white men alike and the lax attitude towards these infractions by law enforcement officials. (One of the rumours they passed on was that

Bill Miner had been seen in Prince Rupert and was probably on his way to Hazelton, though his permanent hiding place was in Ontario!) More relevant to the present day, which has seen a proliferation of land claims by Indians in this region of British Columbia, they spoke of unrest among Indians at Kitseguecla and Kitwanga (down river from Hazelton), of hostility to recently arrived white settlers and of the belief the land belonged to the natives. In the upshot, the two men decided, sensibly, to start their search at Babine Lake. They obtained detailed descriptions of the fugitives but had no photograph (they received one a month later). As yet the local police office at Hazelton was unaware of the undercover operation; the two operatives sent their reports to Ahern in Seattle who, in turn, forwarded them to Hussey in Victoria. They rented "two gentle ponies" for thirty dollars each, loaded their supplies onto the animals, and, on June 12th, set off on the trail to Fort Babine at the top end of the lake, which they reached ten days later. There was considerable activity at the Hudson's Bay Company trading post there with Indians bringing in the winter's fur catch for sale and various prospectors, both white and native, who had been working farther north, coming out of the bush. There were lots of people to talk to and conversations were duly recorded and passed on. As yet, they had found no one who had recently laid eyes on Gunanoot or Himadam. They rented a canoe (leaving their "gentle ponies" in the care of the Hudson's Bay Company manager) and gradually worked their way southward on Babine Lake, one of the longest and largest in British Columbia. They camped where they saw other people, mostly Indian, from whom they gleaned a mishmash of rumours and speculation about the whereabouts of the fugitives. All expressed, however, enormous admiration for Gunanoot and Himadam as skilled outdoorsmen and hunters who would certainly evade all pursuers.

They arrived at the south end of Babine Lake on July 10, from where they walked over the short established trail, or portage, to Stuart Lake. (This portage is the divide between two watersheds: the Skeena draining westward and the Fraser draining eastward.) At this point the operatives were approximately one hundred miles southeast of Hazelton, as the crow flies. After spending a week at the portage talking to the locals and the occasional prospector in vain attempts to gather useful information, the operatives retraced their journey on Babine Lake and reached the Hudson's Bay Company fort several days later. There they spoke to the government mail carrier from Hazelton into the Omineca gold fields (on the Ingenika River to the northeast) whom they assumed to be a reliable person; he said he had not seen the fugitives nor had he met anyone for over a year who had. An equally reliable informant was the Hudson's Bay Company manager who gave it as his opinion, correctly as the subsequent history of relations between whites and Indians in the Hazelton area has shown, that the Indian unrest on the Skeena was linked to the failure of the police to find Gunanoot and Himadam: "If they couldn't find criminals what could they do to us?" Of more immediacy, the manager also linked the unrest to the error of telling the operatives that the government had hired "private men" to search for the fugitives. At Babine they had a minor contretemps involving their horses. As they reported:

> This morning we learned that our packhorses had strayed away or more probably had been driven away by the Indians for the purpose of getting paid to go after them which we learn is done frequently. Learning from the Indians that our horses had been seen 25 miles from here we necessarily had to pay them to go after the horses.[19]

They spent a further ten days at Babine, again talking to many people before returning to Hazelton, which they reached on July 29 after an absence of six weeks. There they were caught up in the local ferment about a possible uprising by the Indians to assert entitlement to the land.[20] The local police official (who was still unaware of the undercover role) told the operatives who talked to him of the fugitives that no police party would ever capture them and that only people travelling incognito in wintertime on snowshoes could hope to track them because in summer the trails were too rough. This remark may have been the genesis of the later plan to launch a winter search. What the operatives did not know while they were re-grouping and planning their future course was that Gunanoot and Himadam had parted company early on, perhaps in the first winter, and remained separated thereafter. The operatives spent nearly a month in and around Hazelton, which was in a considerable state of agitation over a threatened revolt by the Indians, and their daily reports are replete with references to that matter; Hussey read their reports carefully, to judge from the many sections underlined by him, and frequently conferred with the attorney general about a suitable response to any outbreak of violence. During that month the operatives heard many stories about the fugitives' prowess as marksmen, which were true, and much speculation and rumour about where they might be — again, local people not knowing that Gunanoot and Himadam were no longer together. The operatives made day trips or sometimes overnight trips to points in the Kispiox Valley poking around. To the Indians they spoke mostly in Chinook, the lingua franca of whites speaking to an Indian; one wonders where they picked up the lingo. They made an important contact, one which they followed up later. A Kispiox Indian, Tom Lula, just arrived in Hazelton from the coast, told them he had seen Gunanoot immediately after the shootings. Lula claimed that Gunanoot said he had shot both men and that Himadam had done nothing more than get ammunition for him. Occasionally the men, to maintain their cover, obtained temporary employment with surveyors running survey lines on mineral claims, but mostly they walked around, hoping to learn something useful.

Late in August James Maitland-Dougall was appointed chief constable for the Hazelton district. Hussey told him that the Pinkerton men were in the area. Ahern notified the operatives to meet with Maitland-Dougall on his arrival at Hazelton, which they did on August 30. Maitland-Dougall's reliability being unquestioned, Hussey had given to him copies of all the reports filed by the detectives, who by this time had become convinced Gunanoot and Himadam were no longer together and told Maitland-Dougall so; thus the search thereafter was concentrated on one man only. They also told Maitland-Dougall they thought the search should be focussed on the upper Skeena, near Groundhog country, but expressed little enthusiasm for undertaking what would necessarily be a four or five month arduous task in the dead of winter. That, however, was precisely what happened, but first they journeyed up the Skeena Valley to the village of Kisgegas, roughly fifty miles northeast of Hazelton, arriving on September 5. There the two operatives split up; one set off on the trail to Bear Lake, due east of Kisgegas, though he did not reach it. He encountered several prospectors, none of whom had seen or heard of Gunanoot. The other operative stayed at Kisgegas to talk to Tom Lula who, it turned out, had at one time been a constable employed by the federal government on the Indian reserve. He reiterated in greater detail his conversations with Gunanoot and Himadam soon after the shootings, the essence of which was that Gunanoot had confessed to the shooting of MacIntosh, giving as his reason the insults levelled by him at his wife, and of Leclair, though not giving any reason. This was valuable evidence from a reliable witness for any future prosecution. After a week or so in Kisgegas and area, the two operatives returned to Hazelton, reaching it on September 16.

They learned from Maitland-Dougall that Hussey, after a further conference with Ahern, had lost his enthusiasm for the search by Pinkerton's, recommending to the attorney general that the search be called off, but the attorney general's blood was up and, again with the approval of the premier, he authorized it to continue. Not only had Hussey lost his enthusiasm, so had one of the operatives, who asked to be relieved, obviously because he did not relish searching in wintertime. He returned to Seattle and was replaced by a local prospector (whose identity was never revealed) chosen by the remaining Pinkerton man. Hussey was dubious of the choice, fearing the man "under the influence of liquor" might give the show away by "talking too much."[21]

On October 3, Operative No. 28 (the senior man) received definite instructions from Ahern to proceed to Groundhog country to prospect for anthracite coal at the headwaters of the Nass, Skeena, and Blackwater Rivers — a well-known area for that mineral (still true today). Accordingly, the operatives started making arrangements for supplies and having them packed to Fifth Cabin, the telegraph line cabin closest to Groundhog Mountain, about 125 miles from Hazelton. They met one George "Burns" (actually "Beirnes") who had spent the previous winter at Groundhog Mountain where, he said, Gunanoot would definitely be found. He drew a map for them of the area where Gunanoot no doubt would be wintering (though "map" is hardly the right word for what was no more than a rudimentary sketch), and told them: "None of the Indians bother his hunting grounds and he is not going to be molested by any Indian. It would not be safe for officers to put in an appearance there, for it would mean getting shot; whether Simon has someone who keeps him posted or not I am not sure, but believe he is kept posted on all the moves of the officers, and I'll bet he knows you fellows are out looking for coal long before you get there. He may keep away from you, but he will not bother you. If he tries to keep out of your sight, you will only see him at a distance, but I believe he will hunt you up to get provisions, and a drink of whiskey." That Beirnes should be discussing Gunanoot's whereabouts at all is curious, for he was probably Gunanoot's best friend among the white members of the Hazelton community; he may have done so while drinking with the operatives for he had a guilty conscience about his co-operation, asking them not to tell anyone they had information from him.

The operatives spent days trying to find Indian packers who would pack their supplies to Fifth Cabin. No amount of haggling could persuade any of them to go beyond Third Cabin and there was great reluctance to go even that far. Eventually they found someone at Kispiox who after sobering up from a drinking bout agreed to go at an exorbitant rate. Accordingly, they laid in their supplies and provisions weighing in total about one thousand pounds; they rented and purchased sleds and five dogs, and dried moose meat and one hundred salmon for them. For themselves they took the usual items: bacon, flour, sugar, and tea. They would have to rely on shooting game for fresh meat. After frustrating delays, they finally got away on October 18, heading for Groundhog country. They made good time, arriving at Third Cabin, about eighty miles from Hazelton, on the twenty-fourth. As he said he would do, the Indian packer returned to Kispiox. Thereafter they were obliged to relay their provisions, loading about twenty-five pounds on each dog and each man carrying about fifty pounds. In this fashion, they arrived at Fourth Cabin on November 2 in fourteen inches of snow, too soft to use the dog sleds and necessitating further canine and manual relays of supplies from cache to cache. At Fourth Cabin they met a prospector who had just returned from Groundhog Mountain, about forty-five miles to the north, who claimed to have seen Gunanoot at a distance and had also seen children's footprints in the snow (it will be recalled Simon took his children with him). The operatives began to give serious thought to just what they would do if they met Gunanoot. How would they bring him in? Or should they? Or should they just get word to Maitland-Dougall in Hazelton and let him worry about it? They decided the latter would be the best course.

Considering the bad weather the operatives met a surprising number of people camping between Fourth and Fifth Cabins: an Indian trapper and his wife, prospectors, and travellers. None had seen Gunanoot but all had heard of him and were convinced he was in the Groundhog area. One prospector said he was convinced Simon was in the area because near his own cabin he had found snowshoe tracks of an adult, and what appeared to be tracks of a woman and child. The operatives soon ran into difficulties all stemming from the fact that the Indian packer whom they had hired at Kispiox would not travel beyond Third Cabin, forcing them to move their provisions on foot towards Fifth Cabin, near Groundhog Mountain, by establishing caches in successive stages. After discovering an unoccupied shack near Fourth Cabin they bent their efforts towards moving their winter

supplies to it, from which they planned to travel to Fifth Cabin. Bad
weather prevented transporting their main supplies, so with only a few
provisions they set out northward and did reach Groundhog
Mountain, where they found what they believed to be recent
snowshoe tracks. Judging the snow to be sufficiently frozen to support
a sled they returned to their shack, loaded all their supplies onto it,
hitched up the dogs and set out. But they had misjudged; the sled fell
through the river ice and most of their supplies were lost: flour, sugar,
tea, bacon, and dog food. This was a disaster, for the linemen at
Fourth Cabin were themselves short and could offer only meagre help.
(When one speaks of "cabin" with reference to the Yukon telegraph
line, there were in fact two cabins at each point; the linemen were
thrown into close company with each other, and having separate
cabins to eat and sleep in reduced potential tensions. Each lineman
maintained the line over a distance of approximately ten miles north
or south from the "cabin" to a point equidistant from the next
"cabin.") They were compelled to return to Third Cabin to which
point emergency replacement supplies could be packed in. One
operative, #6 (the local man), went back to Hazelton to order
replenishments and #28, who remained, passed his time by moving
such supplies as he could commandeer at Third Cabin northward to
the shack. Among the supplies #6 was to get at Hazelton was rum,
notwithstanding Pinkerton's strict injunction not to drink on the job;
small wonder the injunction was broken in this case. Operative #6
rejoined #28 on December 24 and the two once again travelled north
by sled, moving very cautiously. They arrived at their shack on New
Year's Day, 1910, where they met four Indians travelling south who
had seen Gunanoot in the area a few months previously.

On January 9, the operatives were within ten miles of Groundhog
Mountain in country universally described to them as Gunanoot's
winter quarters. Two days later they discovered the only solid
evidence of his presence. In a campsite, sheltered from snow by the
heavy overhang of trees they found a message written on birch-bark:
"I hunt four weeks only dry one moose. I go way but may be come
back four weeks. S." This had every appearance of being recent, and
was obviously intended as a message. There was no doubt in the
operatives' minds that "S" was "Simon" and consequently they spent
nearly a month searching for further clues. They did discover
another birch-bark message in a similar campsite: "I go hunt moose
maybe I come back. S."[22] Using Groundhog Mountain as a reference
point they carefully searched an area within a radius of fifteen miles

finding only occasional snowshoe tracks. By early February they decided further searching was useless and returned slowly to Hazelton in very bad weather, reaching it on February 25. By coincidence, their return journey was at the very time their Spokane colleague was also discontinuing what had proved to be an equally unsuccessful search for Bill Miner in Montana. In Hazelton they had several de-briefing meetings with Chief Constable Maitland-Dougall, who complimented them on their efforts, even though they had been unsuccessful. He had been galled to learn that in September (when the Pinkerton men were inland) two of Gunanoot's children had been brought to the hospital for emergency treatment. The fact the doctor had not mentioned it to the police until six months later was further indication of the local support for Gunanoot. The services of #6 were now dispensed with and #28 travelled down to Prince Rupert on foot over the frozen Skeena River, the journey taking eight days. He spent two days recuperating before sailing to Vancouver. He went to Victoria as instructed to meet Hussey and the attorney general to report on the expedition. He told them that Maitland-Dougall in Hazelton was doing an excellent job and expressed optimism, like everybody else, that Simon would give himself up within a matter of months.

Gunanoot gave himself up alright — but not until 1919, nine years later, almost thirteen years to the day after the homicides. After consulting his friend George Beirnes and after hiring Stuart Henderson, the best criminal lawyer in British Columbia, and after praying, Gunanoot walked into the Hazelton police office. A police constable from Prince Rupert happened to be relieving the regular duty constable. Gunanoot said, "I am come for my trial." The constable asked his name. Gunanoot said, "Johnson," his baptismal name which he used on formal occasions. The name meant nothing to the officer who told the most famous outlaw in Canada to come back the next day when the regular officer would deal with him. "No, No," Gunanoot protested, going on to say he was Simon Peter Gunanoot and wanted to surrender. The incredulous constable still could not believe who was standing before him but it soon sank in and Gunanoot was lodged in the cells. His surrender and arrest were front page news in every major newspaper in Canada. At his trial in Vancouver in October 1919 he was acquitted. There was not a jury in the land who would have convicted the "noble Indian," as he was referred to often in the newspapers, who over a period of thirteen years had been transformed in the public eye from a vicious killer to a folk hero. His confession to Tom Lula, obtained by the Pinkerton operative, was not used, probably because the prosecutor was not aware of it. The Pinkerton reports had been buried in official files in Victoria. Stuart Henderson may have been aware of it for he emphasized to the jury that there was no reliable evidence positively linking Gunanoot to the crimes. Peter Himadam remained a fugitive for some months longer than Gunanoot and in fact he — and not Gunanoot — holds the record in British Columbia for being a fugitive the longest. He surrendered, but was not brought to trial.

And so, very little of value resulted from the arduous labours of the Pinkerton men — one unused confession and the firing of a B.C. Police officer at Kispiox for drunkenness as the result of reports by Operative #28.

Seven

Dominion Police

In eastern Canada the Dominion Police Force was for many years a patron of Pinkerton's, beginning in the mid-1880s with A.P. Sherwood as commissioner. The force grew out of an earlier body, the Western Frontier Constabulary (the "Frontier" being the boundaries of Upper Canada West, now Western Ontario) which had been founded by John A. Macdonald in 1864 as a protective measure against any repercussions of the Civil War in the United States. Its duty was to gather information on "the existence of any plot, conspiracy or organization whereby peace would be endangered, the Queen's Majesty insulted or her proclamation of neutrality [with reference to the Civil War] infringed."[1] It was this force which Gilbert McMicken headed, and employed, during the Fenian scares of the mid-1860s, carrying out covert and secret investigations. In early 1868, D'Arcy McGee was assassinated in Ottawa; though a Fenian connection with the murder was never directly proved, no one in authority doubted its existence. The murder led to the establishment of the Dominion Police Force later in 1868. The force's original function was to protect federal government buildings and naval yards on both coasts from armed attack and to enforce certain federal laws such as those prohibiting counterfeiting and trafficking in prostitution. Although the force was stated to be national in scope, in practice its activities were concentrated in eastern Canada. Originally the force had two commissioners, one in Ottawa and the other in Montreal. However, that arrangement was short-lived. McMicken became the de facto sole commissioner and in 1869 was officially confirmed in that office. It was during McMicken's de facto commissionership that he worked with Pinkerton's on the famous Reno case.

In 1882, A.P. Sherwood, later Lieutenant-Colonel A.P. Sherwood and, still later, Brigadier Sir Percy Sherwood, became superintendent of the Dominion Police and its acting head. Three years later he became commissioner, a position he held until his retirement in 1918. During his tenure, the national fingerprint bureau (discussed in chapter 2) was founded and during World War I he was in charge of Canada's security and was actively involved in wartime espionage, often with Pinkerton's (as will be seen in chapter 9). In 1920 the Dominion force merged with the North West Mounted Police to form the Royal Canadian Mounted Police. Sherwood became a well-known figure in the Ottawa establishment, and a bit of a social lion as well; he clearly relished both roles. He once declined an invitation from W.A. Pinkerton to speak to the International Association of Chiefs of Police because in his official capacity he was to head the guard mounted for the governor general in opening Parliament.

As with the B.C. Police, so with the Dominion Police; many of its members were recruited from ex-military personnel, but one gets the impression Sherwood subjected prospective members to a more searching inquiry than was the case with the B.C. Police. Unlike the B.C. Police, however, the Dominion force did not engage in general policing duties and perhaps could afford to be more choosy in the selection of its officers. Also, again unlike its B.C. counterpart, the Dominion force did engage in a considerable amount of detective work, limited, of course, by its relatively narrow jurisdiction; counterfeiting, thefts from post offices, and customs fraud are examples. One important function took up a lot of time; keeping track of prisoners on ticket of leave, or "parolees" as we would say today. All prisoners on parole, as today, were required to report, at stated intervals, to someone in authority (not necessarily a police officer) who in turn would advise the Dominion Police.

During his long tenure, Sherwood established a warm personal relationship first with W.A. Pinkerton in Chicago and later with

Robert Pinkerton in New York. The relationship, much the same as that between F.S. Hussey and P.K. Ahern in British Columbia and Seattle, was founded on mutual respect and professional competence.[2] The three corresponded frequently over a twenty-two-year period and after Robert Pinkerton's death in 1907, Sherwood and W.A. Pinkerton continued their correspondence up to and through World War I, until Sherwood's retirement in 1918. They wrote on a wide variety of topics and exchanged all sorts of information, not all of it strictly professional. They constantly kept in touch on matters of mutual interest, motivated by professional courtesy, sending bills only if out-of-pocket expenses were incurred. As Sherwood put it, "I may say that it gives me great pleasure to be able to do something for you in return for the many kindnesses I have received at your hands."[3] They called upon each other for help in locating wanted persons, asked each other for personal favours, and often connected with visits by mutual friends to New York, Chicago, or Ottawa. Once Sherwood asked Robert Pinkerton to lay out the red carpet for a deputy minister and show him the sights of the metropolis, which Pinkerton gladly did. A friend of Sherwood's expressed a desire to visit the famed New York city prison, the Tombs; Robert Pinkerton arranged a tour of inspection for him. It was all very chummy, but always gentlemanly. Occasionally, Sherwood would personally go to New York to interview Pinkerton or his operatives.

Sherwood had occasional dealings with Scotland Yard, officials of which looked upon him as an equal. Now and then a three-way investigation took place involving the Yard, the Dominion Police, and Pinkerton's; trans-Atlantic swindlers were the usual subject of such investigations. The three organizations formed a de facto club, three legs of a stool, none superior to the others. Sherwood wanted to keep it that way. When he learned that a group of people in Ottawa had applied to the appropriate government authority for a certificate of incorporation under the name "Provincial Secret Service Agency" he wrote Robert Pinkerton to tell him. Though the latter's letter has not survived, one can gather its contents, for Sherwood made strong representations and successfully prevented the incorporation.[4]

Though he did not correspond so warmly as the Pinkerton brothers, P.K. Ahern in the Seattle office carried out frequent commissions for Sherwood. In one curious case illustrating the audacity of professional thieves, a man in Seattle telegraphed the postmaster general in Ottawa telling him he had discovered $800 in stolen Canadian currency deposited in a Seattle bank, and suggesting he be appointed agent to take custody of it on behalf of the Canadian government. The postmaster general referred the matter to Sherwood who immediately got in touch with Ahern advising him he would be appointed as agent. It turned out, of course, that the man was a fraud, on the make; Ahern recovered the funds.[5]

Of the subjects which occupied the attention of Pinkerton's and Sherwood, many involved formation or abandonment of romantic attachments combined with flights to the USA or Canada. Sometimes Sherwood's friends or relations were involved. A male relative (Sherwood does not give his name) had become "very intimate" with an American lady whose "social standing" was not "desirable"; Sherwood asked Robert Pinkerton to find out as much as he could about the woman, which he did. The correspondence, however, does not reveal whether the family's fears about the woman's social status were allayed.[6] On the other side of the coin, Sherwood, on behalf of a wealthy friend in Ottawa, asked Robert Pinkerton for full information about an "adventuress" in New York with whom the man's son was living. A firm of private detectives wrote the friend offering evidence of the adultery — for a large fee. Again, the outcome is not known, but Robert Pinkerton was able to tell Sherwood that the detectives were motivated by greed.[7] And in a matter closer to the bone, Sherwood wrote Robert Pinkerton concerning Sherwood's cousin, who had gone to New York to work, had got into extreme financial difficulties, and wound up as a patient in Bellevue, the large New York mental hospital. Sherwood sent some money to Pinkerton in the hope it might help to extricate the man from his problems. Pinkerton got the money to him all right but, sadly, the poor man died soon after; Pinkerton sent Sherwood the death certificate.[8]

The impression one forms of Sherwood through all the correspondence is of a rather patrician figure very conscious of social position (both his own and that of others). It is a view reinforced by a letter to Robert Pinkerton in response to a request from the latter for assistance in some unnamed matter in Quebec City, a request which Sherwood had referred to the High Constable (chief of police) in that city who had botched the business. In a comment typical of an Ottawa patrician, Sherwood told Pinkerton "I think perhaps the matter might have been put in better hands than those of the High Constable, but I know him to be reliable and therefore entrusted him with the matter. But almost everybody left in that ancient city is living in the past ... and therefore have no proper appreciation of time and the necessity of getting a move on though in politics they

are ... up to every trick in the trade both ancient and modern."[9] Such
sentiments are not unknown today. This then is the man who headed
the Dominion Police for over thirty years.

Of the dozens of investigations conducted by the force in association
with Pinkerton's, four are worth mentioning in detail, and of those
four the Alaska Sealing Arbitration and the threatened invasion of
the Yukon are unique. The facts of the other two cases, both in 1904,
are not of any great interest in themselves but what is worth noting is
the level of co-operation between the Dominion Police and
Pinkerton's. Unlike the B.C. Police, who lacked skilled investigators
and, what is more, investigators who could act undercover if called
upon, the Dominion Police in Sherwood's time employed "secret
service" men. Of those men, R.G. Chamberlin, later superintendent,
was the most skilled and a man in whom Sherwood placed the utmost
reliance. His name will appear frequently in these pages. It was he
who happened to be in Vancouver at the time of the train robbery by
Bill Miner and the reason he was there was in connection with a
planned theft from the mail of $10,000 in Bank of Hamilton bank
notes. (Chamberlin was to conclude his law enforcement career as
chief of police of the City of Vancouver.) Sherwood received
information that four Americans who found out about the mail
shipment had through subterfuge conspired to have the mail parcel
taken off the train at Gleichen, Alberta. (Strictly speaking Gleichen
was still in the Northwest Territories, but was soon to become part of
the province of Alberta.) The Dominion Police's information — one
cannot tell its source — was that one of the conspirators would show
up claiming to be the consignee of the shipment, even though the
waybill was from Winnipeg to Vancouver. Sherwood decided to
mount a classic "sting" operation to catch the conspirators and
engaged Pinkerton's, through Ahern at its Seattle office, to carry it
out. The plan was to get to the consignment before the criminals,
mark the package with a code sign usable in evidence, and wait for
the conspirators to appear. To effect this Sherwood at first planned to
employ Chamberlin and Ahern but on reflection, realizing
Chamberlin might be recognized whereas Ahern would be unknown,
instructed Ahern to proceed to Gleichen by himself where he would
be joined by an NWMP officer, in plain clothes, who would act under
Ahern's directions, an interesting example of a Canadian police
officer acting under the orders of an American employee of an
American private detective firm. Ahern went to Gleichen and, posing

undercover as one of the consignees, persuaded the postmaster of his genuineness. When one of the conspirators showed up to claim the parcel the NWMP officer stepped into his role with Ahern standing by, arrested the man, seized the parcel, and eventually all four conspirators were arrested. From the point of view of the Dominion Police, it was a very satisfactory outcome and Sherwood was effusive in his praise of Ahern's — and Pinkerton's — role. For Ahern, who has often figured in these accounts and will continue to do so, acting in an undercover capacity in Canada was a new experience.

The second case was an extradition matter that involved attempts by the Canadian government to extradite a Canadian fugitive from the United States. Isaac Burpee was a merchant in Dawson, Yukon Territory. A friend entrusted him with $600 to pay off the friend's indebtedness at a bank; instead Burpee put the money into his own account. At almost the same time Burpee, who was in partnership, sold off a large quantity of stock and office equipment belonging to the partnership and, on receiving the proceeds of the sale — about $12,000, quite a lot of money — put it into his personal bank account as well and, after withdrawing all his funds, decamped, going "outside." The defrauded friend and the business partner lodged complaints with the police and two separate charges were laid and warrants of arrest issued. At first, the Canadian government declined to involve itself in the affair by applying for extradition — it was learned Burpee had gone to the United States — evidently believing the thefts not to be of sufficient importance to justify the large expenditure of public funds. But pressure was applied in the right place by the right person; the government relented and authorized extradition, if Burpee could be located. At that point the matter was referred to Sherwood who hired Pinkerton's to find Burpee, believed to be in the St. Louis area. Pinkerton's office there did find him; he was arrested to face an extradition hearing.

The extradition was beset with difficulties and delays. Pinkerton's assisted as far as possible, keeping an eye on developments. Flaws were found in the material sent from Canada, but the chief difficulty lay in the reluctance of the district attorney, representing Canada, and eventually of the extradition commissioner, to extradite Burpee on the second charge, that of selling off partnership assets. The extradition treaty made "embezzlement" extraditable and also "larceny or theft" as well as "fraud" by an agent which was made "criminal" by law. The first charge, taking his friend's money, was clearly extraditable as theft but the Americans were dubious about the second, believing the complaint to be civil in nature rather than criminal. At one stage Pinkerton's seriously advised Sherwood that Burpee should be spirited away from Missouri and shipped to California where, it was thought, extradition could more easily be arranged. Sherwood thought about it, but then realized that charges of kidnapping and unlawful confinement might be laid which would prove a major embarrassment. The St. Louis people soldiered on and eventually Burpee was extradited, but only on the first charge and the only one therefore on which he could by law be tried in Canada. He got off lightly. Sherwood and his staff spent a lot of time on the Burpee case, with a rather disappointing result.

In 1897 Pinkerton's carried out an important investigation for the government of Canada arising from the hearings in Victoria, B.C., to decide what compensation should be paid to Canadian sealing vessel owners whose ships were illegally seized by the American navy. The investigation was remarkable, for Pinkerton's, an American agency, was asked by Canada to find evidence in the United States to defeat arguments made by the United States government at the hearing as to ownership of some of the vessels involved; if they were American owned and not Canadian, no compensation would be payable.

Sealing on Pribiloff Islands rookery c. 1895.

NAC PA 51492

Sealing, which became highly commercialized in the second half of the last century, also became highly controversial. Generally speaking, the sealing industry was divided between those who caught the seals on the high seas by shooting them as they floated on the surface of the ocean — the pelagic hunters — and those who went ashore or onto island rookeries to kill the seals by clubbing or shooting them. Of the island rookeries, the Pribilov group was by far the most prolific. Sometimes pelagic sealers would send boats ashore to get their catch. The industry was very lucrative, and vessel owners could make a great deal of money with a good catch. As Canadian sealers started to move into the Bering Strait in pursuit of the seals, they increasingly found themselves at odds with Russia on the one hand and the United States on the other over boundaries within which seals could be taken. As well, sealing was unregulated and there was not much interest in preserving the stock until the 1890s, when it was realized the seals could not be harvested indiscriminately forever.

Beginning in 1886, and continuing until 1889, the Americans seized and confiscated twenty Canadian vessels, virtually all of them based in Victoria. After 1889 and until 1893 the Americans stopped seizing ships but used naval vessels to force the sealers out of the Bering Strait. These actions resulted in predictable protests from Canada and the British government, which in that era conducted Canada's foreign diplomacy. After difficult negotiations, Britain and the United States agreed to submit to an arbitration tribunal five questions relating to sealing in the Bering Strait and the authority of Russia and the United States to control it. The seven-member tribunal convened in Paris in 1892 and 1893 to hear arguments from a battalion of eminent lawyers from Britain and the United States. (One of the British lawyers, incidentally, was Sir Richard Webster who ten years later, as Lord Alverstone, Chief Justice of England, presided over the Alaska Boundary Tribunal in 1903, much to Canada's disadvantage.) In its award of 1893 the Paris tribunal laid down restrictions upon pelagic sealing but did not restrict sealing on land or the islands (regulation of on-shore sealing came later). The tribunal did, however, decree that the seizure by the United States of the twenty Canadian sealing vessels and the pelts onboard was illegal but left the question of compensation to be settled by the United States and Great Britain. After a great deal more wrangling, a further tribunal was set up composed of two judges, one Canadian and one American, which convened in Victoria in November 1896. The principal question to be answered was the ownership of the seized vessels and their value. The most difficult of the two questions was that of ownership. Sealing vessel owners were a notoriously slippery lot. Often they went to great lengths to disguise actual ownership for various reasons: to evade creditors by registering the vessel in someone else's name, or by an American registering a vessel in Canada in the name of a Canadian and flying the Canadian flag to evade U.S. regulations on sealing vessels, or by a partner registering a vessel in his sole name on the pretence that his fellow partner didn't wish to be bothered with the details of ownership, or by placing a vessel in the name of someone who, on its security, could obtain a bank loan which would not otherwise have been granted.

One of the more notorious vessel owners was Joseph Boscowitz who, since his arrival in Victoria many years earlier, had cut quite a swathe financially and socially. He was cantankerous, litigious, and wealthy, and the largest single claimant for compensation from the tribunal. The Americans contended that even if there was only a smell of American ownership in a vessel that would invalidate any claim for it since the entitlement had to be one hundred percent Canadian.[10] Somehow the American representatives at the tribunal learned that Boscowitz might not be all he claimed to be, that he might after all be an American. He had many enemies and it is possible one of them tipped off the Americans. The lawyers representing the ship owners, including Boscowitz, as well as the lawyer representing Canada (nominally Great Britain), then took up the cudgels on Boscowitz's behalf. He had been born in Germany. As a young child he came to Wisconsin with his emigrant father, Aaron Boscowitz. As a young man he left the United States to settle in Victoria and from length of residence had become, so he thought, a British subject and a Canadian. But if his father had acquired United States citizenship while young Joseph was still a minor and still resident in the United States, then Joseph also would have been American, so the American lawyers contended.

It was at that stage that the Canadian lawyers consulted Sherwood who, in turn, called in Pinkerton's to investigate Aaron Boscowitz's status. Sherwood wrote a lengthy letter to W.A. Pinkerton in Chicago setting out the allegations by the United States lawyers and asking Pinkerton as a matter of urgency to make inquiries about Aaron Boscowitz, who had lived in Milwaukee. Pinkerton's discovered that Aaron's name had appeared on a polling list — which certainly was an indication of American citizenship — but there was no evidence he had actually voted. The mere name was inconclusive — he might have falsely declared himself eligible to vote. Far more pertinent, however, was a court record showing Aaron Boscowitz had applied for citizenship but had never actually been granted it. There was, therefore, no proof Aaron Boscowitz was an American citizen, let alone young Joseph, who had left Wisconsin. The arbitration tribunal rejected the American arguments about citizenship and awarded Boscowitz the large sum of $155,000 directly, which was slightly more than half of the total award. Boscowitz could count himself lucky; whether he was aware that only a thorough investigation by Pinkerton's was the source of his good fortune is unknown; certainly Sherwood lauded the agency for its prompt and thorough investigation.[11]

Men of the North West Mounted Police performing gun drill in the Yukon c. 1901.

NAC PA 122800

A plot in 1901 by a secret American organization to invade the Yukon (or, more accurately, a reputed plot) caused great anxiety among senior officers of the NWMP at Whitehorse and Dawson; in retrospect the affair contains elements of opéra bouffe. The Yukon Police District had been established in 1895 and in 1901 there were ninety police officers at Whitehorse among a total population of just under one thousand persons, of whom roughly half were of British origin, the remainder being mostly American. Dawson's population and police detachment were smaller. By 1901 the frenzy of the 1898 Klondike gold rush had subsided, but there was still significant gold mining activity around the two centres. In 1901 the position of the north-south boundary between Alaska and Yukon was unsettled, and remained so until the Alaska Boundary Tribunal of 1903 fixed the demarcation of the Alaska Panhandle. During the 1898 rush, roughly 250 officers of the NWMP enforced Canadian laws and customs and excise regulations. At the foot of the famed Chilkoot Mountain, up which long lines of gold seekers toiled in frightful weather, the force maintained a post at which, among other duties, the police officers ensured prospective miners carried enough provisions for survival on their trip to the goldfields. There were, however, occasional disputes with the Americans stemming from the uncertainty of the boundary, and that uncertainty gave some plausibility to the reported conspiracy, which could be viewed as an attempt to regain lost American territory.

View of Skagway, Alaska, c. 1900.

NAC C 21869

The secret organization behind the plot was the Order of the Midnight Sun, led by H. Grehl and Fred Clark (it was these two men whom Pinkerton's investigated at a later stage of the affair). According to Clark, in a newspaper interview, the Order was first formed in Dawson in the winter of 1900 among disaffected American miners, and soon established branches

Fred Clark, secretary and effective head of the Order of the Midnight Sun.

NAC PA 187297

along the length of the upper Yukon River. As the Order grew and its activities became more widely known, it was decided to move its headquarters to Skagway — beyond the reach of Canadian authorities — along with all the membership and financial records (these were later to excite the attention of the NWMP).[12] Clark was a handsome dog. A.P. Sherwood sent to Fred White, the civilian comptroller of the NWMP, a photograph of him (probably obtained by Pinkerton's) and White remarked upon his "distinguished appearance," both men implying that he seemed to be a cut above the ordinary rabble. The police kept the photograph in their dossier.[13] It was believed that the Order would raise an invading force from Circle City and Eagle City, both in Alaska, and from Skagway, whose merchants had suffered when business dropped off as the initial gold rush had dwindled. Many employees of the White Pass and Yukon Railway running between Skagway and Whitehorse were American, and Canadian officials feared they might form what we would now call a fifth column to infiltrate the Yukon as members of the Order. As a consequence, the police urged Ottawa to enforce labour laws relating to employment of aliens on railways — a federally regulated industry — by insisting that Canadian crews be placed aboard the trains at the border crossing, but nothing appears to have been done.[14]

The first official comment on the threatened invasion came in a letter of September 20, 1901, from Inspector Cortlandt Starnes, in Dawson, to the commanding officer at Whitehorse, Superintendent P.G.H. Primrose. Starnes spoke of information he had received about a conspiracy by a "secret organization [The Order of the Midnight Sun]" and, in a nutshell, described the plot as one which "intended to take possession of the Yukon Territory their plans being to rush Whitehorse, take the smaller detachments along the river [Yukon River] and then, as they were aware that the police in the Yukon only numbers about 200, with their number it would then be easy matter to take the barracks at Dawson. This organization has representatives at both Seattle and Skagway and their plans were nearly complete." Starnes followed this letter up with another a month later which he entrusted to one J.H. Seeley for delivery to Primrose (Seeley will be referred to later in this account). One of the leaders of the "secret organization," H. Grehl, in Dawson at the time of these letters, was said to be recruiting support among American miners; he was placed under surveillance.[15]

Primrose, who had himself heard similar reports, wrote Fred White, who assumed control of the affair, in association with Sherwood of the Dominion Police. Primrose gave his opinion:

> I do not consider myself an alarmist but I always believe in being prepared. I do not think these people could possibly head us off, but at the same time I consider it advisable that the 60 men necessary to bring up to the strength and allow for withdrawals during the winter should be sent in before the close of navigation <u>without fail</u> and also the men necessary to complete each division.[16]

There followed the most bizarre feature of the entire episode. Superintendent Primrose decided to go to Skagway himself to learn what he could of the conspiracy, and took with him J.H. Seeley, whose role in the business was shadowy, to say the least. The latter seems to have been little more than a plausible barfly, though an intelligent one, who had gained Inspector Starnes' confidence by claiming to be a private detective, and persuaded him that he and only he could gain reliable information about the Order. Primrose got drunk en route and upon arrival at Skagway continued his binge. There he insulted the wife of an American army officer who gave him a drubbing. Primrose was arrested, put in jail, charged with being drunk and disorderly, and fined ten dollars by a judge the next day. On learning who he was the Skagway local authorities tried to hush up the matter, but word got out to the local papers, who reported it. Superintendent S.A. Snyder later sent copies of the newspaper accounts to Ottawa.[17] One would have thought if the citizens of Skagway were supporting the plot they would have tried to get maximum publicity out of Primrose's antics. This behaviour by Primrose was a major embarrassment for Ottawa,[18] but provided a momentary diversion from more serious matters; needless to say Primrose learned nothing in Skagway of invasion plans. One would have thought that he had blotted his copybook so thoroughly he would have been drummed out of the force, but he survived. Transferred to Dawson later in 1901, in effect a demotion since the superintendent at Whitehorse was the senior position, he was transferred to MacLeod, Alberta, in 1903, where he served as superintendent until his retirement in 1915.[19] Many months later, in April 1902, P.K. Ahern of Pinkerton's Seattle office, who by then had been retained by the Canadian government, told R.G. Chamberlin, Sherwood's right-hand investigative officer, that he, Ahern, had spoken to a Skagway man who clearly recalled the Primrose arrest. The man attempted to justify Primrose's loutish conduct by speculating that he had deliberately set out to get intoxicated and had spent a lot of money in saloons in doing so in order to get information about the conspiracy from barflies and thus square himself with his superior officer.[20] In view of Primrose's subsequent record with the force, there may have been some truth in the conjecture, but insulting a lady in the presence of her husband was surely carrying the guise too far.

Another NWMP police officer, Inspector F.J. Horrigan, also went to Skagway, sober, where on November 5 he met with the judge of the United States District Court, the United States marshall, and several other local officials. He told them what had been learned of the plans of the Order to establish the Republic of Yukon with the capital at Dawson. The Skagway people dismissed the plans as nonsense. A San Francisco newspaper learned of the meeting and, expressing a similar opinion, editorialized that the whole scheme of the "so-called conspiracy was to again bring the boundary question to the notice of the world."[21] Horrigan's visit made it into the *Ottawa Citizen*, which ran a news story about the plot based in turn on coverage in the *Seattle Evening Times* newspaper on November 20, 1901. The latter cited various grievances held by American miners, alleged corruption by Canadian mining officials, alleged unequal application of the mining laws, imposition of high taxes, and excessive royalties on minerals — and other complaints. The Seattle paper said it was easy for the Order to feed on these grievances but no one in authority gave any credence to plans for an invasion:

> The so-called conspiracy with the object of establishing a republic in the Yukon Territory has been known by the Mounted Police for several months past but it was considered too much of a bubble to be taken seriously; in fact it would be an insult to the better elements of citizens of the United States who are living in the Yukon to assume they would be party to such a scheme. The Mounted Police have dealt with the matter as one of the many subjects for inquiry which come under their attention, and the bubble appears to have been burst by an officer of the force [Horrigan] visiting Skagway in the U.S. territory in search of further information.[22]

While it may have been true that, in the result, the affair was no more than a "bubble," the initial police response was to a credible threat and measures were taken accordingly. Fifty extra police officers were dispatched to the Yukon in dribs and drabs so as not to draw attention to the reinforcement of the garrison. These brought the total strength in the Yukon District to three hundred men, of whom one hundred were stationed at Whitehorse; additional ammunition was shipped in and two Maxim (machine) guns, one placed at Whitehorse and the other at Dawson. Sir Wilfrid Laurier, the Prime Minister, and Clifford Sifton, Minister of the Interior, were both kept advised of the plot and of the strengthening of the Yukon garrisons. The force increased its patrols throughout the district, placed plainclothes officers on board the trains, and put two undercover officers into Skagway.[23] A.E. Snyder, who had replaced Primrose as superintendent at Whitehorse, was not prepared to dismiss the plot as shadow boxing for on January 6, 1902 he sent a lengthy letter to White, the gist of which was that the threat was real but with diligent police work, keeping malcontents under surveillance, for example, the threat could be contained. In response to this White instructed Snyder to "take necessary steps by Palisade or otherwise to protect Whitehorse barracks against attack."[24]

Clifford Sifton, Minister of the Interior.
NAC PA 27943

On May 22, 1902, Fred White, in a memo to Clifford Sifton, disclosed that since January he had "had four men working, confidentially, between San Francisco, Seattle, Skagway and Whitehorse in connection with the Order of the Midnight Sun," and had received reports from all of them; one of these men, R.G. Chamberlin, was at the very moment of his writing in "close touch" with a Pinkerton detective who was interviewing Clark.[25] In addition to Chamberlin, White also instructed Superintendent Charles Constantine, who had headed the Yukon Division when first established, to investigate the Order; he, as well as Chamberlin, consulted Pinkerton's. The remaining two investigators were J.H. Seeley, whose motives were questionable, as exemplified by the large bills he sent in for his services. A protégé of Inspector Starnes, he became a thorn in the side of everyone else. He had travelled up and down the coast as far south as San Francisco and became convinced that the sinking on August 15, 1901, of the CPR vessel *The Islander*, with heavy loss of life, was caused by an "infernal machine" placed on board the vessel at Skagway by one of the conspirators of the Order. White became so exasperated by Seeley's demands for money that finally he instructed Z.T. Wood, the assistant commissioner at Dawson, to make the best deal he could with Seeley and be done with him.

Throughout all the dealings concerned with the Order and the later investigations, A.P. Sherwood of the Dominion Police was kept advised. And he asked a friend, E.F. Drake, who Sherwood described as an "ardent Britisher" to undertake an undercover investigation.[26] Drake was motivated only by his close friendship with Sherwood and, entirely at his own expense (except for seventy-five dollars run up in various bars while ferreting information), travelled from Ottawa to Whitehorse, Skagway, Seattle, and San Francisco, and thence back to Ottawa, handing in to Fred White a comprehensive report of his activities.[27] He concluded that the conspiracy had at one time been real enough and was not a mere newspaper "fake," but was now "dead." Drake reported that, though rumours had it that Clark and Grehl had raised as much as $30,000 to forward the aims of the Order, the actual amount was closer to $10,000 but, in any case, was all spent. The Order never enjoyed any support "south of Skagway" and what support there was came from "Skagway people" who were worried that any new arrangements for the Alaska boundary would work to their commercial disadvantage, and "from the restless dissatisfied element always to be found in a new mining country." Drake's was a sensible appraisal, in keeping with the reports by Superintendent Constantine and R.G. Chamberlin.

Constantine was dispatched to the Yukon where he was to assume nominal command of the Whitehorse Police District. Though his function was essentially military, and, it was hoped, short term only, his arrival, not surprisingly, caused considerable upset among the other superintendents already in the Yukon who felt slighted. He laid out defensive works to protect the Whitehorse and Dawson barracks, and drew plans for the deployment of all the police forces in the Yukon in the event of an actual attack; he drew up a nominal roll of all British subjects who had military experience and who would serve voluntarily in a defence force and he was also to keep a sharp eye on the movement of people over the trail from Skagway to Whitehorse, in effect setting up a spy network. Finally, he was to satisfy himself that the 450 Lee Enfield rifles and the approximately 60,000 rounds of ammunition on hand would be sufficient for the defence of the territory. All these arrangements were made on the specific authority of Clifford Sifton.[28]

But Constantine was not to confine himself to the Yukon if he thought he could gain information about the Order elsewhere and was specifically instructed to consult Pinkerton's if he thought it wise to do so. He travelled to San Francisco and discussed with William B. Sayers, the Pinkerton superintendent there, the progress of investigation into the activities of the Order. Learning of this consultation, White personally informed Laurier of it, and a copy of Constantine's report was sent also to the governor general.[29] Constantine also tracked down what he believed to be the "papers" relating to the Order; that is, lists of members, minutes of meetings, and financial records. In November 1901 (sometime after the Order had moved from Dawson to Skagway) these papers came to the attention of the police, who believed it would be worthwhile to get possession of the papers, if possible.[30] Constantine learned that a Skagway lawyer said to be "very hard up" held the papers and would be willing to sell them (and, presumably, to "sell out" the Order) for a "reasonable amount." Constantine reckoned $500 would suffice and asked for authority to buy them at that figure; White contacted Laurier who authorized personally the expenditure. White didn't hold out much hope that the papers would be useful, telling Laurier:

They may be worthless, but on the other hand they may contain the names of the subscribers to the Fund and, indirectly, be of a value to the extent of placing us in possession of the names of men who are still in the Yukon and could be watched.[31]

White's fourth investigator was R.G. Chamberlin, who was made available by A.P. Sherwood. White personally gave Chamberlin his instructions:

> I have told him that his mission will be to make inquiries on the lines suggested by the reading of the papers I have given him and other information which I have been able to communicate verbally. He is not to tell the object of his mission to any of the mounted police; on the contrary what we desire is to get the result of an independent inquiry by a man versed in detective work for comparison with the reports of others who are employed on the same work, but in other directions.

In other words, a roving undercover commission whose reports were to be tested against those of others, a rather elaborate scheme by White considering that by March 1902 the Order had been pretty much written off as a spent force. What had happened to revive White's concerns? We do not know. Perhaps he acted out of an abundance of caution.[32] Soon after he embarked on his commission Chamberlin travelled to Seattle to consult P.K. Ahern, the Pinkerton superintendent. The two men had not previously met, but were to be associated in future investigations into the Bill Miner train robbery and the Gleichen theft. As Chamberlin reported to Sherwood, Ahern was very helpful. (It was at this time that Ahern spoke of Primrose's peccadilloes in the Skagway bars.) Chamberlin asked Sherwood for permission to hire Pinkerton's to find Grehl and Clark, who were believed to be living in a small town near Yakima in eastern Washington. Sherwood agreed. Chamberlin himself learned of a brother of Fred Clark who he himself interviewed; Clark's brother thought the plot was "fake."[33]

Pinkerton's, learning Clark was working as a house painter in north Yakima, sent an undercover operative — also a painter — who got work on the same job site as Clark. The operative managed to wheedle a considerable amount of information from Clark, some of it already known or suspected by the police, but some new. Clark claimed to be the originator of the idea of setting up a "Republic of the Yukon" while in Dawson where he got together a "small reliable following." On moving to Skagway he claimed to have enlisted support among many "influential people" including two United States senators and other government officials. In Skagway there were perhaps 150 citizens devoted to the cause of the Order, though he claimed the total strength in the United States was between 1,500 to 2,000 persons. Clark refused, however, to divulge the names of any other persons, with two exceptions, who had been associated with the Order. The exceptions were men named Harrington and Burns, both in Skagway, and both men of apparently good reputations. Fred White, on learning of these two, authorized inquiries to be made about them but the official record is silent on the result. In his conversation, Clark maintained he still had all the records of the Order (a statement which gave the lie to the assertion by the Skagway lawyer that he had them for sale), but would not disclose their location or contents. There is no further reference to these papers in the official correspondence. Clark told the Pinkerton operative: "Now, if you will think the matter over carefully, you can see how practical the movement is, after thinking it over, let me know if you are willing to join." In his last conversation with the Pinkerton man, Clark talked of assuming "the obligations of the old Order" and, "if the thing succeeds, give them bonds on the new republic for the amounts due as was contemplated when the money was given." One gathers from these remarks that so far as Clark was concerned the "Order" was not dead. A month earlier, in the Yukon, Constantine had been told the Order might be resurrected under another name, and Clark's remarks support that view.[34]

But it never happened. The Order of the Midnight Sun was indeed dead, never to be resurrected. No invasion was launched. No hostile forces crossed into Canada, nor did an insurrection occur from within, no shots were fired in anger. Notwithstanding, Canadian officials, police, and government spent much time, energy, and money, prodded by the fear that such events might occur. After all the reports from his four investigators were in hand, Fred White summed up to his minister, Clifford Sifton:

> The substance of these various reports points to the conception, organization and manipulation of the Order of the Midnight Sun by a few men without standing or reputation in the community, and solely for the purposes of personal gain.

Yet, and his remark is typical of the ambivalent attitude of the police to the threat, White said there were Skagway merchants who were still "in a state of desperation by business passing their doors" who saw the activities of the Order as a form of salvation if Yukon Territory became United States territory. For that reason, White told Sifton, the force was maintaining surveillance on the most prominent of those merchants who "will still bear watching" but agreed the overall operation should be wound down to end "continuation of large expenditure." Sifton read White's memorandum, initialled it with his characteristic flamboyant flourish, and placed it in the file.

The sun had set.[35]

Eight
On Strike

In the course of preparing this book, the author spoke to many people about Pinkerton's; virtually everyone was familiar, in a general way, with the agency and its work though few were familiar with its particular work in Canada. What was surprising — at least to the author — was the number of people who made such remarks as "Didn't they do a lot of union-bashing and get involved in violent labour disputes?" Pinkerton's has never been quite able to shed that image, even though, in 1937, the company as corporate policy forbade the gathering of information relating to attempts by unions to organize and to bargain; the policy did not, however, preclude the agency from supplying personnel to protect strike-bound plants from acts of violence.

In the closing years of the last century there occurred two episodes which were the nadir of the agency's image, at least so far as unions were concerned. Their effect, combined with recollections of Pinkerton's role in the Molly Maguires affair, was to convince the labour movement and many others that the agency was an anti-working-class organization catering only to the middle- and upper-class segments of society and bent on the destruction of trade unions. Though these events happened over a century ago, this perception has persisted, at least in some quarters, to this very day. The perception has been kept alive, perhaps unfairly, by other much less serious confrontations between Pinkerton's and trade unionists.

Early in 1888 there was a strike against the Chicago, Burlington & Quincy Railroad. The company hired Pinkerton's to guard its rolling stock and other property, and to protect non-striking employees. The strike became violent and protracted with many allegations — unfounded — that Pinkerton's had deliberately fomented the riots and assaults which marked the dispute. The union eventually capitulated, and various union members were put on trial for possession of explosives intended for use in bombs and were convicted on the evidence of undercover Pinkerton operatives. Pinkerton's assignment had not been uncommon, for during the previous twenty years the agency had provided similar services on many occasions, so that if a widespread strike occurred, one expected Pinkerton's to be called in. Though strikes had frequently been bitter, often with pitched battles, there had actually been little loss of life; three dead over the two decades prior to 1892, but in that year ugly and tragic events at the Homestead Steelworks caused grave damage to Pinkerton's image.[1]

The Carnegie Company operated a steel plant on the banks of the Monongahela River at Homestead, a town just outside Pittsburgh. After negotiations for a new labour contract broke down, union members occupied the plant. The county sheriff, at the behest of the owners, issued an ultimatum to the striking men, warning that unless they vacated the steelworks the full weight of the law would fall upon them. The men ignored the warning. The sheriff was unable to muster a force strong enough to overwhelm the strikers, and so the company called in Pinkerton's. Rashly, as it turned out, Robert Pinkerton agreed to supply approximately three hundred armed "watchmen" who were to force their way into the plant, evict the occupying strikers, and restore the plant's operation to its owners. The men were taken by barge to the steelworks and in an ensuing affray between them and the strikers, who with their supporters numbered about five thousand persons, three Pinkerton men and ten strikers were killed. The Homestead riot has settled into the folklore of the American labour movement. The chorus of a popular contemporary ballad typifies much of the public reaction to Pinkerton's role at Homestead, which the agency found very difficult to counter:

God help them tonight in the hour of their affliction
Praying for him who they'll ne'er meet again
Hear the poor orphans tell their sad story
Father was killed by the Pinkerton men.[2]

After Homestead the agency deliberately scaled back its involvement in industrial disputes, probably through the influence of William Pinkerton who, of the two brothers, gradually became the dominant figure. With his predilection for sniffing out crime and catching criminals, and his cultivation of contacts with police forces in North America and abroad, it was he who mainly gave Pinkerton's its international reputation, and by doing so restored its good name following the Homestead riots.

But, even so, the image persists. In late May of 1977 the New Democratic Party of British Columbia held its annual convention, at which one of the delegates was Dave Barrett, a former NDP premier of the province. The convention was told that the current (Social Credit) provincial government intended to hire Pinkerton guards to prevent incidents during a planned pesticide spraying. Barrett denounced Pinkerton's as "anti-union and anti-people." The agency was defended by an official of the Teamster's Union (which represented Pinkerton personnel in British Columbia) who in effect accused Barrett of talking poppycock. Unrepentant, Barrett shot back that when he grew up, "there were two dirty words in [his] family — scab and Pinkerton."[3] Barrett may have had in mind episodes of the sort experienced by two former loggers, neither of whom knew the other, who told the author in separate interviews of industrial espionage in British Columbia logging camps in the 1930s. One, an active member of the International Woodworkers of America, was blacklisted in 1935 (or 1936, he was unsure which) by a logger's agency in Vancouver, B.C., which hired men for the coastal logging operations of the larger companies; he had been reported by a Pinkerton undercover man as a union troublemaker and lost his job. The other had been hired by the same agency. At work he was approached on several occasions by a Pinkerton man who wanted to recruit him to keep an eye on his fellow loggers and their union activities. He was warned that he would lose his job if he failed to co-operate, but he refused and was fired. He put the date of this episode as 1938 or possibly 1939. Since Pinkerton's did not have a Vancouver office until 1944, the operatives may have been sent out from Montreal, which seems improbable, but were more likely sent from either the Seattle or Portland offices. The opening of Pinkerton's Vancouver office in 1944 was vehemently opposed by the Trades and Labour Council, which urged city hall to refuse to issue a business licence. One delegate said, "the agency has been spying on labour since Civil War days."[4]

Memories of the Homestead debacle were still vivid in 1899 when Pinkerton's became involved in a labour dispute in Canada for the first time. It was called in by the British Columbia attorney general to do an undercover investigation of the unrest which occurred in the Kootenay mines of British Columbia late that year. However, neither then nor at any other time did the agency engage in anti-union activity on the scale of that in the American coal and steel industry, and the only instance in which Pinkerton's has even been suspected of supplying strike breakers or "scabs" occurred during the Hamilton Street Railway strike of 1906, which will be referred to later in this chapter.

The Exchange Hotel Bar at Sandon, B.C., frequently visited by miners of the sort investigated by Pinkerton's.

BCARS C-06184

Late in the nineteenth century rich silver lead deposits, and some gold, were discovered in the Kootenay region of British Columbia. A number of mines were brought into production, spawning new towns: Slocan, Silverton, New Denver, and Sandon among them. The Payne mine, the richest of the silver lead mines in the Kootenay, was located at Sandon. Other towns, not directly involved in mining, also sprang up, Nakusp and Nelson, for example. And at Rossland, the scene of the Mah Lin murder, gold mines were brought into production. To facilitate bringing the ore out, railroads were necessary and granting land for rights of way and providing subsidies were never-ending sources of political jobbery. However, the labour difficulties in the Kootenay did not arise from railroad jobbery, but from the confused state of British Columbia politics, with premiers coming into office as leaders of a cadre of personal supporters rather than as heads of a political party. (This system did not change until 1903.) As loyalties to individuals shifted, new groupings were formed, from the largest of which a strong man — a leader — was chosen by his fellows to be premier.

In August 1899 a new government led by Charles Semlin was sworn in. Though not himself particularly strong, he had as his attorney general a strong though erratic man, Joseph "Fighting Joe" Martin. Martin, no doubt with the idea of gaining votes from working men (which would eventually bring him the premiership), introduced legislation, adopted by the legislature, which gave miners an eight-hour day. On failure to comply mining companies were subject to severe penalties. The mine owners vehemently objected to the legislation and pressured the federal government to declare it unconstitutional, but Ottawa refused to do so and the legislation stood.[5] The miners rejoiced, seeing the reduction of the work day — without any affect on their base pay — as their salvation. Turmoil followed when the mine operators threatened to close down all operations and the miners, knowing they had the government on their side, refused to make any concession on wage levels. At that point Alexander Henderson, who by then had succeeded Joseph Martin (who was dismissed because of his contumaciousness), called in Pinkerton's. Henderson was concerned that the mine owners would either shut down the mines completely or keep them operating with non-union workers, and that the regularly employed miners, fearing loss of work, would resort to violence. Henderson therefore decided to have an undercover man visit the mines and take the pulse of the communities. W.B. Sayers of the Pinkerton office in Portland went to Victoria to meet with both Henderson and the premier to lay out the lines of investigation. James Nevins, the Portland superintendent, in a letter referring to this consultation, used language typical of management sympathizers of the day:

[W]e would state for your private information that through reliable sources we have known that the Miners at Rossland were organized into a union, that a number of the miners there employed in the mines, were men who were driven out of the Coeur D'Alene country or left there fearing arrest for complicity in the blowing up of the mill of the Bunker Hill & Sullivan Mining Co. in April last.

We need not say to you that these men are of the most dangerous character and are a menace to any community. Backed by the Union they will commit any crime and influence and terorize [sic] peaceful men and through their agitation will demoralize their fellow workers, who otherwise would be contented and law abiding citizens.[6]

There may have been some truth to the alleged presence of American miners, for as well as passage of the eight-hour law, the government had also passed the Alien Exclusion Act, designed to keep out foreigners and prevent them from working mining claims.

In due course, the operative arrived in Victoria, saw H.A. MacLean, the deputy attorney general, then F.S. Hussey, who gave him letters of introduction to the B.C. Police officers stationed in the mining communities, and set off for the interior, arriving at Nakusp on the Arrow Lakes on November 16, 1899. A typical reaction to the mining situation was voiced by a townsman at Nakusp:

The Government has settled the question of hours and it is only of one of wages. The mine owners are not so very hard on this point and can pay the wages asked but they wish to beat the Government on the law because it is a measure in favour of the working-classes and we will see that the Government backs us up.[7]

Although the operative believed most of the miners were "rabid socialists" he was impressed by Constable Forbes at Nakusp whom he described as "a very intelligent man." Forbes was clearly a moderate, believing for example that the decision to place special constables on the Payne mine property (which had become the flash point of the conflict between mine-owners and their employees) was a great mistake. Forbes was inclined to think that there would be no violence unless a "hot-head" got into a fight with a mine manager.[8]

The operative, visiting New Denver, found there also "a great many socialists" who were "strong talkers who knowing the government is on their side believed they can do as they like."[9] When visiting Silverton he discerned similar elements but added that the miners there seemed to be far more determined to hold out against the companies than their counterparts elsewhere. Because of all the rumours about the company bringing in strike breakers, every boat and train was watched to see if any workers arrived. At the train station at Sandon the operative counted some thirty local miners on the lookout. He met with C.H. Hand, the manager at the Payne mine, who told him that the mine owners throughout the Kootenay intended to amalgamate all the local associations so as to present a common front against union activity and wage demands. The operative reported that many small businessmen resented passage of the eight-hour law because of the labour unrest resulting from it and a consequent loss of business.[10]

At Nelson, he found the general opinion was that there would be no violence and, after some bickering between the mine owners and the union, the wage scale would eventually be settled. The operative met W.H. Bullock-Webster of the B.C. Police, chief constable of the Kootenay District, who also struck him as a sensible steady man and who, like Forbes at New Denver, opposed the use of special constables at mine sites and deplored their carrying pistols. Bullock-Webster was so little concerned about the possibility of violence that his principal complaint was that Victoria would not sanction the purchase of a horse for Constable Forbes to enable him better to patrol his scattered district. The operative left Nelson for Victoria in an optimistic frame of mind, being unable to detect any indication of serious trouble. Bullock-Webster told him "he feels quite equal to cope with any outbreak they [the miners] may attempt and he keeps himself thoroughly posted on the situation." The operative may have left the Kootenay earlier than he intended for he reported "that I was known in the district and someone must have notified the Slocan people as to who I was."[11] He arrived in Victoria at ten o'clock at night and spent two hours talking to Hussey. At one in the morning he met the attorney general, with whom he discussed his findings and observations until 3:00 a.m.; whether the consultation at that unusual hour was due to Henderson's anxiety to learn of the situation in the Kootenay or to his nocturnal habits, one cannot tell.[12]

But the agent's optimism was premature. Six weeks after he left there were at least two nasty incidents at separate mines, the Payne at Sandon and the Enterprise at New Denver, each involving non-union workers brought in to replace union workers who had refused to work at the company wage scale. The union men at the Payne, in trying to deny the non-union workers access to the job site, resorted to invective and "vileness of language" which, the mine manager said in a telegram to the attorney general, justified the deployment of additional special constables to protect the mine.[13] The secretary of the union local, William L. Hagler, was charged with unlawful assembly but no actual violence occurred then or later. Interestingly, Constable Forbes was opposed to a charge being laid against Hagler, believing it would only inflame the situation, but he did think three more special constables should be sent in to prevent physical clashes between the opposing forces. The spread between the wage scale proposed by the company and that acceptable to the union was minuscule, a compromise was reached, and union men returned to work.

In July 1900, just six months after the labour difficulties ended in the Kootenay, there was a strike by fishermen on the Fraser River as the result of a dispute over the price offered by canneries for fish landed at the dock. Though the strike was relatively short-lived, it was bitter. It was followed a year later by an even more bitter and protracted strike over the same issue; in each instance Pinkerton's was called in, though not by the provincial government or the B.C. Police but by the canneries. Their engagement may seem to be outside the scope of this work, but it is worth recalling since Pinkerton's activities were carried on with the tacit approval of the B.C. attorney general, to whom some copies of the agents' reports, though not all, were sent.

On the surface, each of the strikes, in 1900 and 1901, seemed merely to be about wages, but the underlying cause was the resentment by white fishermen of native Indians on the fishing grounds and, worse, active hostility by white fishermen to Japanese fishermen of whom, at the turn of the century, there may have been as many as five thousand. As this is written (1998) the Fraser River commercial fishery for sockeye salmon, the premier species in 1900, and today, has been severely limited. The number of sockeye salmon returning to the Fraser River in 1900 was far, far greater than the current level. The number of Japanese fishermen will appear astonishing but one must remember that fishboats in the era were small and relatively primitive, without the sophisticated gear which characterizes present-day fishing craft. One cannot discern from the official correspondence of the B.C. Police or the attorney general precisely what role Pinkerton's played in the 1900 strike (the records of the canneries have long since disappeared) but that they were on the river looking out for acts of intimidation by striking fishermen and evidence of assaults by white fishermen cannot be doubted.[14] The militia was called out (on much flimsier grounds than was the case in the Nanaimo coal strike in 1913), and the strike ended within a week. In his report to the attorney general of August 4 that year, Chief Constable Lister at New Westminster stated that the settlement affected between "four and five thousand boats on the Fraser River," though many of these went beyond the river's mouth to the Gulf of Georgia into an area roughly fifty miles square.[15]

In spite of the settlement, the presence of Japanese on the fishing grounds remained inflammatory. Just as Chinese miners brought out the worst in otherwise decent occidental miners, so, in the same era, Japanese fishermen, by their mere presence on the fishing grounds, provoked contempt and loathing, particularly when they were willing to fish at prices unacceptable to the whites. These tensions, racial and economic, long-simmering in the British Columbia fishing industry, burst into the open in the Fraser River Strike of 1901, which was characterized by acts of outright violence against the Japanese. An editorial in a Vancouver newspaper during the strike typified community attitudes towards the Japanese:

The vital fact is that through an unfortunate combination of circumstances the catching of fish seems likely to pass out of the hands of the white fishermen and the Indians into the hands of the Japs and practically the whole of an annual expenditure varying from one to two millions of dollars will be lost to the city and vicinity.

The money will be paid out, it is true, but the bulk of it will go into the pockets of the Japs, and stay there. It will not find its way into general circulation through all the various veins and arteries of local commerce. A little of it may, but not much. The Japs do not live luxuriously. On the contrary, they live as economically as they can and save every penny that can be saved, presumably with the purpose of returning some day to the land they love beyond the sea, and living there in comfort on the money made in Canada."[16]

Pinkerton's was hired once again by the canneries. Though one cannot learn the duration nor the precise nature of the engagement, an operative worked undercover, posing as a fisherman. In one of his reports sent to the B.C. Police, the operative spoke of a union man telling him "that if the Japs did go out [fishing] that the committee must see that they did not come back with all they went out with"; other informants told the operative that "violence would be used to stop 'scabs' and Japs from fishing."[17] These were not idle threats, as was demonstrated two weeks later when three separate violent incidents occurred within the space of two days. In one, a boatload of white fishermen overpowered two Japanese fishermen, clubbing one into unconsciousness; the second jumped into the sea. Their boat was later found drifting, without its nets. It was assumed the Japanese had drowned, and a Steveston cannery offered a $500 reward leading to information about the "murder." Later the two Japanese turned up in Tacoma, Washington; they had made their way to shore and, terrified, fled to the United States. Their assailants were never caught.[18]

In the second episode, six white fishermen boarded a Japanese vessel and, at gunpoint, threatened to shoot if the Japanese did not agree to discontinue fishing. The six, however, were arrested on the spot by two police offers who, anticipating trouble, had concealed themselves on the Japanese fishboat. A newspaper, taking the side of the Japanese for once, stated that of the six men only one was British, the others being Austrian, German, West Indian, and Filipino, implying that only foreigners would be capable of such a dastardly act.[19] They were tried on various firearms offences and acquitted by a sympathetic jury.

In the third incident, which happened within hours of the one just described, groups of white fishermen led by two union organizers forced their way onto four Japanese fishboats, destroyed all their gear, grabbed the seven crew members and marooned them on Bowen Island in Howe Sound, albeit unharmed. The two union leaders and others were brought to trial for kidnapping and other charges, and were also acquitted; the prosecutor found a crumb of comfort in the result, for the second jury deliberated four hours before letting the men off; in the earlier case the jury stayed out only briefly; juries were not going to convict white men for terrorizing the "heathen Japanee."[20] The strike ended a week after the marooning of the Japanese and Pinkerton's was not to be involved in fishing disputes again.

The agency's image as a purveyor of strike breakers was not enhanced by the events of the Hamilton (Ontario) Street Railway strike of 1906. In August that year the contract between the Amalgamated Association of Street Railway Employees expired and, after negotiations failed, three prominent citizens, with the consent of the union and the railway company, made recommendations for settlement which were agreed to by both sides, and which were to take effect on November 5, 1906. At the last moment, the agreement was not implemented, each side blaming the other, and the strike was on, ending a month later. That month was marked by violence with dynamite being thrown, rocks being tossed through windows, and people being assaulted, mainly because of the attempts by the company to run their streetcars with strike breakers — many of them, according to the union, from the United States. Just before the strike started, the police reported that a considerable number of Pinkerton men had been brought to Hamilton by the company and quartered in local hotels.[21] But news reports also claimed that other agencies — Noble's Detective Agency of Hamilton, and the Thiel Agency of the United States — had also supplied strike breakers, perhaps as many as one hundred, though the rail company, while admitting having hired people through detective agencies, said they were not operating the streetcars but riding on them to keep law and order.[22] One cannot say from the surviving materials whether the Pinkerton men were in fact brought in to run the streetcars but the mere suggestion that it might be so would be enough to damn the agency in the eyes of many of the general public. The author is inclined to think the agency would not have been interested in bringing into Canada numbers of strike breakers, nor even supplying Canadian personnel through its Montreal office.

After the Hamilton Street Railway strike, there is no record of the agency involving itself in a labour dispute in eastern Canada until recent times, but it did accept three engagements in strikes in British Columbia coal fields, in each case supplying undercover operatives.[23]

The first, a strike in the coal mines at Fernie, B.C. late in 1906, was relatively low-key; the B.C. Police hired the agency to keep surveillance for any breaches of the peace. The operative's expense account complied with Pinkerton's exacting standards for billing: lunch in the dining car for $.50; the cost of a sleeper in the Pullman car, $1.25; and a tip to the sleeping car porter of $.15.[24]

Five years later there was a strike at Coal Creek near Fernie, with the usual features: the company bringing in non-union men who on arrival at a train station would be greeted by as many as three hundred unionized miners shouting and cursing. Pinkerton's was engaged not for the strike itself but to investigate a charge of attempted murder of William Barr in the aftermath of the dispute, which ended in November 1911. In February 1912, someone fired six shots from a Winchester 30-30 rifle through the windows of the house occupied by William Barr and his family; no one was hurt. It was assumed that the shooting stemmed from the recent strike since Barr, a union member, had crossed the picket lines before the strike was officially over to return to work, thereby becoming a "scab." Barr was not a popular figure anyway among the mining community, being single-minded and determined and, besides, being a "bloody old Scotchman" as one of his townsmen described him, who had "deserved all he got." Another said of Barr, "You see he was a scab also his boys [sons]. One of the shots went between him and the old woman [his wife] but he got what he deserved."[25] Barr was a pugnacious man not easily intimidated and not amenable to union dictates if they conflicted with his own inclinations.

The local constabulary of the B.C. Police had no leads to the identity of the gunman, and after investigation, could turn up none. Colin Campbell, by then the superintendent of the B.C. Police, decided to call in Pinkerton's. P.K. Ahern suggested that Pinkerton's supply two men, one to work undercover, the other in the open; Campbell, no doubt on the grounds of expense, decided to send in a B.C. Police constable as an "open" investigator while Pinkerton's would supply the "secret" man. And so it was arranged. Ahern sent up a man experienced in coal mining who worked in tandem with the B.C. Police office. The operative found work at the mine as a track man's helper and ferreted out as much information about the attack on the Barr house as he could, frequenting pool halls and saloons and bars where he drank as much beer as the locals, and attending the motion picture shows, a newly arrived craze. On a more genteel level he called on stationery stores, haberdashers, drugstores, and hardware stores where after purchasing trivial items like shoelaces and sticks of gum, he engaged sales clerks in idle but studied conversation about the Barr shooting. In his inquiries the operative learned of the probable involvement in the shooting of three juveniles — two brothers named Vingallaa and their friend Tony de George — and passed on this information to the local police who interviewed the three; they confessed to the attack and, taken into custody, were placed on trial for the attempted murder of Barr.[26] Their confessions were ruled inadmissible because they were taken without one of the parents being present, and the boys were acquitted. They were, however, convicted of other, unrelated charges of theft and sent away to the provincial jail for young offenders; the jail superintendent, at least, believed them rightly acquitted of the charges of attempted murder, a view concurred with, oddly, by Ahern.[27] Again, in accordance with Pinkerton's billing procedures, the operative's wages received from the mining company were offset against the daily per diem charge of the agency, but the cost of the operative's union dues, heavy underwear, gloves, work socks, and overalls were charged to the B.C. government.

Eighteen months later Pinkerton's was hired by the B.C. attorney general to do undercover surveillance during the Vancouver Island coal mine strike, certainly the most serious labour dispute in the history of the mining industry in British Columbia, and perhaps the most serious of any industry in the province. Pinkerton's had an operative at work among the striking miners from mid-August 1913 until the end of January 1914. The daily reports filed by him are voluminous and form a valuable chronicle of the events of the strike, as well as a revealing social commentary.[28]

Turmoil in the coal fields of central Vancouver Island was common, most notably in the 1880s. A number of issues contributed to a sense of insecurity among miners, who as a class were not fitted for skilled work elsewhere: the hazardous conditions of work — between 1884 and 1912, 373 men were killed in coal mine explosions; the employment or attempted employment of orientals by the companies as a means of keeping wages low (which engendered racial animosity by occidental workers); the provision by the company of low-rent housing to employees and the threat of eviction on to the street in the event of a labour dispute; and the perceived threat of new technology made possible by electrification and the replacement of manual labourers on the coal face by cutting machines. Historically the principal Vancouver Island coal mines had been owned by the coal baron Robert Dunsmuir of Victoria, but after his death his interests were sold and, in 1910, a newly formed company, Canadian Collieries (Dunsmuir) Limited took them over; the new operators believed it to be commercially advantageous to retain the Dunsmuir name, but to many it stank in the nostrils, looked upon as a mark of disdain by management for its employees. The new company's largest operations were at Cumberland (near Comox), north of Nanaimo, and at Extension (just south of Nanaimo). Other operators owned mines at Nanaimo and at South Wellington; thus the main grouping of mines was within easy reach of Nanaimo, with the largest single mine at Cumberland.

In 1911 the United Mineworkers of America, headquartered in the United States, began a campaign to unionize Vancouver Island coal miners. The motive was not entirely altruistic in the sense of bettering the condition of the working man, although that argument was of course often advanced, but was prompted as much by achieving wage parity among Canadian miners on Vancouver Island and their fellows in the United States. According to the union, the lower wages allegedly paid by the Vancouver Island mine operators compared to those paid by American mine-owners gave the Canadian companies an unfair competitive advantage and, in the greater interest of union solidarity, the wages in each country for similar work should be equivalent. The Canadian mine operators, on the other hand, saw this as a ploy by an American-based union to favour American producers at the expense of Canadian and, as a consequence, at the expense of Canadian mine workers who might have to be laid off. The central issue, therefore, during the two years of the "Big Strike," as it has come to be known, was recognition by the companies of the United Mine Workers of America as the bargaining agent of their employees.

The strike began in Cumberland on September 17, 1912. The company had fired a union organizer, prompting the union to stop work and declare a "holiday." This was of course a euphemism for work stoppage; today the equivalent term would be "study session." The company retaliated by demanding each miner sign an individual wage contract; the miners refused and the mine was shut down, throwing two thousand men out of work. The same thing happened at the Extension mine, owned by the same company, and another fifteen hundred men were out of work. The company said it was an illegal strike; the union said it had been locked out. Gradually the mines resumed production by re-hiring those union members who wanted to work — and there were more than a few; by hiring oriental miners who were less enthusiastic about union aims than their occidental counterparts, and who as a large group signed separate contracts with the company enabling it to resume production on a limited scale; and, more inflammatory than anything else, by hiring strike breakers on a large scale. They were hired in British Columbia but the companies went farther afield, bringing men in from the United Kingdom and the United States. The returning strikers, the orientals, and the imported strike breakers enabled the company to achieve near-normal production. But as production levels resumed the United Mine Workers of America members on strike — or locked out — became increasingly frustrated and angry with those whom they saw as "scabs," and vilified and harassed them. To protect them, the company housed them in enclaves: bunkhouses for the unmarried, and married quarters for families. But isolation was not sufficient protection and, at the request of the company, the British Columbia government swore in substantial numbers of men as special constables to maintain law and order; they were vested with the same legal authority as a regular police officer, but for a limited period only. There may have been as many as 120 such "specials" who were employed without much regard to their antecedents and who thereby drew the opprobrium of the unionized miners.

This state of affairs — mining in progress and strike breakers' houses uneasily protected by special police — continued until May 1913. Not all mines were affected by the strikes (or lockouts), but on May Day in Nanaimo the situation altered dramatically. Following a giant rally in Nanaimo attended by perhaps fifteen hundred men, the union executive, that is the international executive, decided to expand the strike to all the coal mines on Vancouver Island, thus escalating the dispute beyond one simply between several thousand miners and a single employer. In response, the companies newly drawn into the dispute resorted to the same tactics as those first involved. As the hot summer months of 1913 dragged on, high temperatures frayed the nerves of employees and employers alike. Union men increasingly harassed and intimidated strike breakers and their families without resorting to actual physical violence, but there were ominous signs in July and early August that the relatively peaceful nature of the dispute could not continue for long; additional detachments of "specials" were sent in to the coal fields and everyone, miner and management alike, awaited the flash point for violence.

Regardless of the justification or otherwise of having sent them into the mining communities in the first place, it was the presence of the specials which proved to be the flash point. They protected strike breakers, therefore they were hated. A party of them on horseback confronted groups of striking miners in Cumberland on July 16, 1913, and rode among them swinging clubs; the miners fought back and there was a general mêlée. Word of this imbroglio reached Nanaimo and Ladysmith, with Extension in between, accounts of it gaining exaggeration the farther south they penetrated. On August 9 several strike breakers attacked strikers in Ladysmith, prompting the strikers to ask for protection from the police, failing which they would themselves do what was necessary. Two days later one of the smaller mine companies at Nanaimo resumed work, though on a much reduced scale. This news sparked massive protests from large, quickly assembled crowds of miners, their wives, and their families in attempts to prevent strike breakers and management staff from working. There was mayhem — pushing, shoving, screaming, stone throwing, horses neighing.

Far more serious rioting occurred the next day, the 12th, and then it was the turn of Extension and South Wellington, and Ladysmith where many miners lived, union and non-union, on the 13th and 14. Again, regardless of the rights and wrongs of the employers vis-à-vis their employees, the situation got completely out of control during those two days: milling crowds of striking miners invading company houses where strike breakers lived, setting fire to many of them (as well as torching the house of the mine manager at Extension), looting houses whose occupants fled into the adjacent woods to escape the wrath of the mob, uncounted physical assaults, shootings and stabbings, ransacking houses of union members not living in company compounds who had returned to work, and, the incident which triggered Pinkerton's engagement, throwing a stick of dynamite into a house lived in by a union member who had returned to work. It landed in his children's bedroom; bravely he picked it up, fuze burning, to throw it out the window; it exploded, seriously injuring him.

During these forty-eight hours of mid-Vancouver Island anarchy, an American from the international union, Joe Angelo, was very much to the fore of events. There seems little doubt that the union he represented was instrumental in fomenting the riots by striking miners as a last-gasp effort to force the mine operators into recognizing it. Even those observers like Lynne Bowen who are sympathetic to the union cause concede that the union, if not the motivator of the riots, sought to take advantage of them.[29]

By the night of the 13th of August the regular B.C. Police officers, aided — or, as some might argue, hindered by the special police — were clearly unable to contain the widespread disorder which threatened a breakdown of civil order on mid-Vancouver Island. The premier of the province, Sir Richard McBride, was absent; the administration of the province was left in the hands of W.J. Bowser, the attorney general and acting premier. It was evident to him, particularly after pleas from the mayor of Nanaimo, that the regular police and specials were unable to cope with what seemed to be a state of anarchy. The Militia Act — a federal act — provided that a province unable to enforce law and order could by the certificate of the provincial attorney general requisition the military in aid of the civil power, and the militia — as it then was — would be called up to bolster the local police forces.[30] Bowser made the decision to call in the military, for which he has been much maligned, and at exactly the same time he decided to call in Pinkerton's to provide an undercover operative to give him an eye — the Pinkerton eye — on what was happening and specifically to discover who flung the dynamite bomb.

Units drawn from six regiments — two from Vancouver, the remainder from Victoria, were sent to Nanaimo, the first to arrive being the Seaforth Highlanders from Vancouver on the morning of August 14, 1913. Militia were posted in all the key areas — Ladysmith, Nanaimo, and Cumberland — and eventually a force totalling one thousand men was stationed on the island under the command of Lieutenant-Colonel A.J. Hall of Victoria. (The commander of the force at Ladysmith, incidentally, was Lieutenant-Colonel A.W. Currie, later to achieve fame as the commander of the Canadian Corps in France.) Units were bivouacked in prominent places for maximum visibility and the men carried rifles with fixed bayonets. Many of the men were mounted; shipping the horses over to Nanaimo on a CPR vessel posed quite a challenge. As well as the militia, there were smaller units of the regular army who had come up from Victoria. One of those who came over from Vancouver with the Seaforths was Oscar Orr, then a lieutenant in the militia, and in later life a prominent and highly respected member of the Vancouver legal community. When the author interviewed him he was, at age 99, the oldest surviving member of the militia force.[31] Though all ranks were issued live ammunition he says it was "gallery ammunition," used in training and less lethal than the regular ammunition. During his stay in Nanaimo not a shot was fired. There was also what he called an "armoured train," a rail car carrying a large field gun — a formidable weapon which had an observable deterrent effect on potential rioters. After two weeks of patrolling the streets of Nanaimo, Orr returned to Vancouver to be replaced by another officer; all the militia were employed in civilian jobs and could not afford to be absent for long stints.

Another officer, Major Walter Bapty of Victoria, attached to the 88th Fusiliers as a medical officer, has left recollections of his experiences. He was inclined to think sending in the militia was a mistake and that the strikers had legitimate grievances. His unit was stationed at the Esquimalt and Nanaimo Railway train station, where a train was kept on standby in order to move troops north or south at a moment's notice. Bapty saw no violence, though his unit took all precautions for dealing with it if it did occur. He and Oscar Orr one day were ordered down to Extension on hearing of reported violence. They rode down carrying swords and pistols, but if violence had occurred it was over by the time they got there; they turned around and returned to Nanaimo.[32] And, as it proved, that experience was typical of later events: the militia effectively put an end to mayhem and mêlée and, a week after its arrival, arrests started of those accused of various criminal offences committed before August 14. At the time, however, further violence was very much a potential and it was for that reason that the Pinkerton man stayed in place for so long. The militia, whose arrival was hardly greeted with enthusiasm by striking miners, was not nearly so unpopular as the special police. Much of the time the military was used to escort accused prisoners to the court house and guard them; the strikers made no attempts to interfere. In one role or another the militia remained in the Nanaimo area for a year.

A Pinkerton man did not arrive in Nanaimo until August 20. After Bowser urgently consulted him by telephone on August 14, Ahern sent up an operative from Seattle the same day, but he did not pass muster. Bowser told him he wanted a "roughneck who could get in among the mob of men and yell and throw a stone occasionally in order to be one of them" and keep the provincial police advised as to the future actions of the mob. Bowser also was anxious to find the person responsible for the dynamite bombing but, in any case, he didn't think the operative was of "a roughneck kind" and another man would have to be sent up in his place. This was done; the new man who fitted Bowser's criteria received the same instructions and entrained immediately for Nanaimo. On arrival, he checked in at a medium-priced hotel under an assumed name, letting it be known he was one of a group of campers from Shawnigan Lake (a resort area north of Victoria) who had come to Nanaimo "to see the fun." As soon as he could, he met surreptitiously with the Deputy Chief Constable (to whom he had been instructed to hand in his daily operational reports rather than, as was usually done, send them off to Seattle in the first instance). To judge from these reports, which are extraordinarily detailed, the operative, though a "roughneck" in appearance, was a well-educated, literate man.

The operative soon dropped the "camper" pose and assumed that of a working man, though not a miner, doing odd jobs around town and, for a couple of weeks, cutting firewood. Consistent with that guise, he moved out of the hotel into a boarding house not far from the town centre where a number of manual labourers were also staying. During

his five-and-a-half months as an undercover man, only twice did he
fear his true identity might be revealed. He bumped into a
newspaperman on the local paper, *The Nanaimo Free Press*, whom he
recognized as a person he had had dealings with during an
investigation in Quesnel, British Columbia; the newspaperman,
however, did not recognize the operative in his rough working clothes.
(The author is unaware of any business Pinkerton's did in Quesnel.)
The other occasion was not long before he left Nanaimo. A miner he
had been hobnobbing with accused him of being a detective or a
special police officer, but the operative laughingly brushed aside the
suggestion, and other men nearby thought it was a joke as the miner
was known to be a blustering type ready to accuse anybody of
anything. Once, to ingratiate himself, he put up cash bail for an
arrested miner, and willingly forfeited it when the man did not show
up for his trial.

However, the operative became aware of union "spotters" who
were spying, not on him, but on their fellows to ensure if possible that
union members hewed to the party line and did not waver in their
determination to bring the companies to heel. Late in December
1913, a news story in the *Toronto Globe* claimed that all the special
policemen in Nanaimo and other mining areas on Vancouver Island
had been supplied by Pinkerton's from the United States. The story
was the subject of heated discussion in a bar where the operative was
drinking with friends. None of his companions put any faith in the
story but, in common with the generally held opinion that Pinkerton's
was anti-labour and anti-union, thought the specials were such
miserable specimens of humanity that they would be the sort
Pinkerton's would readily hire, if asked. The operative heard no more
on the subject. He worked every day of the five-and-a-half months he
was in Nanaimo, though he noted much less activity on Sundays. His
regular routine was to join the ever-present crowd of unemployed and
striking miners who gathered each morning and remained for the rest
of the day at Post Office Square in the centre of town; the operative
referred to it in his reports as the "loafing spot" for "idling strikers."
But of course, with the onset of winter, fewer men showed up, though
there were always some present, even in the most miserable weather.

The operative's specific role was to find the person responsible for
the Ladysmith bombing and, less specific, to monitor the activities of
strikers and their supporters and, as well, the activities of strike
breakers, whether they were union men returning to work or hired
from outside union ranks. With a companion, he went down to

Ladysmith but found no clues or leads. The bombing was a constant source of discussion during the operative's stay, many miners professing to believe the man had injured himself by attempting to hurl a lighted stick of dynamite at striking miners assembled outside his house. In any case no one was ever charged. Perhaps his failure to glean any useful information from the Ladysmith residents soured his opinion of them, for he records:

> The Ladysmith men are a distinctly lower order of people and display the traits employed by the ignorant and savage. Foreigners seem to predominate.[33]

The other task involved "mingling" which the operative did for five-and-a-half months, joining the crowds at Post Office Square, at army encampments, at mine entrances, at the court house, and, often, in bars, the most popular of which, or at least the one most frequented by the operative, being the Vendome. He took some pride in forming a useful friendship with an alderman on the Nanaimo city council, a man named Ferguson, who was also one of the strikers, remarking of him that "he is the one man besides myself who spends the most of his time in front of the bar at the Vendome."[34] In fact, besides the bar, the Hotel Vendome itself seemed to be the hotel of choice since Frank Farrington, an American union leader, kept a room there. If the bars were closed, or the operative and his companions were inconveniently far away from one, the operative could always be counted on to buy a bootleg bottle or contribute to the purchase of one. He made a standing arrangement with the bartender of the hotel where he first stayed by leaving a sum of money to be applied to the purchase of liquor as occasion required. He describes the arrangement:

> These fellows [his drinking pals and informants] I have treated to whiskey almost daily. I am enabled to obtain a bottle at an advance price, from a porter and bartender employed at the Wilson Hotel. The strikers themselves cannot obtain a drop of anything [because the hotel management opposed the strike] and this fact alone helped me out greatly.[35]

Lest the bartender or hotel get into trouble with the police who read his reports, the operative was at pains to state that it would be impossible for just anyone to go in "for a like service." The operative, using liquor to loosen tongues, garnered information, for example, about union meetings and plans by union officers for future action; he also gained useful information about dissension and internal wrangling among members of the union executive.

But it was not always necessary for the operative to "lubricate" the throats of striking miners; he often observed miners freely spending their own money in the local bars, particularly after payment of the strike benefits which were made regularly each week, prompting him to question whether the strikers were as hard up as they claimed to be. Nor was he always merely a listener and observer. As he put it: "I am in a position to argue with them [that is, the striking miners] and show them the folly of some of their acts, without arousing the least bit of anger or suspicion on their part and I do so each day, trying to wean them away from the UMWA, Farrington, all such affiliations."[36] In this, he may have been straying from his mandate or, perhaps, giving it too wide an interpretation. Frank Farrington, a member of the international executive of the union, was the effective leader of the strike. He was one of several Americans whose presence coloured the attitude of the mine owners, who regarded them as more interested in the welfare of their fellow countrymen than that of hard-working Canadians. Three other Americans on the scene from time to time were John Walker, a former head of the UMWA from Illinois, David Irvine, another executive from Illinois, and Joe Angelo, who was sent in 1912 to organize men into the union (he was subsequently sentenced to four years in jail for inciting riots and looting and burning). The operative remarked that there didn't seem to be much sympathy for him when news of his conviction (at a trial in New Westminster) reached Nanaimo.

Not surprisingly, the operative had far less contact with mine management than with striking employees. One he did meet and have a long talk with was Harry Freeman, manager of the Jingle Pot mine, one of the smaller operations in the area, which had settled with the union, according it full recognition. For that reason, Freeman was a bit of an outcast among his fellow managers and apparently did not hesitate to discuss with the operative the strike situation in general and, as a possible solution, arbitration pursuant to the Industrial Disputes Investigation Act of 1907, a federal act. (Many years later the courts declared it unconstitutional.) It says much for the "roughneck's" conversational ability that Freeman spent as much time with him as he did, even to the extent of showing him around the mine. He also demonstrated that ability by becoming friendly with

Parker Williams, one of the heroes of the labour movement and strike, a member of the legislature, later a member of the Workmen's Compensation Board, and later still a magistrate.

True to the historical antecedents of Pinkerton's, and the strongly expressed views of its founder, Allan Pinkerton, the operative heaps scorn on the activities of socialists, the most rabid of whom he equates with the devil himself. But he concedes that some socialists like Parker Williams, whose views are less "radical," are entitled to respect. Thus he notes that "it was advocated yesterday by Socialists in a quiet manner that the wives of the imprisoned men [awaiting trial] take the children and babies to the jail and there demand that the government and soldiers feed and care for the little ones until the 'breadwinners' are released." But the "ultra-Socialists" or "radicals" are dangerous people:

> it is a curious state of affairs when one can hear apparently sane men, old countrymen, mostly, stand and berate their own government and prophecy all sorts of evil ends for the nation and in every way show the ear-marks of ranting anarchists which heretofore one has associated only with ignorant European peoples and any but British born men. Law and order are nothing to these men and their doctrine is one of overthrow for every form of law and government now in existence and the establishment of a form which promises the working man complete control of everything and everybody.[37]

However, these extreme views were local, so to speak, and were certainly not those of the UMWA, which was relatively conservative in that respect, and which brought in from Seattle a well-known socialist, Kate Sadler. The operative spoke admiringly of her. In a two-and-a-half hour speech before an audience of perhaps fifteen hundred, including the operative, she deplored the use of violence during the riots, emphasizing that lasting change in the social order to benefit the working class could come only from the exercise of the franchise and passage of laws favourable to the working man. The operative said she "made a marked impression upon her audience and was cheered repeatedly."[38] Large meetings like that were common during the strike; it was nothing for two thousand people to show up to be harangued and encouraged by union officials to stick to their principles and never yield — the union would undoubtedly triumph by gaining universal recognition (a hollow prophecy). During his time, the operative attended them all.

He frequently comments on the conduct of the soldiery stationed about the area. They were sent to quell disorder, and succeeded. The operative often heard verbal abuse heaped upon them by his companions in the bars and on the streets but always out of earshot of the soldiers. Not so, however, with the womenfolk, of whom the operative records: "I note that the wives of the miners are the most outspoken and bitterest of enemies to the soldiers. They are often cautioned by their men folks when speaking in reckless tones of the soldier." He describes an episode when soldiers escorted a large group of arrested miners to the train station for return to jail in Victoria (the Nanaimo jail being overcrowded). They ran a gauntlet between lines of "crying, cursing and hysterical amazons" and were hard pressed to keep their formation, aided, as it happened, by miners restraining the women. The operative used even choicer language to describe the conduct of a large group of women awaiting the arrival of prisoners at the court house. "Seldom," he says, does it fall to "the lot of a person to mingle with such a vicious ... and misguided lot of human beings of that sex"; the "strings of oaths and foul language which eminated [sic] from the mouths of these mothers and wives would shame a mule driver." But there was never any physical act of hostility during his time.[39]

Initially the army presented a show of force at a time of serious disorder, but as things calmed down the number of men on patrol declined and their function changed. Their role became more that of protecting miners returning to work and strike breakers from physical harm — both in their coming to and going from the mines and in their homes — and guarding prisoners and witnesses on their way to and from the courthouse while the numerous trials were being held in Nanaimo. (Later, trials were held on the mainland.) The business community of Nanaimo wholly supported their presence, and even amongst the miners there was a certain grudging respect; it was the specials they hated. The majority of troops during the operative's time came from Highland Scottish regiments, who of course wore kilts. Some prudish observations by the operative give new meaning to the old, naughty, question of what a Scotsman wears under his kilt:

Regarding the kilties which are the greatest number of soldiers left here and for whom I have a good opinion, one hears a great deal of talk about them and they are called the half clad barbarians. It is this way. It is a positive fact that these men wear no covering over their upper legs and hips

Some of the "Kilties" bivouacked during the Nanaimo Coal Strike, 1913.
BCARS A03194.TXT

other than the kilts. They wear a narrow strip of light colored cloth hung from the front of the belt to the rear and fitting tight over their privates. That is all. Now, their campsite is elevated some four to ten feet above the level of the street and on a slope opposite the post office. These fellows seem to forget these conditions and if engaged in tightening a guy rope on the tent or fixing a peg or lying around in a careless manner, or stoop over, their skirts go up so far behind that all passers by, women, children and the people seated opposite are given a display that one is not supposed to meet with in a civilized land. I myself have seen some shocking displays there on many occasions. If these men were asked to don some sort of a covering underneath or at least asked by their officers to bend a knee or stand sideways to the street when stooping it would help same.

Perhaps typical of the relationship between soldiers and the civilian population was a parade which the operative described. Having already noted in an earlier report that the kilties were given to parading about the streets with a great deal of "noise and display" disrupting traffic, he goes on:

> Some of the "kilties" appeared on the streets wearing
> gorgeous uniforms and bedecked with ribbons and

gold braid and with a massive head-piece of black fur
or feathers and the whole creating a costume which
would attract attention anywhere. Some of the
strikers appeared to take great interest in the makeup
of the kilties and gazed continually at the latter and
not without bringing out sotto-voiced curses from the
kilties in return for the looks.[40]

The day after the operative arrived in Nanaimo, the preliminary
hearings began for the men arrested for indictable (felonious)
offences — which necessitated trial either by jury or by a county
court judge, as the accused chose — and the trials of men for minor
(non-felonious) offences went ahead before the magistrate. The
various court proceedings, some in Nanaimo, and still later in New
Westminster after a change of venue was ordered, went on all winter
and did not end until March 1914. A number of miners involved in
the riots at Ladysmith decided to take their chances before Judge
F.W. Howay (far more competent as a historian than a judge) by
pleading guilty in the hope of getting off with a lighter sentence. It
was a vain hope, since he imposed severe, sometimes maximum
punishment. Worse, he later gave a newspaper interview castigating
all the convicted men and strikers in general for widespread
unlawful behaviour. It was this intemperate and ill-advised outburst
which led the authorities to transfer the remaining cases away from
Nanaimo. The operative had had no part in the investigation of
these offences, all of which occurred before his arrival, but he
certainly heard plenty about them from his companions. There was
the occasional strike-related offence during that winter, usually
assault arising from too much drink, but the operative had also no
direct part in them. Of the men arrested — over two hundred of
them — 166 actually stood trial and of those, fifty were sent to jail,
and as a result of amnesty arrangements reached in March and April
1914, those still in jail were released.[41]

The operative was chiefly concerned with learning of union plans
for waging the strike war. There was a lot of discussion about the
wisdom of a province-wide strike to show support for the Nanaimo
miners, but the latter were not enthusiastic, believing cash
contributions from other unions would be more effective. John Walker,
the American union official, and clearly a moderate, discouraged any
plans to mobilize the general union movement or even to stage a
limited strike (confined to other coal fields in British Columbia for a

period of forty-eight hours, and to be declared a "holiday," as was done in Cumberland in September 1912, thereby triggering the "big strike"). Walker felt that such actions would cause mine management to become even more intransigent. One of the hare-brained schemes talked of as a means of embarrassing the authorities was the storming of the Nanaimo jail to free the notorious Henry Wagner, the "Flying Dutchman," who was awaiting execution for the murder of a police officer at Union Bay near Cumberland in March 1913 during the commission of a burglary. His pending execution caused much local excitement, as did the execution itself which occurred on August 28, two weeks after the militia arrived; some hot-heads advocated a resumption of rioting and of physical violence. Frequently union men proposed putting up picket lines once again, even though such activity had been declared illegal. All these confrontational proposals were abandoned during the Pinkerton surveillance for two reasons: the ever-present military which could not be trifled with and, almost as compelling, the fear that violence or illegal activity would make it probable that even harsher sentences would be meted out to those still facing trial than would otherwise be expected. As the operative put it, "it can be safely stated that everyone will be on their good behaviour until after the coming trials are held."[42]

Because of this hiatus, or truce, or whatever one calls it, the larger mines were able, with the help of strike breakers and union miners breaking ranks, to resume production. In spite of his oft-expressed antagonism to the strike, the operative had an innate sympathy for the miners displaced by strike breakers:

The new miners now being employed are of the lower European class, laborers mostly and ones who will never patronize any business house or good hotel such as the town furnishes to the unmarried class of miners, heretofore. The new arrivals are the sort that huddle together in rooms and hovels, and never patronize anyone outside their own nationality and on pay day send most of their earnings home to the old country keeping but enough on hand to do them until next pay day. I only mention this phase of the local situation because it is so apparent that one cannot observe it without feeling a bit sorry for the actors [that is, the miners] in the drama who are robbing themselves unconsciously of that which has heretofore supplied them so satisfactorily in peace and comfort.[43]

Reliable figures of men working and mine production are hard to come by but by the end of 1913 substantial numbers of men were working and in one case, Cumberland, the mine produced more coal in 1913 than it did the year before.[44] The operative estimated, just before he left Nanaimo, that 150 union members had returned to work at the #1 mine of Canadian Collieries, the largest at Nanaimo, enabling it, he says, to run "almost to its normal capacity." Moreover, he predicted that at the rate which striking miners were returning to work, the mine would have its full complement of five hundred to six hundred men by year end, up from approximately one hundred men estimated by him to be working late in October, and 150 early in November.[45]

The steady dribble of returning men and the consequent resumption of production caused discouragement and frustration among union officials and miners, emotions not improved by news that the Teamsters' Union, despite pleas from the UMWA, had decided to haul coal from the #1 mine to dockside for loading.[46] The strike ran on for another eight months with increasing pressure from the government in the summer of 1914 for settlement. During all that time there were military units in the area; though in reduced numbers, they continued to exercise a deterrent effect on violence. The discontinuance of strike payments by the UMWA in July 1914 and the threat of a European war made the parties more amenable to ending the strike and in August 1914, after the outbreak of war, the strike was over. The union did not gain its main objective — recognition — but the mining companies agreed to re-hire union members without discrimination.

The operative received instructions on January 31, 1914 to end his surveillance. He notified the local police and left that very day for Seattle. There is no hint in his earlier reports of a pending departure. One can only speculate. Had his cover been blown? Unlikely, since the local newspaper, had it learned of such an event, would have made it front page news and, moreover, until now the presence of a Pinkerton man for five-and-a-half months in the Nanaimo coal strike has not been commented on by authors previously writing of the affair. More probably there was nothing further he could do; though the atmosphere remained tense, there was no turmoil and little fear there would be any, at least in the short run. Filing his last report on January 31, 1914, Pinkerton operative 29-S vanished into anonymity.

Nine
Wartime Espionage

The outbreak of World War I brought much Canadian business to Pinkerton's in a new field — espionage. It was mostly conducted in the United States before that country declared war on Germany on April 2, 1917, but there were at least two bomb attacks carried out by German agents in Canada that were investigated by Pinkerton's, notably the explosion at a factory manufacturing uniforms in Windsor in 1915, and investigations by Pinkerton's into the activities of suspected German spies operating in Canada. The agency was employed by Canada to infiltrate the ranks of suspected German spies operating on the American eastern seaboard — New York and New Jersey — and also to investigate suspicious fires and explosions thought to have been caused by German agents involving allied war materiel.

In 1914 Lieutenant-Colonel A.P. Sherwood was still the head of the Dominion Police and was to remain so until 1918. Canada had no spy agency as such, no apparatus for investigating hostile activity by German nationals or sympathizers, and no intelligence-gathering network. By virtue of being head of the only national law-enforcement body, Sherwood became the de facto head of the security and intelligence service of the country. He was not entirely unprepared. As early as 1907, he told the minister of militia: "I still possess and have under safekeeping one book containing a list of persons suspected of being foreign agents." In the context of the times "foreign" meant "German."[1] Even so, the Canadians were better organized to deal with intelligence work than the Americans since Canada was at war and therefore there was greater urgency. In the United States, intelligence gathering was fragmented among various federal agencies and occasionally private agencies such as Pinkerton's were called on. William Pinkerton had scathing words for the intelligence work, or lack of it, of the Americans during World War I, accusing the federal agencies of incompetence and negligence.[2] Pinkerton's in fact was very seldom consulted by American intelligence agencies, an odd circumstance considering the major role it had played in the Civil War fifty years earlier, but was frequently consulted by Canadian authorities for whom they did far more wartime work than for their own countrymen.

Sherwood became in effect the Canadian spymaster, which had important ramifications for Pinkerton's, with whom he had enjoyed a long and cordial relationship. There were two other men in Ottawa closely associated with Sherwood in his wartime role. Commander R.M. Stephens had come to Canada as an officer of the Royal Navy to help establish the Royal Canadian Navy; when war broke out, he effectively became the head of naval intelligence. Vice Admiral C.E. Kingsmill, a Canadian who had achieved distinction with the Royal Navy, was in 1914 the director of the naval service in Canada, in effect the ranking naval officer. He, with the other two, Sherwood and Stephens, formed a triumvirate of Canadian wartime intelligence. On the enemy side stood the German agents in the United States, until 1917 an officially neutral country. From the German Embassy various campaigns of sabotage were mounted, both in Canada and the United States, and espionage carried out. The ambassador in 1914 was Count Johann von Bernstorff who, in 1920, wrote his self-serving memoirs to deny any personal knowledge of the activities of his embassy minions in carrying out these schemes. One of those minions was Captain Franz von Papen, the military attaché to the embassy, who, in later life, became chancellor of Germany and played a crucial role in the events which brought Hitler to power. Another was Captain Karl Boy-Ed, the naval attaché, and still another was Franz Rintelen, also a naval man. These are the men who were to figure principally in the events about to be described, though von Papen, after the bombing in Windsor in 1915, was, later that year, after pressure from the United

States government, recalled by Germany. After the United States entered the war, of course, all embassy staff were recalled.

But Pinkerton's efforts on behalf of the Canadian government during the war — their engagement ended in 1917 — were not always covered with glory, at least according to some Canadian officials (Commander Stephens for one). But Pinkerton's enjoyed the confidence of Sherwood throughout, notwithstanding questions raised in the United States about Pinkerton's loyalty to the allied cause, and about its integrity as an investigator for Canada. The question was raised most prominently by Sir Cecil Spring-Rice, the British Ambassador in Washington who on June 7, 1915, wrote Sherwood, knowing of his connection with Pinkerton's, to say he had received "various warnings that Burns [another large detective agency] and Pinkerton's are both in German employment or that members of the agency are doing work for German government agents." He went on to say he had been informed that Burns was "particularly dangerous" but in any case "high authority" had warned him of the dangers of hiring any agency for espionage since "they generally give away information to both sides."

Sherwood reacted immediately by getting in touch by phone with William Pinkerton from whom he received, three days later, a letter signed by Pinkerton and his nephew, Allan, the principals of the firm, a copy of which they sent to Spring-Rice. To say that they were affronted is an understatement. Acknowledging the seriousness of the accusation, considering its source, the two Pinkertons assured Sherwood that "this agency nor any of its branches has not knowingly done one iota of work directly or indirectly for the German government or German Agents or representatives." Such a suggestion was unthinkable particularly in view of the "close friendly relationship this agency has had for half a century with Scotland Yard." The two men reminded Sherwood that in the last year the agency had "done a great deal of work both through Washington and through your office" in a satisfactory manner "without serious leakage." They said they had heard similar rumours before but no "definite connection" had ever been made between the agency and the Germans, and if it could be demonstrated, the two brothers said "that either the principals, the General Management, or our Superintendents, have knowingly accepted work for German interests" then Pinkerton's would "return every dollar paid to us by either yourself or the [British] Embassy in Washington." The current rumour is "too ridiculous even for consideration" and as the agency is regarded in the USA as "agents of the allies," the only explanation is that the rumour was deliberately set on foot to "throw suspicion and distrust" in the mind of Spring-Rice.[3] In this letter, Pinkerton's does not say outright there has been no "leakage," but no "serious" leakage, implying some may have occurred. The very nature of the work makes it inevitable that some leakage will occur, that the identity of an undercover investigator might be discovered and revealed. Pinkerton's reference to the large amount of work they had performed on instructions both from Sherwood's office and "through Washington" is noteworthy. It was precisely because Pinkerton's had done so much work for the British through its embassy in Washington that Spring-Rice's letter was so worrisome; the nature and extent of that espionage are, however, outside the scope of this work.

Hardly had the first shots been fired after the outbreak of war in August 1914, when Pinkerton's was called in. Two police officers of the North West Mounted Police travelling east on a passenger train spotted two fellow passengers whom they believed to be German military reservists endeavouring to make their way back to Germany, although in conversation they said they were merely travelling to Philadelphia to visit an aunt, whose name they gave. The two were taken off the train at North Portal, Saskatchewan, and detained while inquiries were made through the commissioner of the NWMP, A.B. Perry. Perry referred the matter to Sherwood who in turn hired Pinkerton's in Philadelphia to do an investigation of the aunt. She existed all right, but Pinkerton's learned she had close ties with groups in the United States who were promoting German interests. On the strength of this information, the two men were interned.[4] Not long after, Perry hired the Thiel Detective Agency to investigate a group in Edmonton believed to be raising money for the German war effort. The agency filed a report later shown to be suspect as a result of which Perry in the succeeding years was to have a jaundiced view of hiring private agencies where national security was concerned. During the war he was not in a position to impose his views on others, let alone Sherwood, but that changed with the reconstruction of the NWMP to become the RCMP in 1920 which would, apart from normal policing, maintain a security and intelligence service, obviating any need for private agencies such as Pinkerton's; he also thought that the police, in any case, could do a better job of detection than a private agency.[5]

Pinkerton's role in active wartime espionage began on the eastern seaboard of the United States early in 1915 with a relatively minor job of surveillance in Boston and a major piece of work in New York City. Those investigations, which were concluded at virtually the same time, in May 1915, were followed by three engagements in Seattle, two of which were to establish the cause of a fire and an explosion, which destroyed munitions and were believed to be the work of German agents. Those inquiries were followed by a major investigation into a bomb explosion at Windsor, Ontario, which was proved to have been carried out by saboteurs hired by Germany. Pinkerton's was continuously and actively engaged in several locales from February 1915 until well into 1916; thereafter it performed other investigations, though not continuously, until 1917.

As with some other episodes, the materials relating to the Pinkerton investigation in Boston in May 1915 are incomplete or unclear. Only one report has been preserved but it suggests it was part of an ongoing inquiry into the shipments from Boston on American vessels of war materiel, principally cotton, destined in fact for Germany but disguised on a ship's manifest as consigned to other countries. The inquiry was launched by Lieutenant-Colonel Sherwood, who kept Commander Stephens notified of its progress.[6] Contemporaneous with that investigation, Pinkerton's carried out in New York City a much longer and more complicated counter-intelligence operation. Its purpose was to shadow and keep under constant observation members of an alleged German espionage ring believed to be plotting the bombing of American plants and factories supplying war materials to the Allies, and spying on the movement of British vessels in and out of port at New York and Hoboken, New Jersey and on their cargoes. It was believed this information was then relayed to U-boat skippers. It was the Canadian, not the British government, however, which hired Pinkerton's; there is no indication in the dossier that any of Pinkerton's reports were sent to British officials. Commander Stephens, though, was kept advised of the course of the Pinkerton inquiries and received copies of the operatives' reports which, in great detail, spanned the period from February 10 to May 29, 1915. According to the authors of a book on Canadian naval forces and German sea raiders, a Pinkerton operative talked his superior into launching the undercover operation, but there is no suggestion of this in the official file.[7] Sherwood was not one to be easily talked into something he didn't think useful, and he must have considered the lengthy investigation worthwhile otherwise he would have called it off long before it in fact ended. Threaded among the Pinkerton reports are letters from Pinkerton's to Sherwood as well as correspondence between Stephens and Sherwood. From marginal notes made by him on one of the reports, Stephens was clearly keeping tabs on the progress of the operatives' work and on the names of the various suspects; he also instructed his private secretary to keep the reports "together" and not to file them, so that he could easily examine them when he wanted.

The specific targets of the surveillance, and the infiltration of their ranks by Pinkerton operatives, were a number of German seamen who had served on German vessels owned by the North German Lloyd and Hamburg-Amerika shipping lines which were tied up in Hoboken. They were effectively interned by the presence of British cruisers patrolling in international waters off the American east coast, and their crews, in effect, were marooned. The shipping companies, not wishing to continue paying wages to the crews (which they were obliged to do), endeavoured to find temporary employment for them elsewhere. (For example; the owners of one vessel, whose ship's complement was about 250, managed to place all but 56 in shore jobs.) They were employed as labourers in packing plants, steel mills, and other industrial enterprises. Some continued to occupy their old shipboard quarters, unpaid, and others lodged in boarding houses operated by German-Americans.

One such boarding house in New York City, run by a Miss E. Seithen, became the focus of the Pinkerton investigation. There were constant comings and goings of German nationals who sometimes boarded for a brief period or used the house as an accommodation address or storage depot for their trunks and baggage. Living there, or, if not in daily residence, storing personal effects there, were two wireless operators, Otto Pfeil and Frederick Bertrom, who were close friends of a certain Paul Von Heiden who, though he lived elsewhere, was in constant contact with the two. Von Heiden had secured work at a packing plant in Jersey City, New Jersey, owned by the big packing outfit Swift & Co., which was believed to be selling its food products to the British. These men were thought to be the nucleus of a larger spy-ring and became the focus of the Pinkerton surveillance, though their associates were often shadowed as well. During the long operation, Pinkerton's assigned at least four operatives who, as occasion required, shadowed the supposed members of the spy-ring as they patronized bars, restaurants, cabaret shows, and movie theatres. Sometimes one operative would shadow another when in company with one of the suspected members of the ring.

At first, however, Pinkerton's assigned operative #68 who took the name of Frank Steickternott. If not of German birth, he was of German descent and spoke the language like a native. He made an initial approach to the Seithen household on the pretext that he was one of the many Germans stuck in New York because of the British blockade. Insinuating himself into the confidences of Miss Seithen, the operative learned the details of the background of the three suspected men. Sherwood followed Pinkerton's advice that the encouraging start of the operation warranted placing the operative in the house as a boarder and, accordingly, the operative persuaded Miss Seithen to let him move into the front parlour, the only room available in the crowded dwelling. Once ensconced there, he began sweet-talking and making eyes at her. She was hardly a temptress, a stocky thirty-year-old woman weighing two hundred pounds. (The operative in all his reports was very careful, following his training, to give a full physical description of each person whom he met or talked to during his investigation.) He employed the time-honoured blandishments of buying copious quantities of good German beer (or schnapps), taking her out to dinner or to movie shows or to the theatre. The operative once recorded that he "took some drinks to the house and got Miss Seithen half full"; in view of her bulk, it must have taken a considerable amount of beer to make her "full." Whether all this led to physical intimacy the operative does not say, although there are one or two hints in his reports that it did. When a boarder in a room immediately next door to hers moved out, she was "very anxious" that he move into it. He did. He also says that he affected jealous rage when Miss Seithen spoke of any close friendship with another man. In any case, maintaining his pose as a German working for the Fatherland in some unnamed fashion (so secret, he told her, he could not disclose it), he met numbers of other Germans and beguiled Miss Seithen into telling him vast amounts of information about all of them. She told him also that she was considered by the group to be "too talkative" and he must try not to reveal her as the source of his information, much of which related to the travels to and activities in other cities such as Chicago; Scranton, Pennsylvania; and Alton, Illinois, of various Germans actively working on plots to destroy factories or to have British vessels sunk by U-boats in the Atlantic. It was she who told the operative of "people working in the Canadian government and at Canadian ship companies" to learn details of Allied ship movements and cargoes. That statement in the Pinkerton report caught the eye of Commander Stephens.

One threat to a factory was taken very seriously. In mid-February while drinking in a bar with Von Heiden the latter confided to the operative that he was not working at the Swift plant to make money but "to wreck that dump." Later that same day the operative spoke to one Sturtz, another boarder at the Seithen household, who showed the operative a bomb he was making for use at "Von Heiden's place." It was made of a two-foot-long section of two-inch galvanized pipe with appropriate wiring and, inserted in a receptacle, dynamite. When the bomb was primed, Sturtz said, he would deliver it to Von Heiden. The operative drew a sketch of the device which he enclosed with his report.[8] When Pinkerton's New York office saw this, they wrote to Sherwood immediately, saying that Swift & Co. had better be notified; moreover it was possible that Swift would pay for the continued investigation of the bomb threat rather than the Canadian government.[9] One cannot tell the result of that suggestion but after approval from Sherwood Pinkerton's got in touch with the Swift manager who confirmed that Von Heiden worked for them in the cooperage department, but had been pestering his foreman to transfer him to the "engine room" (that is, the steam plant). The manager agreed that a bomb planted there would indeed put the plant out of commission; Von Heiden and some others in the cooperage section were fired that same day. Whether the local police were contacted is not mentioned; probably not, since the espionage investigation was still going ahead and would be compromised by any public knowledge of the affair.

In mid-March, Stephens began to express to Sherwood his reservations about "contradictory statements" appearing in the reports of operative #68, the boarder. They were contradictory in the sense that different people gave different versions of the same subject, but Stephens was inclined on principle to doubt the utility of private agencies. By coincidence the operative was thinking about the merits of a trip to Chicago to join Sturtz who had gone there. His story to Miss Seithen and others that he was engaged in top secret war work for Germany, without ever giving any details, was beginning to wear thin and Miss Seithen and others began pressing him to do something obviously useful in Chicago, with Sturtz, who would pay his expenses. Encouraging him to go, she buttered him up: "You could do more good by being directed by Government officials than from private people [whom #68 claimed to be working for]. I do not think the work you are now doing fits your spirit and independence." There were, she said, other "places where you would be best fitted by your personality" and thus "our Fatherland would derive more benefit out of you."[10] And so he went, arriving about the first of April, staying at the Kaiserhof Hotel. He contacted Sturtz who gave him twenty-five dollars, which the operative told him was a paltry sum. Sturtz was vague about just what sort of work was expected of him, telling the operative to wait for instructions; the operative replied he could hardly survive on twenty-five dollars and might have to pawn his belongings.[11]

In the meantime, Pinkerton's had placed another boarder in the Seithen household. He was told by Miss Seithen that the boarder who had just gone to Chicago was a detective. She knew he was a detective because "he had asked too many questions" and she wouldn't have him back, therefore the new man could have his room. On reading this report Pinkerton's realized the usefulness of #68 was over; he was taken off the case and hence forward #91 carried the burden. Sherwood, who of course was advised, approved of the change and concurred that #91 should continue in his undercover role as replacement for #68 saying "there is no doubt she [Miss Seithen] is in touch with a dangerous element." Sherwood's comment on the general situation is interesting, reflecting as it does his confidence in Pinkerton's: "We have practically dropped all this shadowing business and are content to keep in touch with the situation generally which from all appearances is quite satisfactory."[12] It turned out Pfeil had become suspicious of the operative #68's prying and had his trunks removed to the office of the German consul for safekeeping. As of May 10, Pinkerton's had only one operative at work, at Hoboken, observing the German vessels. Pinkerton's were not convinced his presence was really necessary but in view of the sinking of the *Lusitania* on May 7, it might be wise to maintain surveillance a while longer. This was done. On May 29, operative #91 filed a report to note that "the Hamburg-Amerika Line are going to give all the men employed on the boats full pay from now on as all the men were dissatisfied." This caught Stephens' attention, for in a marginal note he left instructions to "extract the item." There were no further reports; it seems this news persuaded Stephens and Sherwood that the surveillance should end.

Was it worth the candle? Was anything achieved? Did anything valuable come out of it? Who knows; it was war time and often measures taken which at the time seemed sensible proved futile in the end. The only discernible result was the prevention of a bombing at the Swift plant, which could have been very serious causing many casualties, and could have interrupted food shipments to the Allies.

There was no discernible effect on German efforts to get their interned ships released, nor on British efforts to sink enemy vessels. The war went on.

The first of the three Seattle jobs related to a German freighter, the *Saxonia*, which was moored at Eagle Point, on Puget Sound, awaiting consignments of freight before heading out to sea. The British Consul at Seattle, learning the *Saxonia* might clandestinely load torpedo heads stored in barrels or kegs, informed the British Embassy, who in turn informed Commander Stephens in Ottawa, who then wrote Sherwood on the subject. The Consul had placed "one of his own men" to keep surveillance on the *Saxonia* and Pinkerton's was instructed to watch a dock in Seattle from which a coastal vessel sailed at regular intervals for Eagle Harbor. (This vessel was the only method of transporting freight from the docks at Seattle to Eagle Harbor.) It was assumed that if any torpedo heads were illicitly consigned to the *Saxonia*, they would be carried on it. Accordingly the operative kept a sharp eye on cargo transported to Eagle Harbor but noticed nothing suspicious and nothing consigned to the *Saxonia*. All his reports were sent to Sherwood who forwarded them to Stephens. Rumours of torpedo heads were just that — rumours.[13]

More serious was an episode hardly a week later on May 22, 1915.[14] There was a serious fire at a dock owned by the Northern Pacific Railway in Tacoma where armoured vehicles destined for Russia awaited unloading from railway cars. Two of the vehicles were destroyed in the fire, which badly damaged one of the railway cars. Since all munitions for Russia were shipped from west coast ports to Vladivostock to avoid the menace of the U-boats on the Atlantic, many people concluded right off the bat that the fire had been deliberately set by incendiarists working for Germany. All consuls and vice-consuls on the Pacific coast were under standing orders to send word to the admiral superintendent at the naval base at Esquimalt, near Victoria, of any suspected German involvement in matters which might affect British shipping on the Pacific. This officer, Rear Admiral W.G. Story, on receiving from Lucian Agassiz, the British vice-consul at Tacoma, a telegram suggesting a "German plot to destroy the Allies' Pacific coast shipping," sent word to Commander Stephens and through him to Sherwood. Agassiz had elevated a suspicious fire in Tacoma to become part of a concerted attack on the whole of allied shipping on the Pacific — a considerable feat. One who believed Germans were responsible was Charles Roediger, a 22-

year-old Canadian employed by the Customs Service, but detached from his normal duties to work as an undercover agent for Agassiz. In that capacity, he went to the dock immediately after the fire and concluded that the "fire was of incendiary origin and no doubt was perpetrated by some German." Agassiz initially had discounted any German involvement but Roediger persuaded him otherwise and Agassiz, on the twenty-fourth, sent the telegram to Story. Partly because all Pacific coast naval intelligence went through Story and partly because of his confidence in Pinkerton's, Sherwood contacted Ahern, still head of the Seattle office, who dispatched an operative to the scene of the fire. On May 26, he examined the damage, interviewed railway officials, the watchmen who had been on duty at the time of the fire, and the local police. He carried out a second inspection two days later on the twenty-eighth. A railway switching engineer working nearby had noticed smoke coming from one of the railcars on the dock but saw no suspicious persons or loiterers. Railway employees broke open the sealed door of the car and extinguished the fire. Every local official investigating the fire concluded it had started spontaneously among some oily cotton waste in the railcar. The Pinkerton man agreed; to conclude otherwise, he reported, would be "absurd." That report brought him into open warfare with Roediger. Whether it was because the latter was a brash young man, whether professional jealousy was at work — on both sides — or whether Roediger was suspicious of American private detective agents is not clear but he was scornful of the Pinkerton operative, named Robinson, who doubted there was any German sabotage on the Pacific coast. Robinson, Roediger said, was "inclined to throw cold water on anything which does not come from the Pinkerton headquarters," accusing him of "four flushing" by trying to "discredit everything we may turn into you [that is, to Story]." That letter, along with the Pinkerton reports, was passed on to Sherwood and Stephens in Ottawa.

It was no coincidence, therefore, that early in June, Stephens, who was not enamoured of using private agencies in security matters, met with Sherwood to express personal concerns about the value of Pinkerton's work on the Seattle case. But it may or may not have been a coincidence that a day or two later, on June 7, Spring-Rice sent his telegram to Sherwood questioning Pinkerton's bona fides. Stephens, who also received a copy of the telegram, wrote Sherwood the following day: "It was curious we should have been discussing the matter on Saturday. I would not presume to offer any opinion on

Pinkerton's in face of your experience of them, but the attached report from Mr. Roediger of 29 May about the burning of Russian automobiles at Tacoma does seem to give some reason for enquiring into the matter as it contradicts Pinkerton's report of 28 May in several material particulars."[15] Sherwood came down on Pinkerton's side. In a handwritten memo to Stephens he described Agassiz as "an unduly excited personage judging by his reports [which of course originated with Roediger]," going on to say that "if this govt were to undertake to watch all the ships loading for G.B. and her allies everywhere we would have no men for fighting purposes." After observing there was no evidence of enemy action in the fire, he advised "Don't let us be stampeded into folly by making him [Agassiz] secret service manager for the Pacific coast."[16] Allan Pinkerton himself was drawn into the controversy. On June 16 he wrote Sherwood that Roediger was entirely too young and incompetent for the work he was asked to do, and that Agassiz was a "talkative man ... inclined to believe everything that is brought to him." Pinkerton was firm: all the evidence was against a deliberately set fire and there were no German saboteurs in the Pacific Northwest.[17] Although Admiral Story, in Esquimalt, weighed into the argument on Stephens' side — as might have been expected — Sherwood and Pinkerton's came out on top; no evidence of a German connection with the fire was ever discovered.

Still, the doubters were given fresh cause, for on May 30, 1915, six days after the dock fire, a scow loaded with thirty tons of gunpowder, also destined for Vladivostock, exploded in Seattle harbour.[18] Newspapers said the explosion could be heard fifty miles away. A watchman supposedly on board was never found, but whether he was blown to bits or, having primed the detonator, escaped, was never established. The explosion caused extensive damage to buildings on shore, though no one was killed or injured (except perhaps the watchman). Agassiz on this occasion reported the matter in the first instance to Stephens and not to Story, who was thereby miffed, complaining that British consuls in the United States were not reporting to him as they had been told. The usual officials were notified, Stephens and Sherwood, and by June 1 Pinkerton's had been called in; Charles Roediger was assigned by Agassiz to determine the cause of the explosion. Robinson was not assigned but the operative who had kept a lookout for torpedo heads was; it is probable that Ahern, in view of the poisonous relationship between Roediger and Robinson, deliberately kept the latter off the scow case. Relations between the two men nonetheless were rancorous. Suspicion centred on a man named Smith who had left Seattle soon after the explosion; Agassiz, convinced he was the culprit, blamed Pinkerton's for not having him apprehended before he left town. In any case, the Pinkerton operative, on instructions from Ottawa, embarked on lengthy inquiries about Smith's activities in the Seattle-Tacoma area for the two-week period prior to the explosion when he was known to be in the area. The detailed descriptions of his movements, the conflicting stories he gave to a variety of people — store proprietors and hotel keepers, for example — about the reasons for his presence in Tacoma, his purchase of lengths of fuse, his knowledge of the German language, and his disappearance from Seattle right after the explosion, all cast suspicion on him. The operative's lengthy reports were handed into Agassiz who sent them to the Admiral in Victoria. Unlike the dock fire, in the scow case Agassiz approved of Pinkerton's, telling the Admiral the operative had "worked hard" in establishing "beyond doubt" that "Smith ... is the man who is responsible for the explosion." Smith was tracked down in the eastern United States by United States federal agents and by Pinkerton's and was arrested for complicity in the explosion.

He was placed on trial along with Franz Bopp, the German consul in San Francisco, Baron Von Schack, the vice-consul, the military attaché to the consulate and several others, all charged with conspiracy to violate United States neutrality laws by destroying "munitions of war and property of the entente allies."[19] This was a reference to plots to blow up Canadian ships leaving Canadian ports and Canadian railroads. Obviously this aspect of the trial was of great interest to Sherwood and his colleagues, particularly Stephens, heightened by learning that one of the co-conspirators, a Dutch national, had apparently fled to Canada. There is no record he was arrested but even if he had been it is questionable whether anything could have been done with him: he had committed no crime in Canada and conspiracy was not an extraditable offence. In addition, they were charged with the specific offence of blowing up the dynamite laden scow in Seattle harbour. The trial took place in United States District Court — a federal, not a state court — where only federal crimes were triable. Hence, the most that could be made of the explosion was that it constituted restraint of trade under the Sherman anti-trust laws, whereas the conspiracy charge was far more serious since it constituted an unauthorized "military enterprise."

Smith turned state's evidence (in Canada we would say "Queen's evidence"), that is to say, he agreed to testify against his fellow conspirators in return for his own immunity from prosecution. He had made all the plans for the explosion but another co-conspirator had set it off — no doubt the supposed "watchman" who could not be found. Some of the other witnesses had been turned up by Pinkerton's as a result of its inquiries in the Seattle area. All the accused were convicted and sentenced to terms of imprisonment. Allan Pinkerton's assurance to Sherwood in 1915 that there were no "German saboteurs in the Pacific Northwest" was clearly wrong.

The investigations of the two episodes — the railway dock fire and the scow explosion — were not well handled. Too many people were involved, sometimes working at cross-purposes: local police, fire department officials, United States agents, the British vice-consul and his undercover man, Charles Roediger, and, of course, Pinkerton's. For three weeks after the scow explosion Pinkerton's denied any German involvement, but was forced to concede its error, by which time Smith had left Seattle, making his eventual apprehension more difficult and costly. Through it all, however, and of great importance, the agency never lost Sherwood's confidence.

In June of 1915 there was a massive explosion at the Peabody plant in Windsor, Ontario, a manufacturer of military uniforms and accoutrements employing some six hundred women. This occurred at the same time as the planned but aborted bombing of the Windsor Armouries. Inquiries by the local police and by Pinkerton's, who were called in by Sherwood, immediately centred on Albert Kaltschmidt, a resident of Detroit. He was a German national married to an American with interests in legitimate business firms in Detroit as well as in a plant in Windsor, The Tate Electric Co. But Kaltschmidt used his business ventures to disguise his schemes as a German agent plotting acts of violence against factories and military installations on both sides of the border, and bridges linking the two countries. He was not acting on his own, but under orders from von Papen at the German Embassy, which financed his activities. It was the presumed connection between the Windsor explosion, plotted by Kaltschmidt with the backing of von Papen, that led to the latter's expulsion from the United States at the end of 1915. The presumed connection was verified by the discovery amongst von Papen's papers, seized from him on his arrival in England, of a cheque for $1000 payable to Kaltschmidt dated March 1915. The cheque was not sent by the embassy but through an intermediary in New York City. Kaltschmidt was interviewed about this revelation and refused to say anything about it, or about his relations with von Papen.[20] Kaltschmidt himself remained immune from prosecution by Canada, since the type of offence had been declared by United States courts to be non-extraditable, and since the United States government had as yet no hard evidence of Kaltschmidt conspiring against an American target. He was also immune in that country until the declaration of war in 1917.

The Windsor bombing was planned by Kaltschmidt, who enlisted William Lefler and Carl Respa as co-conspirators. Lefler was not known as one sympathetic to the German cause, but had worked for Kaltschmidt's factory in Windsor until the outbreak of war when Kaltschmidt, as a German national and as someone unable to legally cross into Canada, was forced to give up his interest in the factory. Lefler was a bit of a loser and seems to have been merely a catspaw attracted by the prospect of money offered him by Kaltschmidt if he, Lefler, would plant a couple of suitcases of "stuff," meaning dynamite, to be detonated by a clock as timer. Lefler later testified the dynamite had been brought over to Windsor by Kaltschmidt in small quantities on a number of occasions under the cushion of the rumble seat of his coupé. As to how Kaltschmidt was able to cross over the border so often without being arrested, Lefler could only speculate he was bribing the border customs officers. In any case, Lefler agreed to "plant" one suitcase at the Peabody Factory and the other at the Windsor Armouries, where several hundred servicemen were quartered, in return for $200. Kaltschmidt gave him twenty-five dollars as an advance but Lefler never saw the rest; Kaltschmidt welched on him. Carl Respa was also a German national who, before emigrating to the United States, served a stint in the German army. In the United States he worked in factories where electrical fittings were common, and it was he who designed and assembled the timing mechanism of the two bombs. He also had been promised $200 by Kaltschmidt and he also was short-changed, though, unlike Lefler, his heart was in the enterprise so that Kaltschmidt's failure to pay him as agreed did not rankle quite so much.

The two men crossed into Windsor from Detroit at will. No one questioned them. They assembled the bombs at the Tate Electric Co., Lefler's workplace, placing them in suitcases. The bomb they placed at the Peabody plant was smaller than the one at the armouries, seven sticks of dynamite as opposed to twenty-seven in the armouries bomb.

In the dead of night of June 20, 1915, they placed the Peabody bomb in an aperture at the front of the plant (which they had previously scouted) and hid the armouries bomb just outside the rear wall of the massive structure, setting the clocks to explode at 3:15 a.m. on the morning of the twenty-first. Respa returned forthwith to Detroit, but Lefler stayed on in Windsor. He suffered pangs of conscience, and began to think of all the people who would likely be killed in an explosion at the armouries (the Peabody plant would be empty at the planned time of the explosion). He returned to the armouries, disconnected the timing mechanism, and went home. Testimony at his trial established that the bomb, had it exploded, would indeed have reduced the armouries to rubble and caused many casualties. Kaltschmidt was not to learn until later that Lefler had defused the bomb on humanitarian grounds; he was outraged by what he perceived as betrayal, not appreciating the irony that his plans had been thwarted by a man whom he had cheated. The bomb at Peabody's did, however, explode on time, causing some damage — though not crippling — to the factory premises which was soon repaired; after only a brief interruption, production of soldiers' uniforms resumed. There was no doubt in the minds of the police and the military that the Peabody explosion and the "apparently" attempted explosion at the armouries were the work of German saboteurs. Only six weeks earlier the *Lusitania* had been torpedoed off Ireland without warning by a German U-boat with heavy loss of life; any outrage therefore was undoubtedly the work of Germans. And the authorities were right: soon after the explosion Kaltschmidt was identified as the evil genius behind it.

In efforts to track down the perpetrators, hundreds of the military were called out, not just locally, but from elsewhere in Ontario; police reinforcements were stationed at strategic points along the border, guards were placed on bridges and at the Michigan Central tunnel, and Lieutenant-Colonel Sherwood was officially notified. He dispatched some of his officers to Windsor and contacted Superintendent W.H. Jenkins of Pinkerton's Detroit office. Initial investigation and area searches turned up approximately sixty sticks of dynamite in several locations. Having been instructed by Sherwood to work on the investigation, Pinkerton's assigned Frank Dimaio, one of its most skilled detectives, to the case. He, it may be recalled, was the Pinkerton expert in the crimes of the Black Hand.[21] The start of Dimaio's investigation coincided with a news story in a Detroit paper that a watchman at the Tate Electric Co. plant at Windsor by the name of William Lefler had found seven sticks of dynamite in the yard of the plant. Dimaio and a detective of the Dominion Police interviewed the man. Something in his demeanour convinced them he knew far more about the origins of the dynamite than he initially stated and, finally, after persistent questioning, he admitted that the dynamite was part of a cache brought into Windsor by Albert Kaltschmidt, who had hired him and another man (subsequently identified as Carl Respa) to carry out the bombings. Lefler was arrested and Dimaio tried unsuccessfully on several visits to the jail to garner additional information, though Lefler eventually gave the police a complete confession, which was admitted into the evidence at his trial. But Lefler did give Dimaio valuable information which led ultimately to Respa's arrest. Lefler said a man named Schmidt had been convicted and sentenced to imprisonment in Kingston Penitentiary for an attempt to blow up the bridge at Nipigon, Ontario, and that his wife's brother was Carl Respa, who was living with her in Detroit (Lefler provided the police with the address). Dimaio called on the woman under the guise of a penitentiary official inquiring if she was managing all right, and learned that Respa was boarding with her, though he was absent at the time. She also took in other boarders. Dimaio then got an undercover agent to secure work at the Ford Motor Company in Detroit; he became a boarder and met Respa soon afterwards. In the meantime, Lefler stood trial and on July 29, 1915 was convicted and sentenced to ten years imprisonment. In his confession he implicated both Kaltschmidt and Respa, though the former was the ringleader.

The trick now was to lure Respa into Canada. The police would dearly have loved to get Kaltschmidt into Canada but never really tried, assuming he would be careful not to be caught over the border. The "star boarder," the Pinkerton man, ingratiated himself with Mrs. Schmidt, her brother Respa, and other family members. He became very much *en famille*. One day he suggested a jolly family picnic on a small island in the St. Clair River where there was a popular picnic beach. Mrs. Schmidt and Respa, believing the island to be American since it was such a well-known spot, readily agreed. In fact, the island lies within Canada.

The operative passed on these arrangements to Superintendent Jenkins who in turn notified the Windsor police. On the day chosen for the picnic, August 29, 1915, the Schmidt family boarded the ferry to the island; also aboard were Jenkins and two Canadian policemen, all in plain clothes. As the ferry approached the dock, Respa spotted a

Canadian flag and became excited, refusing to disembark. The operative reassured him that the flag was simply flying as a goodwill gesture by Americans towards Canada. Respa was pacified. When he stepped on to the dock one of the passenger policemen who had already disembarked stepped forward: "Charles Respa you are under arrest." Respa tried to escape but was collared and put aboard the ferry to the Canadian shore. On the way he dropped into the river a letter which was subsequently recovered. It was written in German to one Boeninghausen in Hoboken, New Jersey, who was well known as an active supporter of Germany. A translation of the letter dated August 28, the day before Respa's arrest, was produced in court at his trial. It was concerned with clandestine arrangements to keep Respa's whereabouts concealed, but the most important feature of it was Respa's request to his friend to arrange an alibi by telling anyone inquiring of him that he had been in Hoboken for the previous four months and had never left.[22] Respa was placed in the cells in Windsor under exceptionally heavy guard. This highly successful Pinkerton operation, which occurred only two months after the British Ambassador questioned the agency's bona fides, was followed by further valuable undercover work.

Respa was arraigned immediately after his arrest but there were various delays in the court proceedings, requests for adjournment by his lawyers, unavailability of judges, and procedural difficulties, the result being that he didn't come to trial until March of the following year — most unusual since trials in that era generally proceeded expeditiously. It became important to forestall any perjured alibi evidence suggested by Respa in his letter to his associate in Hoboken. Pinkerton's learned that two men from that city had travelled to Detroit expressly for that purpose, and notified the Ontario police. Pinkerton's then were instructed to place the men under surveillance and learn, if possible, their plans. The two checked into a Detroit hotel where they met Kaltschmidt. The Pinkerton operative booked the room immediately next door to that of the Hoboken men and watched and listened over a period of ten days. Whether the room walls were paper thin or whether there were open windows in the two rooms close to each other is not clear, but the operative heard a great deal. Lawyers, hired by Kaltschmidt who agreed to pay the two men $1000 for their testimony,[23] came to the room and rehearsed with the two men the testimony they would have to give to support an alibi, and prepared written statements which the two could memorize, details of which the operative was able to hear. The essence of the fabricated evidence was that suggested by Respa in his letter — that he had been in Hoboken for four months and couldn't have been involved in the bombing.[24] If the two men testified at Respa's trial, the Pinkerton man would have been called as a witness. As it turned out, Respa did not try to establish an alibi at his trial; although his lawyer obtained a court order permitting him to examine potential defence witnesses at Hoboken under oath for use at the trial, he did not proceed with it. Pinkerton's was retained to have one of their men present at the examination, had it occurred.[25] The Hoboken men did not perjure themselves and the operative remained incognito. Still, it was a good piece of work by the agency.

Another matter of concern for the prosecuting lawyers was the admissibility of the confession Respa had made within hours of his arrest, giving full details of the plot. There were a number of police officers present when Respa confessed, so many that it might be argued the confession was the result of third degree methods and hence inadmissible. A Pinkerton man visited Respa in his cell three days after his arrest; he does not say in his report why he went but one can infer the prosecution wanted a confession from Respa free of any taint. And Respa did give the operative full details of his involvement. The operative stood ready to testify to his conversation with Respa if necessary, but the court ruled that Respa's first confession was admissible, holding that he made it voluntarily free of any coercion.[26]

Respa stood trial early in March 1916. Though not in manacles, he was heavily guarded and extraordinary precautions had been taken in view of his apparent attempt to break out of prison a few months earlier. Pinkerton undercover men circulated among the spectators and sat in the public gallery keeping an eye open for "suspicious characters" loitering about the courthouse. There was a stir in the courtroom when the prosecution called Lefler to the stand to testify against his fellow conspirator, which he did with apparent willingness. The jury was out for barely half an hour, finding Respa guilty as charged. He was sentenced to life imprisonment. The presiding judge characterized him as a "hired incendiary and assassin"; the Windsor newspaper reported that he took "his medicine with stoicism."[27] Kaltschmidt, meanwhile, freely roamed the streets of Detroit. He airily dismissed the reports of his having been indicted in Ontario as a co-conspirator, sending messages of condolence to Canadians who were to be pitied for not having thrown off the British yoke. He continued to attend pro-Teutonic gatherings, and to judge from transactions in his bank account in October 1916, he was still financing clandestine operations. He continued to be under surveillance by Pinkerton's, one of whose operatives managed to gain access to his banking records.[28] Even though he couldn't be extradited to Canada, one would have thought he would have been prosecuted in the United States for violation of the neutrality laws. In view of his cocksure attitude following the bombing trials in Windsor, he was evidently confident of immunity on both sides of the border.

But all that was to change with the Americans' entry into the war. Dimaio, still with Pinkerton's, had kept himself informed on all aspects of Kaltschmidt's activities. When a declaration of war on Germany was imminent, Dimaio contacted the United States district attorney in Detroit to turn over to him the Pinkerton dossier on Kaltschmidt who, with several relatives and associates, was arrested on the very day of the declaration and charged with making explosive devices intended for blowing up factories making war supplies in the United States and in Canada. Kaltschmidt was also charged with plotting to dynamite the Grand Trunk Railway tunnel between Port Huron and Sarnia. Lefler was brought over to testify against Kaltschmidt, presumably having volunteered to do so. (Respa did not appear.) It came out that Kaltschmidt had received a total of $77,000 from the German Embassy to finance his operations. Convicted, he was sentenced to a lengthy term of imprisonment, and after serving four years was released for deportation to Germany. In 1927, he was given permission by the United States to make a two-month business visit; he overstayed his leave and was again arrested and deported. He did not return.[29]

Canadian Explosives plant at Nobel, Ontario. Site of a bomb attack investigated by Pinkerton's.
NAC PA 24489

Late in November 1915, while arrangements for Respa's trial were going forward, there was an explosion at the munitions factory of Canadian Explosives Ltd. at Nobel (named after the Swedish explosives giant), a small town seven miles north of Parry Sound, Ontario. The explosion destroyed four small buildings scattered about the property which were used to dry explosive material; the fact that all were destroyed simultaneously suggested an incendiary device had been placed in each. The explosion went off in the early evening and, although about seven hundred people were employed at the plant, there were no injuries. A nearby military unit was called out to cordon off the plant, and other units were put on standby. (It was learned a bomb had been placed at the plant two weeks earlier and had been defused, but it was not believed to be the work of saboteurs but of a disgruntled employee with a grievance.) That the explosion was the "work of alien enemies," as the *Toronto Globe* put it, was doubted by no one and it seemed probable it had been an inside job carried out by a pro-German employee. Materials relating to Pinkerton's involvement are sketchy, but it seems the agency through its Toronto branch was put on the case soon after the blast, probably at the instance of Lieutenant-Colonel Sherwood.[30] The Pinkerton operative concentrated on learning which of the many employees, male and female, were of German or Austrian origin, and if not of either, had expressed sympathy for the German cause. Working openly and not undercover he identified a number of workmen with demonstrable German backgrounds, narrowing down the list of those to a handful of men whom he considered suspect because of their Germanic background or their savoir faire which, he thought, would make them capable of plotting an explosion, though he had no proof whatever of their guilt. In wartime, niceties are often ignored; the men were fired but never charged, and the explosion remains as one of the many unsolved wartime mysteries.

Another possible act of unsolved sabotage, which followed hard on the heels of the Nobel explosion, was the spectacular fire on the early morning of February 4, 1916, which destroyed the Parliament Buildings in Ottawa, leaving standing, as if by some miracle, only the splendid library. Seven people died in the conflagration. It was difficult to persuade the man in the street that the Germans were not involved; parliamentarians, newspapermen, ordinary citizens, all cast about for likely perpetrators of the "outrage." The *Halifax Herald* newspaper ran a cartoon showing a grinning skull wearing a Prussian helmet hovering over the burning buildings, captioned "Did Bernstorff [the German Ambassador in Washington] pay for this job?" The fire fell squarely within the jurisdiction of the Dominion Police, who were responsible for protection of all federal buildings, and Sherwood took charge of directing the inquiry into the fire's origin. Unlike the majority of his fellow citizens, he did not believe the fire resulted from sabotage, but felt it must have stemmed from some accidental cause. With full confidence in his men, he simply didn't believe an arsonist could have slipped past the guards. Still, there were persons suspected of complicity who had to be checked. One of these was a Belgian pianist who, the evening before the early morning fire, had given a concert in Ottawa and left town abruptly afterwards for another concert. On learning that he was to journey by train to Windsor, Sherwood contacted Pinkerton's Detroit office. Accompanied by a Canadian police officer, James Smith, who had been one of those instrumental in the arrest of the bomber, Carl Respa, the Pinkerton man searched the train, found the pianist, and detained him for questioning. He was absolved. A Royal Commission set up to probe the causes of the fire concluded in its report of May 16, 1916 that there was "nothing in the evidence to justify [a] finding that the fire was maliciously set."[31]

Early in 1916 Pinkerton's mounted a surveillance operation in Buffalo, New York, which was to last five months. It was conducted throughout by operative #24S. There is nothing in the official material to offer any clue as to what specific event prompted it.[32] Two years earlier there had been a flurry of rumours that the German-Americans in the city were plotting to raise an army of German patriots to invade Canada. Though such stories proved groundless, there was indeed a sizable community of German-Americans and German nationals in the city. Commander Stephens did not receive copies of Pinkerton's espionage reports unless there was a shipping or naval element, but since Buffalo, though not a deep sea port like New York or Boston, was on Lake Erie and a considerable volume of shipping went through it, he received copies of all the reports of this operation. That he read them is clear from his marginal notes. There is no doubt that the operation was connected in some way with the ever-increasing likelihood that the Americans would enter the war and that it was desirable to gauge the reaction of German-Americans to such an eventuality with whatever ramifications their reactions might hold for shipping on the Great Lakes.

The operative's first report is dated February 9, 1917, but from Sherwood's marginal note on a copy he sent to Stephens it seems that the operation had already been underway, though one cannot say for how long. In any case the operative spent the next five months as a barfly, wandering from one bar to another, all haunts of German nationals, naturalized Americans of German origin, Austrians, Poles, and Hungarians. He does not say what pose he assumed but undoubtedly he took a German name — if he didn't already have one — and spoke the language fluently and colloquially. He set off around noon each day, staying up late, sometimes until three in the morning, often visiting half-a-dozen establishments in the course of a day, taking pains to record whether particular bars were or were not well patronized. He joined in the conversation and noted all the bar talk and gossip as the beer flowed. He must have had the constitution of an ox. The principal topics of conversation, or at least those which he most commonly recorded, ranged all the way from plans to invade Canada with an army of German patriots raised in the United States (as well as plans to foment an uprising by German partisans should the United States declare war on Germany) to condemnation of prohibition and its champion, Billy Sunday.[33] It wasn't just that prohibition would throw a lot of brewery employees out of work and deny the pleasures of drink to bar habitués, but that most brewery workers were "either Germans or of German descent."[34] On one occasion the operative, with many others, went to hear a speech by a female Swiss socialist in which she "condemned the Kaiser and the Prussian Militarisms in unmistakable terms"; he observed that many Germans in the audience walked out in protest.

But the single most common topic of discussion was whether the Americans would declare war on Germany, and the ramifications for German individuals, German enterprises, and, in particular, German shipping. Early in March 1917, the operative reported that most of his fellow barflies doubted the United States would go into the war because of the large number of citizens of German origin, yet by mid-March opinion had shifted, most believing war between Germany and the United States was inevitable. On the other hand, the president of the German-American Alliance, a prominent organization, had, six weeks before war was declared (on April 2, 1917), sent President Wilson a letter assuring him he would have the support of "three million German-Americans to fight for the United States against any enemy." This assertion did not sit well with the operative's drinking pals.[35] German nationals were understandably worried about the very real prospect of internment and those who were naturalized worried about conscription, which was bound to follow a declaration of war.

The topics mentioned in the many reports which caught Stephens' attention, for he noted them, related to shipping both deep sea and on the Great Lakes, and the employment of aliens on vessels. Even before the outbreak of war, vessel owners on the Great Lakes and in New York, so the operative reported, refused to hire German aliens or even naturalized Germans because marine insurance companies had refused to insure vessels which employed German crew members. There was, however, some relaxation of the prohibition since naturalized Germans, after the outbreak of war, did find work on Great Lakes vessels.[36]

Most of the barroom talk before the American declaration of war was bluster-liquor talking. The operative never heard any reference to an actual attack or plans for one. As he observed: "There are no indications anywhere to show that any concerted plans are in progress to get all the Germans or Reservists together in case of trouble or start a revolt of any kind."[37] Once war was declared the bluster disappeared, or at least any public display of it. Germans stopped talking about the war and some bartenders took down the German flag and other Teutonic emblems decorating their premises. Gone, also, were portraits of the Kaiser, to be replaced in virtually every bar by the American flag. Even the head of the German-American Alliance in Buffalo, who had expressed support for the United States, no longer talked of the war. And at an annual picnic convened by a number of German organizations, the "Wacht am Rhien," which on former occasions was played constantly by a brass band, was no longer heard. The operative described an amusing scene that occurred just a few days after the declaration of war:

At Bauer's hofbrau, Pine Hill, there was also a large crowd of Germans. The piano player at this place, in a moment of forgetfullness, started to play the "Wacht am Rhien." I noticed several strangers who were in the place sort of held their breaths; so I went to the piano player and told him to follow this up with "Star Spangled Banner" which he did — and everything passed off okay. I know this piano player well. He is an American and is not even of German Descent and he did not play "Die Wacht am Rhien" intentionally. There were no signs of any group of Germans being together at this place or uniting their efforts to bring harm to this country or its Government in any way.[38]

He filed a report on July 4, 1917, the final one for an operation that marked the end of Pinkerton's wartime espionage for Canada. In retrospect, it was an extraordinary operation, with little apparent purpose, but such was the nature of wartime espionage. Pinkerton's first wartime engagement on Canada's behalf was in 1914. For three years it had been the eyes and ears of the Canadian government in the United States in security and intelligence matters. Lieutenant-Colonel Sherwood, in spite of doubts expressed by the likes of Commissioner A.B. Perry of the NWMP and Commander Stephens, remained loyal throughout to Pinkerton's, on whose expertise he relied. His reliance stemmed from an association which began in 1885 and was warmed by a close personal relationship with William Pinkerton in Chicago and, later, Allan Pinkerton, grandson of the founder, in New York. It is perhaps a fitting coincidence that Sherwood's tenure as commissioner of the Dominion Police, and spymaster, ended in 1918, just a few months after Pinkerton's completed its last assignment for him; the conjunction of those events marked the end in Canada of personalized espionage, if one can use that phrase, and the commencement of an institutional model resulting from the merger of the Dominion Police with the NWMP in 1920 to form the Royal Canadian Mounted Police.

Ten

Politics and Politicians

So far we have been looking at Pinkerton's role in the investigation and detection of crime (with some exceptions, specifically the Fenian raids, the Reno and Anderson extradition, and wartime espionage). This chapter will deal with episodes which were politically oriented, though in some of them crime was certainly involved.

There are two broad categories of Pinkerton's political work: retainer of Pinkerton's by a politician for personal reasons, and retainer by a politician with some specific objective in mind. The most notable example of the latter category was the hiring of Pinkerton's by the then-attorney general of Manitoba, Clifford Sifton, in the aftermath of the famous 1896 Dominion election in which the Manitoba Separate Schools question was the burning issue. To unseat elected Conservatives because of suspected election frauds in the hope that in resulting by-elections Liberals would be returned in their stead, he engaged the agency to supply detectives to do an extensive investigation. The affair, ultimately reaching the House of Commons, is a splendid example of parish-pump politics and venal political behaviour which no doubt could be multiplied many times over in that era, but this one is fully documented and can be savoured to the full.

Separate schools in Manitoba for Roman Catholics — and the funding of these schools — had bedevilled provincial politics for years prior to 1896 and were to do so for many years afterwards. In 1890 the Liberal government of Thomas Greenway abolished public funding of Roman Catholic separate schools, a decision reviled in Quebec and controversial elsewhere. Proponents of separate schools launched a constitutional challenge but the Privy Council upheld the legislation. The issue did not go away, however, and the federal government on which the courts conferred jurisdiction to pass remedial legislation was drawn into the argument, trying to find some remedy which would be palatable to Ontario Protestants and which would placate Quebec Roman Catholics. There were several Cabinet crises over the issue along divisive religious lines. A bill drawn in 1894 by Minister of Justice Sir Charles Hibbert Tupper (known as "Sir Hibbert" Tupper to distinguish him from his father "Sir Charles") amounted to a toleration of separate schools, though it did not provide public funding. Sir Charles Tupper, who became prime minister on May 1, 1896, tried desperately to get his son's bill passed but failed when it was blocked in Parliament by Wilfrid Laurier (whose behaviour in the affair hardly does him credit) and his Quebec caucus, and by the likes of D'Alton McCarthy, a Protestant and member of the Toronto establishment. Tupper dissolved Parliament and called a general election for June 23, 1896. Laurier won 49 of Quebec's 65 seats, decisively defeating Tupper, whom he succeeded as prime minister in July. Having opposed the Conservative remedial legislation he cynically put forward a scheme not much different but for which he and not Tupper could command support in Quebec.

There were seven parliamentary ridings in Manitoba, and of those four were won by Conservatives, two by Liberals, and the seventh by D'Alton McCarthy, who had run in Brandon riding as an independent. Though Clifford Sifton was prominent in the campaign he was not a candidate, remaining as provincial attorney general in the Greenway administration. Within days of the general election, however, he vowed, in effect, to reverse the election results by unseating three of the Conservatives for breaches of the Controverted Elections Act and engaged the leading trial lawyer of the day, H.M. Howell, a Liberal (and a future chief justice of Manitoba) to act for the government in taking the necessary steps. But which government? Manitoba or Ottawa? That question became the source of Sifton's future embarrassment. As attorney general he could commit provincial funds to pay for the prosecution of controverted elections, but not being a member of the Ottawa government he had no authority to commit it to any expenditure for the same purpose. In a letter to Laurier, Sifton said that he had "conclusive evidence of an organized system of tampering with ballots which constitutes the most colossal crime against honest elections which I have ever had any knowledge of." He went on to say that "skilled detectives" were at work whose "purpose is to promptly but secretly push the inquiries and secure evidence upon which to convict the guilty parties." But to do so, he went on, would incur an expense beyond the "financial competence of my department," and therefore it was the "plain duty" of the Laurier government to pay it, though in the meantime Sifton himself would personally bear the expense. Laurier replied that "I feel confident that you will unearth the most odious conspiracy that has taken place for many long years, and we will most willingly furnish the necessary funds for the service."[1] According to Sir Louis Davies, another federal Cabinet minister, the government did eventually pass an Order-in-Council to authorize payment of the election expenses. Sir Hibbert, who became Sifton's most vociferous critic, was compelled to shift his criticism from saying there was no authorization for the expense to arguing there should have been no authorization when the matter was wholly within provincial jurisdiction, which meant the province had exclusive responsibility for payment of costs of the administration of justice.[2]

On direct instructions from Sifton, Howell hired a team of three Pinkerton detectives from the agency office in St. Paul. It was by no means the first time Howell had had dealings with Pinkerton's; as a Crown prosecutor at Criminal Assizes, he later testified, he had hired the agency to do the investigation in "five or six" murder cases. Regrettably there was no reference by him — it was hardly germane to the electoral proceedings — to the specifics, though he did say one case had been in the town of Holland. Official records of this work by Pinkerton's have not been preserved, but the reference by Howell is valuable, affording as it does a further illustration of the reliance of provincial law enforcement officials on the agency's expertise in cases of serious crime. The three detectives fanned out through the contested ridings: Marquette, Macdonald (which had been taken by one Nathaniel Boyd), and Winnipeg (taken by Hugh John Macdonald, son of the late prime minister), scouring every polling district within the ridings. They worked undercover, adopting various stratagems. Howell, when testifying before the Public Accounts Committee, recalled that one of the detectives represented himself as a picture seller. Howell, or other lawyers working for him, then travelled to the place where the Pinkerton men had been and took, or endeavoured to secure, sworn depositions. If a ballot had handwriting on it, Pinkerton's employed a handwriting analyst in an attempt to identify the writer.[3]

The detectives turned up a variety of "irregularities" — a euphemism for outright fraud. There was the time-honoured method of plying doubtful voters with strong drink to assist them in making up their minds. At a time when a person could act as "agent," casting a ballot on behalf of someone prevented by physical incapacity or illness from voting in person, it was found at one polling station that twenty-four votes had been cast on behalf of the same person. In another case of fraud the Conservatives had hired a card-shark and got him appointed a deputy returning officer. He kept in his pocket ballots marked for the Conservative candidate, and when a well-known Liberal voted and came to deposit his ballot in the box, the sleight-of-hand expert substituted the Conservative ballot. At some polls, the number of ballots cast would sometimes exceed the number of names on the voters' list. Other times the fraud would be more blatant; by sleight of hand the ballots would simply be destroyed, and on one occasion, when two well-known Liberals came for their ballots, an assistant of the deputy returning officer surreptitiously substituted a blue pencil for the obligatory black pencil in the polling booth so that the ballots, when marked blue, were declared invalid. These types of election fraud were common in the nineteenth century in all provinces and nobody worried very much about them; they were a fact of life. If a Liberal was elected by fraudulent means in one riding, so was a Conservative elsewhere and the two results were cancelled out, or "sawed off" as the phrase had it, by politicians. Only in extreme cases would they wind up in court. In the case of the 1896 Manitoba election, Sifton was out for blood and there were to be no saw-offs.

There were two aspects of the Pinkerton investigation: the prosecution of the deputy returning officers and their assistants for fraudulent practices, and, in consequence, the use of evidence gathered by the Pinkerton men to support the efforts to oust the three Conservatives.

Gathering the evidence was one thing, securing a conviction was another. Howell acted as prosecutor in all the cases against deputy returning officers, but he was up against another fact of electoral life in Manitoba in that era, that there would be many Conservatives on juries sworn to hear the testimony. (Had roles been reversed, a

Conservative prosecutor would have had to contend with a jury composed of Liberals.) Howell readily agreed, when asked, that there was "political bias [amongst juries] on both sides," and that he did not "think that the angels are all on one side." In fact, he said at Portage la Prairie, the jurors came in "swarms," with the "Conservative jurymen [in] one pack and the Liberal jurymen in another pack."[4] The upshot was that only one of the many deputy returning officers was convicted; the unlucky man was sentenced to six months in prison. In one instance the charges were thrown out by the Grand Jury so that the case never went to trial at all; one of the Grand jurors proved to be the brother of Nathaniel Boyd. There were an astonishing number of witnesses involved in the various prosecutions; Howell testified he had never had a case with so many witnesses; one thousand of them, he said, of whom 175 actually testified at the various trials.[5]

But the process was different in attempting to invalidate the elections: those proceedings would not be heard by a jury but by a judge who was less likely to be affected by political affiliation, be it Liberal or Conservative. In the result, Boyd lost his seat in Macdonald and Hugh John Macdonald in Winnipeg; the petition to unseat the incumbent in Marquette was dismissed on technical grounds. The case of Hugh John Macdonald was particularly sad. He hadn't wanted to run in the first place but had been talked into it. No one really believed he had any knowledge of, or would have condoned, the frauds committed by the local Conservative machine on his behalf. Even Howell defended him, saying he was convinced Macdonald had no knowledge whatever of the frauds committed by his supporters. Sir Hibbert Tupper tried to persuade Sifton to allow Macdonald to quietly resign his seat; Sifton refused and, determined to humiliate Macdonald, a decent man, insisted that the court proceedings should continue; thereafter he and Tupper were at daggers drawn. By December 1896, Sifton had achieved two-thirds of his objective: Boyd and Hugh John Macdonald had been unseated and in the ensuing by-elections Liberals replaced the former incumbents. In August 1896, Laurier asked Sifton to resign his provincial position and join the federal Cabinet. Sifton accepted, but a seat had to be found for him. McCarthy obligingly resigned his seat in Brandon, and Sifton was elected. Thus of the seven Manitoba seats, five were Liberal and two Conservative.

All that was known publicly at the time of the electoral investigations was that "skilled detectives" employed by Sifton had turned up evidence of massive frauds on the part of electoral officials.

Few people knew that the "skilled detectives" were Pinkerton operatives. Even fewer people knew that Sifton himself had financed the investigation. He personally paid for the entire cost of the electoral investigation in the expectation the federal government would recoup him for Pinkerton's expenses, which amounted to just under $2,000,[6] and Howell's and other lawyers' fees, all of which came to about $19,000 — a substantial amount for those times. Pinkerton's at that time charged out their operatives' fees at six dollars per diem; Howell charged out his fees at $2.50 per hour. He submitted a bill for the entire sum to the office of the minister of justice for reimbursement. As was the procedure then (and still is) an official in the department scrutinizes the bill to decide if it conforms to departmental standards, disallowing items that do not conform, with the result that Sifton's bill for $19,000 was reduced to about $11,000, leaving him responsible for the difference. The Pinkerton bill was not reduced since it was an out-of-pocket expense; the $11,000 was paid out of public funds without being charged to any parliamentary appropriation.

These financial dealings involving the payment of money out of unappropriated funds lay concealed; Sifton had to make good the deficiency with a loan from his bank whining that his parliamentary indemnity would be taken up to repay it. Early in 1898 Sir Hibbert Tupper, who had many reasons to loathe Sifton, learned from the report of the auditor general for 1897 that the government of Canada had paid to Howell's law firm nearly $11,000 to pay for prosecutions of electoral fraud in Manitoba. Tupper asked himself: "Why is the government of Canada paying out $11,000 'for expenses in connection for prosecution for election frauds in Manitoba including $4,000 transferred from unforeseen expenses?'" He would then have noticed that the expense was buried in the public accounts for the Northwest Territories; Manitoba had not been part of the Territories since 1870.[7]

To modern readers, the attempt by a government in the 1890s to disguise an expense not authorized by a parliamentary appropriation which should properly have been paid by the provincial government may seem trivial in the extreme; at the time it was an important principle: there can be no expenditure of public funds without sanction from Parliament, and any deviation from that principle, which seemed to favour the reigning party, attracted severe criticism. Laurier's letter of assurance to Sifton early on that he would sanction the expense ran up against that principle and when the attorney general of Manitoba, as loyal a Liberal as could be found, thought he should be reimbursed because of his party loyalty, he was surprised to learn that not everyone agreed with him. Certainly not Sir Hibbert Tupper who had found out, one does not know how, that Sifton had hired Pinkerton's for his political purposes and charged the expense clandestinely to the federal and not the provincial treasury. Tupper's discovery led to the affair being referred to the Public Accounts Committee of the House of Commons which convened hearings at which all the principal participants testified — Sifton, Howell, Sir Louis Davies, E.L. Newcombe (the deputy minister of justice), and officials of his department, all of whom were cross-examined vigorously by Tupper at great length. In August 1899, over a year after the hearings of the committee, it formally concluded that "the circumstances ... amply justified the expenditure of the sums disbursed by the government and the government was acting in the public interests in the course which it had pursued in regard thereto."[8]

By that date, however, Tupper had raised the whole matter again, this time in the House of Commons. It came up in an unexpected manner. In 1898 there had been allegations of misfeasance by government officials in the Yukon involving the taking of bribes, allocation of mineral claims to government officials and speculation by them, and the granting of valuable placer leases to friends of the government. Sifton, the minister responsible for Yukon affairs, refused for a long time to make any investigation by appointing a commission of inquiry, telling Laurier it would amount to an admission of guilt to do so. The alleged scandals, or rather the controversy about inquiring into them, lasted well into 1899 when on March 30 Tupper linked Sifton's attitude to his handling of the election frauds in Manitoba. The Laurier government had appropriated public money before it had any legal right to do so to pay for Pinkerton detectives, Tupper argued. The government went "to fish for evidence" and at an expense of $18,000 caught "one miserable creature" (a reference to the single conviction). Why then, Tupper thundered, does not Sifton employ the same fishing tactics in the Yukon where the evidence of skullduggery, he claimed, was far more convincing than the election frauds. The answer of course, Tupper said, was that Sifton protected his friends in the Yukon but hounded his opponents in Manitoba.[9] That was a theme on which Tupper played with every variation imaginable in almost interminable debates in March and May of 1899, during which there were constant references to Pinkerton's role.

He did not blame them — they were in the detective business after all
— but the government which hired them. At the conclusion of a five
hour speech by Tupper on May 16, a government member rejoined:

Of Tupper young and Tupper old
Two belted knights of the Tory fold
Of Tupper schemes and Tupper bluff
Thank the Lord, we've had enough.

There were many members of the House, some on the
Conservative side, who would have muttered "amen to that." Tupper
left federal politics in 1904 to move to Vancouver to practice law.
There he began to meddle in provincial politics and was soon at odds
with the youthful, recently elected premier, Richard McBride, a fellow
Conservative, a relationship which was partly responsible for McBride
hiring Pinkerton's in 1906 to spy on Tupper and other Conservative
stalwarts. McBride, a highly personable figure, became premier of
British Columbia in 1903 at age 32, the youngest person to head a
provincial government (the record still stands), and became leader of
the first government in British Columbia formed on strict party lines.
In his first administration he held only a bare majority of seats in the
legislature, which made him all the more vulnerable to attacks made
upon him in 1906, which arose out of the government railway policy.
Construction of railways and selections of routes and terminals were
always fruitful sources of political jiggery-pokery and litigation. In
1903 the Grand Trunk Railway announced plans to extend its line to
the Pacific Coast, not to the lower mainland but to the more central
part of the province. The Laurier government, wishing to see the
project proceed, asked the McBride government to make a land grant
of six million acres for the purpose. McBride refused, but knowing the
company wished to place its terminal on Kaien Island, on which the
city of Prince Rupert now stands, made a deal through the
commissioner of lands and works with a Victoria lawyer acting for an
American speculator. Ten thousand acres on the island were sold to
the American for one dollar an acre; he in turn sold the land for the
same amount to the railway company and turned over these proceeds
to a business associate who he knew had an interest in adjacent land;
thus the two would benefit from any development by the railway. This
deal was kept secret until, in 1906, details leaked out provoking a
storm of criticism with the usual accusations of bribery and corruption
on the part of government officials. McBride yielded to demands by

the leader of the Opposition for a formal inquiry, and a select committee was constituted. Tupper, though not in the legislature, was also one of those who demanded an investigation, an action which did not endear him in McBride's eyes. Tupper had specific reasons for his mistrust of the government's behaviour. He had in 1904 represented three South African War veterans who had applied for homestead land on Kaien Island; when told the land had been withdrawn from settlement which later wound up in the hands of the American speculator, Tupper was convinced there had been payoffs, and said so publicly.

The select committee, which divided along party lines, three Conservatives and two Liberals, exonerated the government, and McBride, and the commissioner of lands and works, concluding no bribes had been offered or received and no improprieties had occurred, a finding later concurred in by the legislature with the two Socialist members supporting McBride. Yet the affair would not go away. Tupper and a coterie of Vancouver Conservatives continued to snipe at McBride. Tupper thought McBride should resign, telling a correspondent "I firmly believe our party will do well to spew the McBride government out of its mouth." Another disaffected Conservative, though not so strident as Tupper, was W.J. Bowser, a member of the House but not of Cabinet. (It was he who, as attorney general in 1913, hired Pinkerton's for the Nanaimo coal strike.) He was also a Vancouver lawyer and an old Dalhousie law school chum of McBride. In the fall of 1906 McBride, sensing the possibility of a palace revolt, secretly hired Pinkerton's through the Seattle office to spy on Tupper and Bowser and other disaffected party chieftains in Vancouver in order to keep abreast of any plot to oust him from office. In the upshot, the commissioner of lands and works, under severe pressure, resigned his office, and Bowser was brought into the Cabinet early in 1907 as attorney general; the crisis was averted.[10]

It is doubly regrettable that this tantalizing episode, the only known instance of a provincial premier hiring American detectives to learn if a hostile cabal existed, is so inadequately documented. No reference to it is to be found in McBride's personal or official papers at the British Columbia Archives and Records Service, nor in the files of official papers of British Columbia premiers. We do not know how long the surveillance lasted nor its cost, nor the contents of the Pinkerton reports which McBride received. Probably the Pinkerton detectives shadowed Bowser and Tupper and others to learn what haunts they visited and what companions they met. Both B.R.D. Smith (as this is written, the head of British Columbia Hydro) and the eminent Margaret Ormsby are the only two authors of whom this author is aware who have written of the episode. Smith, in the course of his research, examined the Pinkerton reports, then in the possession of one of McBride's daughters, citing them in his thesis, but does not now recall their contents.[11] This author interviewed the daughter twice who, with the help of her son, searched high and low for the reports; they had disappeared. McBride paid Pinkerton's out of his own pocket, which was never a deep one (he was a virtual bankrupt when he died). He obviously valued their help for he became a fan of the agency, so to speak, and a good client utilizing their services on three subsequent occasions of delicacy, quite apart from such police investigations as the Bill Miner and Simon Peter Gunanoot manhunts.

The first of these occurred in 1911 when he asked the agency to inquire into the activities of Arthur E. O'Meara, a lawyer turned Anglican cleric, who had taken up the cudgels as an activist in British Columbia on behalf of the native peoples in their pursuit of land claims based on aboriginal or "Indian" title. Though O'Meara became an ardent spokesman for the interests of Indians generally and for the advancement of their claims to ownership of land within their traditional boundaries, he had a particular interest in the claims of the Nishga people to lands within the Nass Valley. As early as 1910, he prepared a statement and had it printed, based on interviews held with the Nishga chiefs in which he outlined the propositions put forward as the legal basis or framework of land claims.[12] In 1911 (soon after the Pinkerton investigation concluded) he attended a meeting with Laurier and two members of his Cabinet in Ottawa to discuss the claims, which the Nishga were to pursue for another eighty-five years, culminating in a treaty (still to be ratified) between them and the federal and provincial governments in 1996.[13]

Beginning in 1908 discussions took place between Victoria and Ottawa about referring the notion of Indian title or rather the question of its existence to the Supreme Court of Canada on a constitutional reference. The province hired the country's most eminent constitutional lawyer, Eugene Lafleur of Montreal, and he with E.L. Newcombe, the Deputy Minister of Justice, spent days trying to frame the questions to be submitted to the court for an opinion. The consultations received some impetus from an assurance given by

Laurier to Joe Capilano, a prominent native from the Vancouver area, that Laurier favoured such a reference.[14] In the course of drafting the questions, Lafleur learned that "some self-constituted champions of the Indians desire to be heard on the reference."[15] One of these "champions" was O'Meara, who on May 16, 1910, wrote McBride asking for information about the wording of the questions to be submitted to the court; McBride temporized because of the absence of the deputy attorney general who, with Lafleur, was handling the negotiations for the province.[16]

McBride was wary of O'Meara and his zealousness in supporting what McBride believed to be absolutely insupportable claims by the native peoples. In April 1910, O'Meara had given a speech in Vancouver on the subject. It received much advance publicity and even more afterwards. The government was sufficiently concerned about what O'Meara might say that a shorthand reporter was sent to the meeting to transcribe the speech.[17] The speech anticipated all the arguments that have been put forward by British Columbia Indians during the last twenty-five years:[18] the use of the land from time immemorial and the applicability of the famous Royal Proclamation of 1763, one of the cornerstones of the Indians' legal position on land claims. It was hardly an inflammatory speech, judged by present standards but the government viewed it with deep suspicion. On December 14, 1910, McBride and his Cabinet met with O'Meara and other representatives of the Nishga who urged the government to proceed with the reference.[19] McBride made it plain that he was not convinced that any such concept of Indian title existed and indeed he later scuttled any possibility of British Columbia applying to the court for a ruling.

It was against this backdrop that O'Meara arrived in Victoria early in 1911 to represent the Songhees Indians who were, and still are, the principal native group in Victoria and its immediate environs and who were embroiled in a dispute over compensation for reserve lands that were taken from them, so they argued, by illegal means. At that point McBride, who had become almost paranoiac when it came to O'Meara, thought it time to call in Pinkerton's to shadow him, possibly with a view to securing evidence of seditious behaviour. Conduct which led specifically or by implication to the overthrow of established forms of government was one form of sedition, and O'Meara's argument that unoccupied Crown lands in British Columbia belonged to the Indians was, from a certain point of view, seditious.

The Pinkerton man arrived in Victoria on March 16, 1911.[20] In his first report he sets out

In compliance with instructions from Gen'l Supt Ahern I called on Attorney General Bowser in the Parliament Buildings, and was informed by Mr. Bowser that one Rev. Cannon [sic] O'Meara, Pastor of the Church of England, Victoria, B.C. who used to be an attorney-at-law, was causing trouble between the government and the local Indians and was trying to get the Indians to endeavour to recover lands now in the City of Victoria, he helping them with his law knowledge; it is being rumoured he was taking means to take the matter to the English courts. The object of the operation is to ascertain just what action this man is taking in regard to recovery of the lands he claims belongs to the Indians.

(While with Bowser the operative picked up another piece of business, unrelated to Indian land claims, concerning peccadilloes allegedly committed by a Justice of the Peace at Port Renfrew on the west coast of Vancouver Island to feather his own nest.)

The operative worked undercover but he does not say in his reports what his cover was. He had obviously been influenced by his instructions, for reading his reports one would think he was shadowing a dangerous character and not a mild-mannered cleric who just happened to espouse the cause of Indians. O'Meara had rented a house in Victoria which the operative kept an eye on, but since he was seldom there the operative inquired of his whereabouts from various Anglican clergymen at Christ Church Cathedral, and at several parish churches. All spoke disparagingly of him as an agitator in the Indian cause. But there was no sign of O'Meara who, according to one of the Anglican divines, was in Vancouver.

This line of ecclesiastical inquiry proving unproductive, he broadened his horizons by going into hotels (respectable ones, of course). As he says:

I started to make the rounds of the most prominent of the hotels, sitting around the lobbies and getting into conversation with the usual people of the city who pass their time in the lobbies a great deal and who are as a rule fairly well posted on current events to see if I could get in touch with some of the O'Meara crowd. As it was Sunday I could not approach O'Meara with the same prospect of success that I might hope to on a weekday and not many of his followers seemed to be around.

Later in the day he attended a service at one of the Victoria churches hoping that O'Meara might be found there or at least some reference be made to him. One has to visualize the Pinkerton operative — possibly an Episcopalian, the American equivalent of Anglican — on his knees with prayers on his lips, but with eyes on the congregation. But no sign of O'Meara. The following day the operative met O'Meara for the first and only time outside his residence. The operative does not say what his pretext was in talking to him, but talk he did, though O'Meara divulged nothing more than that he was engaged on behalf of the Indians. Following that unsatisfactory interview, the operative called on one of the influential Anglicans in Victoria, revelling in the name of Beaumont Boggs, who, like everybody else the operative spoke to, disapproved of O'Meara's activist views. With that the investigation ended. Pinkerton's was paid out of the provincial treasury. The abrupt ending of the investigation was a clear indication of its uselessness. O'Meara continued to represent Indian interests for another fifteen years.

Before the O'Meara investigation started, McBride, in an entirely unrelated matter, received death threats, starting in mid-February 1911. One has to try to put one's self into his position. He was impecunious, married with six daughters, and his death would cause severe financial hardship on his family. It is, in a way, small wonder that O'Meara's tactics made him nervous. He at once contacted Ahern at the Pinkerton office in Seattle for help. Ahern dispatched an operative to Victoria on the "first boat" to consult with F.S. Hussey, still head of the B.C. Police, and Attorney General W.J. Bowser. On arrival the operative met Hussey, Bowser, and Premier McBride. Bowser outlined the position. The threats had allegedly been made by John Watt, an elderly mining promoter who was embroiled in litigation over petroleum leases claimed by him which had been invalidated. The litigation arose from the granting of licences over the same area to conflicting licensees for exploration of coal and petroleum; Watt and an associate were the applicants for the petroleum lease. The legal dispute, which was about how the licence dispute should be adjudicated, began in 1901, two years before McBride became premier. It wound up in the courts, with the Court of Appeal ruling against Watt in 1906. The matter dragged on unresolved for years. Watt brooded over his misfortune all that time until, in 1911, he applied to the Cabinet for an order-in-council establishing his entitlement. The prospect of a favourable resolution of the problem seemed to perk him up but prior to the application he had made death threats against McBride, who for some reason he held responsible for his misfortune; the threats were made indirectly, to his brother-in-law, who informed McBride. The brother-in-law also disclosed that Watt habitually carried a revolver. The operative saw McBride on February 14; the Cabinet had scheduled a hearing for March 1 to hear Watt's appeal. The operative was to keep Watt under surveillance at least until that date.

Watt was staying at a local hotel but went about town a good deal. He ate breakfast at the same restaurant each day and lunch and dinner at other establishments. He called frequently on his lawyer and his surveyor in preparation for the hearing. The operative struck up an acquaintance with him and became quite chummy. He doesn't say in his reports how he managed this, but Watt spoke freely and often about his difficulties while expressing optimism that his claims would be restored to him one way or another, if not by the Cabinet, then perhaps through intervention by the federal government or even by the American federal government, since American interests were involved with him. The Cabinet hearing was held as scheduled but a decision was postponed. This did not discourage Watt; indeed, he seemed to take heart, for he spoke favourably of McBride, who he described as "a very good fellow generally" and said he was in fact "good friends with him." Never, so the operative reported, did he utter any death threats against McBride or threats of violence of any kind.

Almost in the same breath that he was praising McBride, Watt cursed the latter's old *béte noire*, Sir Hibbert Tupper who, surprisingly, comes into this narrative. Tupper represented in court the successful claimants in opposition to Watt, who, as unsuccessful litigants sometimes do, vented his rage against Tupper, telling the operative: "There is a man that it would be good enough if he had a piece of cold lead put right through him." Although the operative didn't really think Watt was uttering a threat he was prepared to carry out he still thought that if he was driven to a "sudden and violent mood" by an adverse decision from the Cabinet, he might be capable of violence, but not against McBride. After a month of this surveillance the operative was told the job was over. No reasons were given. Watt had not received a ruling. There is no indication Tupper was warned of Watt's malevolence. From the suddenness of McBride's and Bowser's decision to drop the investigation one can infer some settlement of the disputed claims had been reached.[21] In retrospect, Watt's threats were idle ones only, uttered by an angry man.

The final matter on which McBride sought help and advice from Pinkerton's — it was not a formal engagement — related to the suicide of his private secretary, Lawrence Macrae, in September 1914. The death provoked widespread rumours in British Columbia that Macrae had been spying for Germany and had been suborned by Aldo Von Alvensleben, a suave, handsome German national who had lived in Vancouver since 1904. A member of an aristocratic family, he apparently had access to a good deal of money and became a respected member of the Vancouver business and social community, with membership in the posh Vancouver Club, and ownership of a mansion.[22] (In a later generation, a Von Alvensleben was executed as one of the plotters against Hitler's life in July 1944.) Among his business interests were a coal-mine in Nanaimo, which became strikebound in 1913, and a trust company with financial connections to Germany. At the outbreak of war, Von Alvensleben fled to the United States and Macrae's untimely death soon afterwards seemed to some people to give credence to stories that there was cause and effect: the rumours of spying, McBride's known business association with Von Alvensleben, and Macrae's death. All this caused McBride enormous distress. But Von Alvensleben himself may have been a spy. According to author Martin Kitchen, when Von Alvensleben was in the United States after the war started, he headed up a unit to destroy bridges over the Pitt River in British Columbia.[23] McBride's distress was compounded by the strain he had undergone just a month earlier when, on the brink of war, he had purchased two submarines in Seattle without any authority from Ottawa or his own government. They were being built for Chile, which had defaulted on payment, and McBride, in hectic arrangements which had to be concluded before the war started lest the Americans impound the vessels, signed a cheque for $1,150,000 of provincial funds which he handed over, and the submarines stealthily sailed from Seattle in darkness to the naval base at Esquimalt. And then, hardly a month after pulling off a great coup in snatching the submarines from under the noses of the Chileans and Americans, to be told he had been harbouring a German spy in the person of his private secretary was almost more than he could bear.

In early 1913, in a move he must often have regretted, McBride subscribed for $500 worth of shares in Von Alvensleben's trust company, but, in a letter to a correspondent who, like many others, was suspicious of McBride's association with Von Alvensleben, claimed never to have received them (and hence would not have been called upon to pay for them).[24] Not long after he fled Canada, Von Alvensleben, staying at the Ritz Hotel in New York, had the gall to contact McBride. Although only McBride's reply has been preserved, it is clear from it that Von Alvensleben asked for his help in securing safe passage in and out of Canada; McBride telegraphed him, curtly, "Military authorities control situation and impossible for me to interfere."[25]

By mid-September 1914, a great many rumours circulated in B.C. that Macrae's death was somehow connected with a plot by Von Alvensleben to steal plans for the defence of the naval base at Esquimalt, and of the Pacific Coast in general. The stories then reached Seattle, for on November 7, Ahern of Pinkerton's sent McBride copies of two articles which had just appeared in the *Seattle Daily Star*. They asserted that Von Alvensleben, then staying at a Seattle hotel, had, with his brother, obtained the plans of the base at Esquimalt and that the brother had left the United States for Europe with them only to be caught by the British who, when they discovered the plans, shot him. The newspaper reported that when word of this reached Victoria, "the Secretary of a high British Columbia official committed suicide." When Von Alvensleben read this he told the newspaper the story was nonsense; his brother was alive, never had the plans and was serving in the German army; the newspaper printed the substance of his remarks.[26] But the rumours intensified. In December a Conservative friend sent McBride a copy of a scurrilous article about Macrae in a magazine published in Vancouver, *Technical Press Limited*, repeating the canard that Macrae had passed on to the Germans the Esquimalt plans. McBride immediately fired off a rocket to the Vancouver magazine, blaming the Seattle newspaper for the "rumour that was gaining currency in British Columbia" which cast a "cruel reflection about a dead man who, although he committed suicide, was always a faithful servant and true and loyal to his country." The allegations, he said, hurt him very much personally, and he was prepared to have the government spend money to track down the source of the rumours and, if necessary, sue those responsible. Simultaneously McBride wrote Ahern asking for his help in determining the identity of the informant who passed on the "wholly and absolutely unfounded" stories to the Seattle newspaper which, McBride said, the government intended to sue.[27] Ahern wrote once more to offer help because, he said, he knew all the newspaper people, but McBride seemed to back away from any lawsuit for he replied that he would consider the matter further before taking any action.[28]

By early January, McBride, who by then had given up any idea of a lawsuit against the Seattle paper, became so worked up that he issued a "public statement" which he sent to over fifty newspapers circulating in British Columbia; not all the papers, however, ran it. In it McBride — after referring to the "persistent rumour" which linked his "late Secretary" with spying and which suggested that the "discovery of his complicity therein was the cause of his death" — expressed astonishment that "in British Columbia where Mr. Macrae was well known any heed would be paid to it." McBride went on,

> It is a painful subject for me to discuss, but in justice to the memory of one who never betrayed a trust or was disloyal to his country in thought, word or deed, I must state most emphatically that the rumour is without the slightest possible foundation. The circulation of such stories wilfully or otherwise is a cruel reflection upon my late Secretary and painful in the extreme to relatives and friends. Mr. Macrae had been suffering for some many months with a nervous ailment and his untimely death cannot in the slightest degree be regarded as a reflection in any way upon his honour as a man or a citizen.

Not even that quelled all the rumours, and when McBride learned from a member of his staff that the Vancouver police chief was supposed to know where the story had originated, McBride wrote him for verification; it was not true, the chief replied, but the story was "common talk in the city."[29] And there the matter ended. Current political events overshadowed the Macrae affair. Starting with unfounded charges in February 1915 that McBride had financially benefitted from the submarine deal, his popularity declined and he resigned the premiership in December that year, to be succeeded by Bowser.

At the same time as McBride and Bowser were dealing with the activist Rev. A.E. O'Meara, Sir James Whitney, the premier of Ontario, and his attorney general, J.J. Foy, were dealing with another clerical activist, though in a different field, the formidable Dr. S.D. Chown, general secretary of the Department of Temperance and

Moral Reform of the Methodist Church, in a matter which led to Pinkerton's being called in. Chown's great task was to seek out and eradicate vice, wherever it was found and whatever its character — drinking, gambling, or whoring — and the reclamation of those engaged in such sinful activities, all with a view to uplifting the moral and social character of citizens, thereby bringing them closer to the Almighty. Such was Chown's influence that when he spoke politicians generally listened.

Late in 1909 Chown received reports about the "disorderly character of several houses" in Arnprior, a town with a population of roughly five thousand, about sixty miles west of Ottawa.[30] He wrote the attorney general without receiving satisfaction and then went to the top, in a cleverly phrased appeal to the premier. He began by complimenting Sir James on a speech he had recently delivered to the Canadian Temperance League which, Chown said, gave "great pleasure to a very large number of your supporters." Chown pronounced that he was "always delighted through the agencies that have been placed at my command by the Church, to prepare public sentiment to accept, and even to demand, the things the Government might wish to give us for the country's good." He then shifted his attention to Arnprior where, so he had been informed by "a very cool level-headed man" that the "social evil was allowed to run riot in the place with no attempt to enforce the law against it." (In that era, it was not uncommon for local officials to tolerate informal red-light districts so long as no nuisance was caused to others.) Chown told the premier that his complaints had so far fallen on deaf ears, and suggested "a reliable officer from the outside should be sent in [to Arnprior]." The letter worked: there was a flurry of consultations and exchanges of memoranda between the premier, the attorney general, the deputy attorney general (J.R. Cartwright), and the superintendent of the Ontario Provincial Police (J.E. Rogers). It turned out that the "cool level-headed man" Chown referred to was the Methodist pastor at Arnprior, Melvin Taylor, who joined the discussions with a long letter to Rogers, levelling much the same accusations as Chown: flagrant violation of prostitution laws, unwillingness of local officials (amongst whom, of course, would be the chief of police), and requesting an independent investigator. But it was all based on second- or third-hand information and Taylor, when asked to name his informants, declined to do so until he was notified of the scope of any investigation. After expressing exasperation with Taylor's refusal to name names, Cartwright and Rogers decided to call in Pinkerton's anyway, and an operative was dispatched from Buffalo, arriving January 11, 1910. Rogers gave him his instructions: he was to work undercover to find out if there were any "houses of ill fame, streetwalkers or women who accept money from men." He was specifically told to get the information "without getting in touch with Melvin Taylor at any time." Rogers, if he could secure the names of alleged prostitutes would send them to the operative at Arnprior. He did not secure them because Taylor wouldn't supply them.

The operative who appears to have adopted the pose of a travelling salesman visited all the bars, poolrooms, hotels, restaurants, and barbershops, where he struck up an acquaintance with many of the denizens, inquiring unobtrusively about loose women and bawdy houses. One local informed him of a house on a certain street which was said to contain women taking money, anywhere from two dollars to five dollars a visit, which on investigation proved to be non-existent — there was no such street. One elderly local spoke of "two or three old hags" in town that no "white man would go after"; one of them was named "Frozen Foot," but in any case they had long since moved out of town. It may be, he said, that they went to a house in McNab Township some miles away ("McNab" was the founder of Arnprior), for the night constable at Arnprior told the operative there were a couple of women "who entertained men," but they never came to Arnprior. The operative reported that wherever he went in Arnprior — the movie hall, hotels, and restaurants — and from his observations on the streets, all the women appeared to be respectable. This impression was confirmed by the Arnprior chief of police whom the operative first met in a Chinese restaurant after a hockey game. The two struck up an acquaintance as the result of which the operative called on the chief at his office in the "town hall. He had been drinking and was making considerable noise at the time I saw him." This is a delightful capsule vignette: the chief of police sitting in his town hall office rowdy with too much liquor in him. However, the operative spoke to him on other occasions when he was sober; there were no loose women in Arnprior, an opinion he had expressed to the Crown Attorney before the investigation began. Finally, the operative concluded that "it would be a waste of time and money [for him] to remain in the town longer." He filed his last report giving Arnprior a clean sheet and returned to Buffalo.[31]

Rogers, the superintendent, accepting the operative's opinion, told Chown there was no substance to his charges but did not at first tell him he was basing his opinion on an investigation by Pinkerton's.

Perhaps he should have, for Chown on February 25 again expressed his hope that an independent investigation would be undertaken. Cartwright then told him of Pinkerton's involvement. Chown somewhat grudgingly accepted the conclusions of the operative, although stating in his reply "that better results would have been obtained had your agent taken advantage of the offer of information on the spot." In other words, the operative should have consulted Melvin Taylor. Chown was elected general superintendent of the Methodist Church soon afterwards, and in 1925 was to lead it into Church Union. No more vice was heard of in Arnprior — at least officially.

Pinkerton's was later to be associated with Ontario politicians and with the Ontario Province Police in two significant investigations: the ugly riot at Verner, Ontario, on Dominion election day in 1917, and the notorious scandal in 1924 involving the provincial treasurer, Peter Smith, and a well-known Toronto financier, Aemilius Jarvis. The Verner riot, pitting francophones against anglophones (to use current phraseology) sprang from the tensions created by the Military Service Act — conscription. In May 1917, at a time of heavy casualties on the western front and diminishing enlistment at home, the prime minister, R.L. Borden, reluctantly concluded conscription was necessary and announced to Parliament his intention of passing the Military Service Act. He was hotly opposed on the issue by Laurier and his Quebec caucus, supported as they were by an overwhelming percentage of the francophone population of Quebec. Borden decided only a coalition government could succeed in imposing compulsory military service and, with enormous difficulty, and after endless negotiations with possible candidates for a Cabinet position amongst the ranks of anglophone Liberals who accepted conscription as a necessary evil, cobbled together a Union Government, as it was styled. Late in August 1917, Parliament passed the Military Service Act, though it was not immediately implemented. Borden decided to go to the country on the issue and a federal, or, as it was then styled, a Dominion election, was called for December 17.

Verner, a small community near North Bay, had a large francophone element. But it was not merely the existence of that element that triggered the ensuing riot but rather the conduct of the enumerator in preparing the voters' list, and in conducting the poll on election day. Added to this was the fact that none of the local election officials were francophone, a clear break from local tradition though not strictly an infringement of electoral law. In 1916 there had been an enumeration and that list, with minor exceptions, was to govern the right to vote in 1917. Notwithstanding, the enumerator, mistakenly and unwisely, prepared a supplemental list of voters including many francophones so that the latter assumed, quite understandably, that they could vote. They would, of course, have voted against the Unionist candidate. On election day these persons came to vote, including the Roman Catholic parish priest, only to be told they were not on the 1916 list and had no vote. Though disgruntled, they caused no trouble at that stage. Later in the day a railway worker on the CPR who had only three months earlier moved from New Brunswick to Verner — an anglophone and a known Unionist supporter — was permitted to vote by the poll clerks who overlooked his absence from the voters' list on the grounds he was a peripatetic, and should be allowed to vote in the place where he was on polling day. News of this ruling soon became known and enraged those francophones who had been led to believe they could vote but were denied the privilege.

A group of scrutineers who left the polling station after the polls closed was set upon and attacked by a mob estimated by the police at about one hundred persons; a number of scrutineers were badly beaten, requiring medical treatment. The mob was composed of "Frenchmen," as they were referred to in the official correspondence. Local politicians and senior police officers, though officially they could not condone such violence, later came to hold a tolerant view of the motives prompting the riot: absence of "Frenchmen" among polling officials, denial of the vote to many francophones and yet allowance of the vote to an anglophone outsider who favoured conscription. The mayor of North Bay telegraphed the minister of justice to report the riot and to ask for a swift response because the "feeling in district and at North Bay very intense." The minister referred the matter to Lieutenant-Colonel Sherwood, who at once realized it was not a matter of federal jurisdiction but lay within the function of the Ontario attorney general who, in turn, contacted J.E. Rogers, superintendent of the Ontario Provincial Police. Late in December, Rogers, in consultation with his political masters, concluded that a form of what today we would describe as plea-bargaining, an accommodation, should be arrived at. As one of them, Charles McCrea, the legislative member for Sudbury, told Rogers, "I think Storie [an inspector of the Ontario Provincial Police at North Bay] can arrange matters to have one or more of the Frenchmen charged and plead guilty to assault and let that be the end of the matter, for while it is easy from a long distance to theorize on the French and English side of the question, local communities have, in the last analysis, to live it down and face the divisions created. An amicable adjustment of the matter with convictions, as suggested, to satisfy the law, would be perhaps the best thing in the long run." This pragmatic advice from McCrea, who was a highly respected Roman Catholic, is noteworthy on several counts: the francophone point of view deserved respect, particularly since the enumerator, an anglophone, ignored electoral law; the riot was a blot on the good name of the community; and persons were injured and therefore some retribution had to be meted out, but not much. Let us try to heal divisions, but in a mild fashion, charging only a few of the guilty.

But which "few"? Before the days of high-speed cameras, identifying individuals in a riotous mob of one hundred persons was extraordinarily difficult. Rogers decided he had better call in Pinkerton's to put an agent into the field to answer the question. It is not clear from the material whether the agent was a Canadian employee of Pinkerton or whether he was an American brought in by a Canadian branch of the agency. He took up his task in Montreal, where he received instructions, but he might very well have come from the United States; the fact that he filed his reports under "#29" indicates he was an American, since it was customary for Pinkerton operatives working out of the United States to use numbers, unlike Canada, where initials were commonly employed.

It was not a successful operation; everything went wrong. He made his headquarters in Sturgeon Falls, posing as a labourer looking for work. He tried to get a job at the mill of the Lake Superior Paper Company, which he called on daily, and only near the end of his month-long assignment did he obtain work, as a cleanup man in the yard. He could hardly stay in a hotel in his guise of a working man, yet in most boarding houses, which were like dormitories, he could have no privacy for the preparation of his reports; he eventually located one where he could have his own room. He found the townspeople uncommunicative for the most part, perhaps because he was not a francophone. He called on all the local hotels and other gathering places but did not speak to one person who identified any of the rioters. He learned towards the end of January 1918 that the police had charged, and issued warrants for the arrest of, a number of alleged rioters; obviously they had sources other than the Pinkerton man. On February 1, nine men appeared in court on charges of assault. They pleaded guilty, and were fined fifty dollars each and assessed court costs. Thereafter, the situation cooled down and the Pinkerton man reported that the "Verner matter seems to be very quiet." The day following that report the operative was told by a local that "detectives were working on the case to obtain the names of the people who were in the affair," one of whom worked in the mill.[32] Two days later he reported a conversation he had with a townsman of Sturgeon Falls who described the anglophones as "yellow" because they had "engaged detectives to work among the people to find out who was mixed up in the Verner affair." That was the end of operative #29M: he left town, after working only a week at the mill.

Yet his reports of his conversations with francophone members of the community — the "community" consisting of Verner and nearby Sturgeon Falls, also with a large francophone community — are disturbing. One man told him the "three English men" sent from Sturgeon Falls to man the poll at Verner should have been killed by the mob because they denied the vote to "Verner people who had been voting for the last 30 years." Still, the Verner people derived a measure of satisfaction by forcing the anglophones to cry uncle by making them "give three cheers for Laurier."[33] Another told the operative the English poll-keepers got all they deserved as "they had no business to go and be poll-keepers in a French town." The same man said the rioters had prepared themselves for an attack by picking up "broken pieces of bricks" from an abandoned hotel, because they expected "any trouble that would come along." These sentiments were repeated by another man who said the "voters at Verner had a hard time to vote," and when denied a vote "had voted by force, which they used on the poll keeper."[34] A few days after the Pinkerton operative left, Superintendent J.E. Rogers of the Ontario Provincial Police wrote his inspector at Sudbury, within whose jurisdiction the Verner affair lay, instructing him to take no further action "regarding any persons not yet prosecuted. I think the Government are satisfied with the results and feel perhaps if we pushed the thing further it might look like persecution and take away the good effect of what has been accomplished. This, of course, is strictly confidential."[35] But matters remain "confidential" only for so long under archival rules, and Rogers' letter conforms to what Charles McCrea had earlier sensibly urged — try not to inflame local sentiment. It seems they succeeded.

At the time the Verner investigation was going on the train of events started that led, in 1924, to a lengthy investigation by Pinkerton's and the subsequent sensational trial of Peter Smith and Aemilius Jarvis for conspiracy to defraud the Ontario government. Prior to the Great War, Ontario issued large numbers of bonds which, as an inducement for their purchase, were free of provincial succession duties. These could pass from one estate to another, and so long as transfers were done before maturity, each inheritance was free of duty. As the succession duty rate rose on other bond issues and assets, the province lost potential revenue and, in 1917, the Conservative government headed by Sir William Hearst passed legislation enabling the province to buy the duty-free bonds before maturity and cancel them. This measure was supported by all parties. In 1919 the Hearst government was defeated by the United Farmers of Ontario Party led by E.C. Drury, who brought Peter Smith, a prosperous farmer from Stratford, into the Cabinet as provincial treasurer, the senior portfolio. Soon after taking office the Drury government made arrangements through Smith for the repurchase and redemption of a substantial number of bonds held by investors in England, and to that end enlisted the services of Aemilius Jarvis or, as the prosecutor alleged later at his trial, it was the other way around, with Jarvis coming forward with proposals for redemption. He was a man whom any Torontonian would describe as being of impeccable character. Born into an old Ontario family of credit and renown, Jarvis had prospered as a stockbroker and financier. But it was his social standing that left people aghast at his later arrest. He had attended the proper school, Upper Canada College; he was a member of the proper clubs, among them the Hunt Club; he was a director of large corporations; he was a prominent member of the Royal Canadian Yacht Club; and for three years was a very busy president of the Navy League of Canada.

Jarvis, Smith, and Drury, the newly elected premier, agreed that Jarvis should go to London to buy up, if prices were favourable, as many of the outstanding bonds held there as he could. So as to give no inkling that in reality it was the government of Ontario making the purchases (such knowledge, it was believed, would have driven up the price and hence cost Ontario more), Jarvis went ostensibly as a principal — that is, on the pretext he was purchasing the bonds on his own account. There was a side agreement between him and the government, confirmed by an order-in-council which set out the prices which the government was prepared to pay Jarvis for such bonds as he was able to buy. Jarvis interpreted that to mean he should be paid that figure in any event, whereas later the prosecution argued it was only a maximum. It turned out that Jarvis made fortuitous purchases on a large scale which, after Smith authorized payment of the maximum in every case, earned him a profit of about half-a-million dollars. The prosecution later argued that Jarvis and Smith had reached a corrupt arrangement by which the proceeds would be split between them and a third man, Andy Pepall, who had accompanied Jarvis to London.

The matter lay dormant for three years. In 1923, the Drury government went out of office, defeated by the Conservatives led by Howard Ferguson. The new provincial treasurer, Colonel W.H. Price, found what he considered to be gross incompetence in the preparation of the provincial accounts, and, more disturbing, evidence that the province had lost inordinate amounts of money on the redemption of the duty-free bonds. In a debate in the Legislature early in March 1924, Price disclosed the Jarvis transactions and the large profits made by him at the expense of Ontario taxpayers. There was a great deal of talk among the politicians, and speculation in the press, that some form of skullduggery had been afoot; Ferguson refused to set up a royal commission and instead convened the Public Accounts Committee to delve into the allegations; it began its hearings on March 12, 1924. There were various accusations of irregularities by officials of the former government including Peter Smith, but no link between him and Jarvis amounting to criminal behaviour emerged until nearly the end of the committee hearings, when it was alleged some funds from the sale of the duty-free bonds in 1920 had gone into Smith's personal bank account and that he had received a cheque for $4,000 directly from Jarvis's brokerage firm. As he left the committee room on April 14, Smith was arrested and charged with conspiracy to defraud Ontario by taking secret commissions on the sale of the bonds. Later the charges were more clearly articulated and Smith and Jarvis were both charged as conspirators in a scheme to defraud the government by, in Jarvis's case, taking more money than he was entitled to, and in Smith's, taking money which he was not entitled to at all.

There were many in Ontario who at the time believed that Ferguson's motivation in pursuing Smith and Jarvis was revenge — a political vendetta. Smith had been a Cabinet minister in the Drury government and Drury had accused Ferguson of malfeasance when Ferguson was a Cabinet minister in the earlier Conservative administration led by Hearst. Ferguson never forgave Drury, so the reasoning went, and Smith was the means of getting at him. Some credence for this view may be found in the fact of Pinkerton's engagement. At about the midpoint of the hearings and before Smith's arrest, Pinkerton's was called in to monitor the movements of

Frank C. Biggs and his contacts with Smith.[36] Biggs had also been in the Drury Cabinet, holding the twin portfolios of Public Works and Public Highways and was a close friend of Smith's besides. Ferguson held him in as much contempt as he did Drury and Smith. Pinkerton's engagement was not primarily to gather evidence against Jarvis and Smith — though, of course, anything they turned up would have been welcomed — but to try to establish if Biggs was involved in the fraudulent scheme. Such a motive does not appear in so many words from the Pinkerton reports, but it seems the only reasonable explanation of the investigation. Though the engagement lasted for barely two weeks, Pinkerton's deployed a veritable squad of undercover operatives — nine of them — to shadow Biggs in Toronto and Dundas, his home just outside Hamilton, and Smith in Toronto and Stratford; as well, an operative was engaged in Detroit, and another in Los Angeles.

Working in teams and in shifts, one group of operatives kept watch on Biggs, and another on Smith. Biggs' every move was noted: his stays in Toronto where he put up at the King Edward Hotel; his journeys to his home in Dundas; his car journeys (he drove a brand-new McLaughlin-Buick automobile); and his visits to the Parliament Buildings and to the hearings of the Public Accounts Committee. He went to Chicago, apparently to attend a family funeral, lodging en route at Windsor, but did not stop at Detroit, or so it seemed, since the operative on separate days inquired for him at approximately seventy-five hotels and apartment hotels. Nonetheless, an operative interviewed senior officials of over a dozen banks in Detroit to ascertain if any accounts were maintained singly, or jointly, by Smith and Biggs. He drew a blank; he does not say how he was able to gain such supposedly confidential information.

Similarly with Smith: he was shadowed continuously both in Toronto and at his home in Stratford until his arrest. The surveillance continued, notwithstanding that a week earlier he realized what was going on and confronted an operative, who was on foot. Smith stopped his car alongside him, and the operative then described what happened:

> Smith called me and said "How's things". As I turned a man jumped from the Ford sedan and pointed a large camera at me. I turned my back on him and the cameraman maneuvered around while Mr. Smith asked where he might see the boss, as he wanted to talk to him. He stated that he

knew what we were here for and that he had done nothing wrong and that our presence there was but a waste of time. While I listened to all this, the cameraman moved to my side and snapped my profile. Mr. Smith endeavoured to draw me into friendly conversation, but without success. He stated that he was not sore at us, and that he knew that we had to earn our money the same as everyone else. He then excused himself and drove off, the photographer's car following.[37]

Smith may have warned his friend Biggs who, when in Hamilton a week later, drove "around a few blocks" in an apparent attempt to shake his pursuers. Occasionally the paths of the two men crossed. They stayed at the King Edward Hotel for a few days at the same time with rooms on the same floor.

The Pinkerton investigation in Los Angeles related to Andy Pepall, the associate of Jarvis who also made a lot of money out of the sale of the bonds — more, in fact, than Jarvis — but who conveniently moved to California. He was not tried at the same time as Jarvis and Smith because the charge, conspiracy, was not extraditable. The Ontario government made unsuccessful attempts to persuade the U.S. government to deport him and, although details are lacking in the Pinkerton reports, no doubt their services in Los Angeles related to these attempts.

That the purpose of the Pinkerton investigation was politically motivated is further reinforced by the fact that all the reports, though handed in to the Ontario Provincial Police in the first instance, were sent directly to Colonel W.H. Price, the provincial treasurer, and not to the attorney general as was customary in criminal investigations. In any case, no evidence was turned up then or later of any involvement by Biggs; it cost the Ontario government just under $2,000 in Pinkerton's fees to establish his innocence. Jarvis and Smith stood trial before a judge and jury in Toronto in October 1924 and were convicted. Jarvis was sentenced to six months imprisonment and Smith was sentenced to three years. In addition, the judge levied an enormous fine of $600,000 to be paid by the two of them. In Jarvis's case, the fine was reduced later to $60,000 and Smith, $100,000. Later trials followed, that of the deputy treasurer under Smith who was convicted, and Andy Pepall, extradited on a charge of theft, who was acquitted. He returned to the U.S. the same day.

Epilogue
The Modern Pinkerton's

The appointment of J. Edgar Hoover as the head of the Bureau of Investigation in 1924 heralded an expansion of its activities which had profound effects on Pinkerton's fortunes. Of greater significance, however, was the death of William Pinkerton in 1923, which marked the end of effective control of the agency by a handful of people. It was the beginning of a new era for Pinkerton's. Changing times and economic growth dictated transition from a personal style of management to a corporate one. Gone were the days when master detectives of private agencies held sway over law enforcement, when crime detection had a kind of chummy atmosphere in which the hunter actually knew the hunted, and vice versa. Similarly, from the point of view of the criminal, the days had passed when deals could be made on a person-to-person basis. As crime became more institutionalized and offered less scope for the individual criminal to operate on a large scale, so did the function of private agencies like Pinkerton's change or, rather, suffer, because publicly funded law enforcement bodies forced them out of the criminal investigation field. William Pinkerton was the last of the great detective entrepreneurs. (Sherlock Holmes would have been proud of him.) He knew every criminal in his time of any consequence either personally or by reputation, and vowed to bring all of them to justice — if retained by someone to do so. On the other side of the coin, criminals endeavoured to stay out of his reach, but should they fall into his clutches or into the hands of the regular law enforcement bodies as a result of his investigation, they could count on his disinterestedness if they could show they were simple working-men — in the criminal field — who caused no real harm.

On the death of Robert Pinkerton in 1907, his son Allan became joint principal of the agency and, on William's death, became sole principal until his own death in 1930. It was during their joint tenure that security and guard services burgeoned. In 1910, a separate division, Pinkerton's Protective Patrol, was established to provide uniformed patrol men. Allan and his uncle were also joint principals of this enterprise, which had five offices, amongst them one in San Francisco where in 1915 the Panama-Pacific Exposition was held. Pinkerton's was hired to do the security work, the first occasion on which a single organization took complete control of the site of a major exposition. Pinkerton's assembled a corps of operatives and guards from across the United States and deployed them effectively, with the result that criminal activity on the grounds was minimal, notwithstanding the very large crowds (300,000 on opening day alone). In an interview, W.A. Pinkerton proudly observed that when it was learned his agency would guard the exposition grounds, thieves, pickpockets, and burglars who talked of their chances of making a killing always asked, "What does the EYE say?" Pinkerton, the "Eye," let it be known that nothing was to be attempted, and virtually nothing was.[1]

On Allan Pinkerton's death in 1930, his son Robert became the principal of the agency at the youthful age of 26. During his tenure the difficulties of shifting from an investigative to a security body became acute. As well, Pinkerton's was dogged by troubles in the labour relations field. The Homestead Riots in 1892 had made the agency pull in its horns in the United States, and in Canada, as we have seen, Pinkerton's objectivity was called into question as a result of its role in the Fraser River fishermen's strikes in 1900 and 1901, its alleged role in the Hamilton, Ontario, street railway strike of 1906 and, most notably, its role for nearly six months in supplying an undercover agent in the protracted strike in the coal mines on Vancouver Island in 1913 and 1914.

In 1936, a United States Senate sub-committee held hearings on the practice of management hiring private agencies to supply undercover people to report on union activities. The inquiry was a consequence of the passage in 1935 by Congress of the ground-breaking Wagner Act — part of Roosevelt's New Deal legislation — which gave to trade unions having a stated number of members in an industrial plant the right to bargain for a labour contract, free of intimidation by employers. The sub-committee members, Senators Robert M. LaFollette Jr. and Elmer D. Thomas took a jaundiced view of industrial espionage, believing that it constituted an infringement of the right of a labour union to organize and of the concomitant right of an individual to join one. Robert Pinkerton, his vice-president Asher Rossiter, and a number of Pinkerton officials from various offices throughout the United States were summonsed to testify. They were all subjected to aggressive questioning by LaFollette and Thomas, who made no attempt at impartiality. The sub-committee's report condemned the employment of private agencies in industrial disputes.[2] Clearly the tide was running against such practices and Pinkerton's, along with other agencies, could no longer withstand the current.

Robert Pinkerton headed the agency for thirty-seven years until 1967, and was the last of his family to do so. In that period investigative work declined sharply and security work accelerated. The agency supplied uniformed guards, sometimes armed but mostly unarmed, for all manner of activities and institutions: horse racing and other sporting events, exhibitions and fairs, commercial plants and factories, etc. As a reflection of these changes in its function the name "Pinkerton's National Detective Agency" disappeared in 1965 to become "Pinkerton's, Inc.," a sad break with tradition but no doubt a practical decision. In 1982 the Pinkerton family sold the business to a conglomerate, American Brands Inc., which had formerly been the American Tobacco Company. Operation of the Pinkerton business by the new owners was markedly unsuccessful and in 1988 American Brands sold it to California Plant Protection (CPP), a California security company headed by Thomas Wathen which under his guidance had become the fourth largest in the security guard business; Pinkerton's was second. Immediately afterwards, Wathen merged Pinkerton's with CPP. Wathen was well-versed in the guard business. He graduated from university in police administration, and held a series of posts as a security officer, including stints with the United States Air Force and the Department of Defence. He joined CPP in 1963 and a year later became the owner and chief executive officer. In the ensuing years CPP grew significantly, and though its operations were confined to the state of California, its annual revenues by 1988 had grown to $250 million; in the same year Pinkerton's revenues were $415 million.

CPP acquired Pinkerton's for $95 million, of which, as previously noted, the principal asset was the name, valued at just under $55 million, and "Pinkerton's, Inc." continued as the name of the merged corporations. The head office of CPP had been at Van Nuys, a suburb of Los Angeles, and it became the headquarters of the "new" Pinkerton's. Amongst other assets was the rich archival collection of dossiers, photographs, and memorabilia relating to nineteenth and early twentieth century bandits, thugs, and murderers. This priceless material was moved from Pinkerton's former head office in New York City to Van Nuys and, more recently, to Encino, Pinkerton's present headquarters. CPP acquired "old Pinkerton's," as it is now commonly referred to, as a private transaction, but two years later the merged corporation went to the stock market with a public offering by Wathen of 36% of his shares in the corporation. The company has since been trading on the NASDAQ Exchange, and Wathen has divested himself of still further shares and as of 1997 held 34% of the 8,355,765 common shares outstanding.[3]

The "new" Pinkerton's is experiencing a revival of interest by clients in detective work, or "investigation" as it is now termed. "Operatives" have become "investigators," but their function is still the same, the detection of crime. Of the roughly 250 offices (the number changes from time to time) fifteen to twenty percent are devoted exclusively to investigation services. As the company recently stated:

> Investigations is the oldest part of Pinkerton's business and dates back to 1850. With the expansion in both calibre and scope achieved through late 1991 acquisitions, it is also becoming the newest area of growing importance to clients already using our security services as well as other organizations. We have embarked on an active campaign to more closely integrate the service and product offerings of the Pinkerton Investigations Division into the security operations which comprise most of our business.[4]

As part of its investigation services, Pinkerton's has set up its own "hot-line" called "Alertline" enabling employees of clients, and vendors of products or services to clients, to report anonymously suspected incidents of such crimes as pilferage or embezzlement as well as incidents of sexual harassment and racial discrimination.

But investigations are still carried out by Pinkerton's in the good old fashioned way, hiring "secrets," as they are termed (a phrase once applied to men doing industrial espionage), to carry out undercover surveillance. Pinkerton's long-standing policy of not doing investigations for divorce purposes ("over the transom" work as it was once referred to) still applies. Nor will it do investigative work for persons accused of crime; it does, however, do occasional investigations on instructions from district attorneys. Both in Canada and in the United States it does a considerable number of "due diligence" investigations for lawyers and others involved in large commercial transactions. Factory owners engage Pinkerton's to supply undercover men when inventory thefts are suspected, and companies will hire a Pinkerton undercover agent if a key employee is suspected of using illegal drugs or is abusing alcohol. If a male nurse, for example, is suspected of theft of drugs from a hospital pharmacy, Pinkerton's will hire a male nurse and have him taken on as an employee to keep the suspect under surveillance. At any one time, Pinkerton's will have several hundred "secrets" in the field, all of whom are paid a per diem, as was the case with their earlier counterparts. Approximately five percent of the total revenues of Pinkerton's comes from investigations. Based on the total 1997 revenues of just over $1 billion, that would amount to $50 million. This scale of revenue makes Pinkerton's one of the leaders of the security industry, but it faces competition from an estimated ten thousand other firms in the United States which provide protection of one kind or another. The vast majority of these firms are small scale, and Pinkerton's chief competition comes from firms of similar size, principally Burns International Security Systems Inc., and Wells Fargo Guard Services. It is interesting to note that both these firms, like Pinkerton's, reach back into American history.[5] It is calculated that the security industry in the United States is worth $12 billion annually.

In Canada, Pinkerton's is by far the best known and largest firm in the security guard field. Its first major work in this country — "high profile" we would now say — was to provide security for the great horse race between the American-owned "Man-of-War" and the Canadian "Sir Barton" run at the Kenilworth Race Track in Windsor on October 12, 1920. The race was staged by the flamboyant Toronto race track operator and gambler, A.M. Orpen, who hired Pinkerton's firstly to maintain order among the very large crowd expected and, secondly, to prevent patrons from taking photographs, since he had sold the exclusive photographic rights. The one-on-one race was widely publicized and some thirty thousand excited spectators watched Man-of-War win easily, earning his owner $75,000 — a huge purse for those days — as well as a gold cup worth at least $5,000, and gaining acclaim as the "Greatest Race Horse on the Continent." But there was some unpleasantness which drew the attention of the Ontario attorney general. A spectator complained of outrageous behaviour by a Pinkerton man who had forcibly taken his camera and destroyed the film after he had, admittedly, photographed the race. The deputy attorney general indignantly wrote Orpen about the alleged assault and Orpen, in turn, sent the letter to Pinkerton's, whose Chicago superintendent replied (operatives had been supplied both from that office and Toronto). In protesting that Pinkerton's would never tolerate violence by its operatives, he pointed out that Orpen had himself hired a number of men to circulate to prevent on-track betting, since Orpen didn't want any informal wagering to cut into his official bets, and that probably one of these men had been responsible for the episode, if it occurred. The deputy attorney general, angrily rejecting any such explanation, threatened to prosecute Orpen, but nothing came of it. Still, it was not an altogether happy introduction for Pinkerton's security work in Canada.[6]

The Canadian headquarters, which supervise the employment of some four thousand to six thousand personnel across the country (the figure fluctuates depending on what special events are occurring), are still in Montreal. The Montreal office also acts as the research and resource base for the other Canadian offices. At one time, Pinkerton's was hired by the RCMP to do guard duty at embassies in Ottawa, and one of their men was killed during the invasion of the Turkish Embassy by a group of Armenian terrorists. (The RCMP now supply their own people as guards — not, however, because of that incident.) More recently Pinkerton's supplied security services to the Royal Oak gold mine at Yellowknife, Northwest Territories, which was the scene of the most violent strike in Canadian labour history in 1991. Nine men were killed by an underground explosion deliberately set; a mine employee was convicted of their murder. The mine was kept operating by "replacement workers" as management referred to them, or "scabs" as the union described them. Pinkerton's had nothing to do with them, their role being purely protective. (As of March 1993, however, another firm replaced Pinkerton's at the mine site.)

Pinkerton's is very conscious of the difficulties in providing security services to a job-site where relations between employees and management become easily inflamed, as was the case, for example, with the 1991 postal strike in Canada in which Pinkerton's was heavily involved. The agency has imposed very strict guidelines for its personnel involved in labour disputes, guidelines which are intended to ensure neutrality and even-handedness. As a matter of policy, Pinkerton's people (although hired by management) will meet with both union and management representatives as well as with local police in an attempt to defuse any explosive situations by telling them precisely what the agency will be doing and how it will do it. The fact that many of the Pinkerton's employees are themselves unionized makes it easier to convince a striking union that the agency really is neutral and is simply doing its legitimate work as an organization licenced for that purpose. Gone are the days when Pinkerton's itself supplied a work force. Pinkerton's still does work for governments in Canada, but security only, not investigations. The federal government through the Department of Supply and Services puts out to tender contracts with private agencies for the provision of security for government buildings, particularly sensitive ones like National Revenue or Department of National Defence, and Pinkerton's (as this is written) gets the lion's share of that business. In Quebec, Pinkerton's has long provided security for the major hospitals and colleges; a notable example was the prolonged strike at the Veterans' Hospital at Ste. Anne-de-Bellevue, for which Pinkerton's was called in.[7] As of this writing, Pinkerton's, Inc. has more than 250 offices in twenty-three countries, employing some 47,000 persons. It will take on work in countries in which it does not have a physical presence. It is a commentary on the times that the services of bodyguards and protection personnel are so much in demand. This type of market could never have been envisaged by Allan Pinkerton, though he was known to lament that had he had anything to do with Lincoln's subsequent "protection," John Wilkes Booth would never have shot him.

Eco-terrorism, political terrorism, plant vandalism, personal security for vulnerable émigrés or refugees from regimes determined to annihilate opponents: there seems no end to the categories of violence from which persons at risk seek protection by private agencies, conditions which would seem to ensure that Pinkerton's will continue to be called in.

Bibliography

Public Documents and Records

Attorney General's Papers, British Columbia Archives and Record Service ("BCARS") *seriatim*

British Columbia Police Papers, BCARS *seriatim*

Canada Sessional Papers 1898 *et seq.*

Debates, House of Commons 1898 *et seq.*

McBride Papers, BCARS *seriatim*

Macdonald Papers NAC *seriatim*

Premier's Papers, BCARS *seriatim*

Royal Canadian Mounted Police (Dominion Police) Papers, National Archives of Canada *seriatim*

Statutes of Canada *seriatim*

Unpublished Sources

Bapty, Walter, M.D.; unpublished memoirs 1959, manuscript in possession of daughter, Laura E. Williams

Dye, James E., scrapbook in possession of Kenneth Dye

Huntington Library, San Marino, California, manuscript collections L.N. 486 and 487, BR. Box 189(53)

Paul, P. Gale: The S.S. *Iroquois* Tragedy 1911 unpublished thesis, Department of History, University of Victoria, February 22, 1988

Pinkerton Archive, Encino, California

Pinkerton Archive, Montreal, Quebec

Pinkerton's, Inc. Annual Reports, Pinkerton Archives, Encino, California

Smith, B.R.D., "Sir Richard McBride" unpublished Master's Degree Thesis, Queen's University, 1959; Add. MSS 2217 BCARS.

United States Senate Proceedings Before Sub-Committee of the Committee on Education and Labour, Washington, D.C. September 25, 1936 (copy held at Pinkerton Archive, Montreal)

Newspapers and Periodicals

The Advocate

The Detective, The Detective Publishing Co., Chicago, Illinois

Detroit Free Press
Fernie Free Press
Hamilton Spectator
Nanaimo Free Press
Nelson Tribune
New Westminster Daily Columbian
Omineca Herald
Ottawa Citizen
Ottawa Journal
Portland Oregonian
Revelstoke Mail-Herald
Rossland Industrial World
Rossland Miner
Rossland Record
Seattle Evening Times
Thorold Post
Toronto Daily Leader
Toronto Globe
Toronto Telegraph
Vancouver News-Advertiser
Vernon News
Victoria Daily Times
Windsor Evening Record
Yukon Sun (Dawson)

Published Works and Articles

Anderson, Frank W. *Bill Miner: Stage Coach and Train Robber*. Surrey, B.C.: Heritage House Publishing Co. Ltd., 1982.

Bernstorff, Count. *My Three Years in America*. New York: Charles Scribner's Sons, 1920.

Betke, Carl, and S.W. Horrall. *Canada's Security Service: An Historical Outline 1864-1966*. Ottawa: RCMP Historical Section, 1978.

Bowen, Lynne. *Boss Whistle: The Coal Miners of Vancouver Island Remember*. Lantzville, B.C.: Oolichan Books, 1982.

Canadian Almanac. Toronto: Copp Clark Company Limited.

The Canadian Encyclopedia. 2nd edition. Edmonton: Hurtig Publishers Ltd., 1988.

Cole, J.A. *Prince of Spies: Henri Le Caron*. London: Faber and Faber Limited, 1984.

Dafoe, John W. *Clifford Sifton in Relation to His Times*. Toronto: Macmillan, 1931.

Dictionary of Canadian Biography. Toronto: University of Toronto Press, 1966 et seq.

Dugan, Mark, and John Boessenecker. *The Grey Fox: The True Story of Bill Miner, Last of the Old-Time Bandits*. Norman: University of Oklahoma Press, 1992.

The Encyclopaedia Britannica. 11th edition. Cambridge: 1911.

Friedman, Morris. *The Pinkerton Labour Spy*. New York: Wilshire Book Co., 1907.

Hadley, Michael L., and Roger Sarty. *Tin-Pots & Pirate Ships: Canadian Naval Forces & German Sea Raiders 1880-1918*. Montreal: McGill-Queen's University Press, 1991.

Hall, D.J. *Clifford Sifton*. Vancouver: University of British Columbia Press, 1981.

Howay, F.W., and E.O.S. Scholefield. *British Columbia from the Earliest Times to the Present*. Vancouver: S.J. Clarke Publishing Co., 1914.

Kakalick, James S., and Sorrell Wildhorn. *The Private Police Industry: Its Nature and Extent*. Rand Corporation, 1970.

Kelly, William, and Nora Kelly. *Policing in Canada*. Toronto: Macmillan, 1976.

Kitchen, Martin. *The German Invasion of Canada*. The International History Review, vol. VII, 2, May 1985.

McGrath, William T., and Mitchell, Michael P. ed., *The Police Function in Canada*. Toronto: Methuen, 1981.

McLaren, John P.S. *Recalculating the Wages of Sin: The Social and Legal Construction of Prostitution in Canada 1850-1920*. University of Manitoba Canadian Legal History Project.

Marquis, Greg, *Policing Canada's Century: A History of the Canadian Association of Chiefs of Police*. Toronto: The Osgoode Society, 1993.

Morn, Frank. *The Eye that Never Sleeps: A History of the Pinkerton National Detective Agency*. Indiana University Press, Bloomington, 1992.

Mount, Graeme. *Canada's Enemies: Spies and Spying in the Peaceable Kingdom*. Dundurn Press, Toronto, 1993.

Murray, Peter. *The Vagabond Fleet*. Sono Nis Press, Victoria, 1988.

Norris, John Mackenzie. *The Vancouver Island Coal Strike 1912–1914*. Paper delivered at B.C. Studies Conference, University of Victoria, October 1979.

Oliver, Peter. *Public & Private Persons: The Ontario Political Culture 1914-34*. Toronto: Clarke, Irwin & Company Limited, 1975.

Ormsby, Margaret. *British Columbia: A History*. Toronto: Macmillan, 1958.

Pinkerton, Allan. *General Principles of Pinkerton's National Police Agency*. Chicago: G.H. Fergus.

————————————-, *Thirty Years a Detective*. New York: G.W. Carleton & Co., 1884.

Robin, Martin. *The Bad and the Lonely*. Toronto: James Lorimer and Company, 1976.

Rowan, Richard Wilmer. *The Pinkerton's — A Detective Dynasty*. Boston: Little, Brown & Company, 1931.

Siringo, Charles A. *Pinkertonism and Anarchism: Two Evil Isms*. Austin, Texas: Steck-Vaughan Company,1967

Stonier-Newman, Lynne. *Policing a Pioneer Province: The B.C. Provincial Police, 1858-1950*. Madeira Park, B.C.: Harbour Publishing, 1991

Strothers, French. *Fighting Germany's Spies*. Toronto: McClelland, Goodchild & Stewart, 1919.

Talbot, C.K. *Canada's Constables: The Historical Development of Policing in Canada*. Ottawa: Crimcare Inc., 1985.

Varkaris, Jane, and Lucile Finsten. *Fire on Parliament Hill*. Erin, Ontario: The Boston Mills Press, 1988.

Voss, Frederick, and James Barber. *We Never Sleep: The First 50 Years of the Pinkerton's*. Washington, D.C.: Smithsonian Institution Press, 1981.

Williams, David Ricardo. "Judges at War." *The Law Society of Upper Canada Gazette*, September-December, 1982.
——————————————*Just Lawyers: Seven Portraits*. Toronto: University of Toronto Press/Osgoode Society, 1995.

———————————— *With Malice Aforethought: Six Spectacular Canadian Trials*. Victoria: Sono Nis Press,1993.

Wormser, Richard. *Pinkerton, America's First Private Eye*. New York: Walker Publishing Co. Inc.,1990.

Notes

PREFACE

[1] Webster's Third New International Dictionary, 1986.

[2] Although today it is commonly believed that the term "private eye" is short for "private investigator," this is not the case. In fact, the term "private eye" first appeared in the English language in ———, while the term "private investigator" was not used until 196— [*Webster's Ninth Edition Collegiate Dictionary*]. The term "private detective," which Webster's lists as synonymous with "private eye," first appeared in a Trollope novel in 1868 [*Barnhart Dictionary of Etymology*, 1988]. The notion of the "private eye" was popularized by author Dashiell Hammett, who was himself a former Pinkerton's operative.

CHAPTER 1

[1] Most of the historical material in this and the succeeding chapter has been drawn from the various historians of the agency noted in the Bibliography. But there are specific additional references which follow.

[2] Pinkerton's established an office in Toronto in 1910 and at various times had offices in Ottawa and Winnipeg, though not always continuously. Criminal Information Bulletins 2-43 PNDA Toronto Office, Pinkerton Archive, Montreal.

[3] See, for example, Horan, p. 25.

[4] It is a curious fact that the origins of the famous detective agency which dealt with crime in an exact manner should be the subject of uncertainty.

[5] Letter Allan Pinkerton to W.H. Lamon, November 24, 1867, Huntington Library, Manuscript Collection LN487; Operatives Reports, March 30, 1887, Huntington Library, Manuscript Collection BR box 189 (53), San Marino, California.

[6] Letter Allan Pinkerton to Ward Lamon, October 31, 1867, Huntington Library, Manuscript Collection Item LN486, San Marino, California. There are two other aspects of this fascinating letter worth noting. Pinkerton wrote on the letterhead of "Pinkerton's National Police Agency." Premier Richard McBride of British Columbia in 1907 became interested in the affair for he asked Pinkerton's to send him the details of it, which they did. The Premier had great confidence in Pinkerton's; his provincial police force frequently consulted the agency, as he himself had personally done, and was to do again in the future. GR 441 vol. 402 p. 232 BCARS, Premier to Ahern, May 20, 1907.

[7] See footnote 5, *supra*.

[8] For Pinkerton's exploits with the Reno gang, and his role in their extradition from Canada to the United States, see chapter 3.

[9] For a discussion of the rather shadowy role of Pinkerton's spying for Canadian authorities on Fenian leaders in the United States, see chapter 3.

[10] There is a fascinating aftermath to the Molly Maguire episode. Many years later, William Pinkerton and Sir Arthur Conan Doyle were fellow passengers on a

trans-Atlantic voyage and struck up a shipboard acquaintance. Pinkerton told the novelist about the Molly Maguires. Conan Doyle was so struck by the story that he made it the basis of one of his Sherlock Holmes novels *The Valley of Fear*. In the novel, Holmes solves the mystery of an attempted murder, the background of which clearly is the Molly Maguires affair (though that name is not given). However, the novel is remarkably faithful to the actual events, though names have been altered — but not that of Pinkerton. There is one significant difference between fact and fiction: no one attempted to assassinate James McParland in real life, but in the novel John McMurdo [James McParland] who survived the murder attempt later falls from a ship and is drowned; Holmes does not doubt he was pushed overboard by an assassin. Oddly, Pinkerton was annoyed with Doyle who, he felt, had presumed to turn to advantage private conversations without Pinkerton's consent, conduct unbecoming a gentleman.

[11] Annual report of Pinkerton's, Inc., filed with the Security and Exchange Commission, December 28, 1990, and Thomas Wathen in conversation with the author, November 3, 1989.

[12] Worth in 1886 disembarked at Montreal in possession of jewellery, cash, and securities stolen in Belgium. Acting on a tip, Montreal police apprehended him but he talked his way out of his plight and escaped to the United States with most of the loot. For a slightly different version of the return of the Duchess, see Box 25, Pinkerton Archives; it suggests Worth may have received some money as well as immunity.

CHAPTER 2

[1] Pinkerton, *Thirty Years a Detective*.
[2] Pinkerton, General Principles (1867). The essence of these was incorporated into printed instructions found in the Pinkerton Archives.
[3] Talbot, *Canada's Constables* (q.v.).
[4] Morn, pp. 54-55; *The Detective*, June 1915 issue.
[5] Friedman, Morris, *The Pinkerton Labour Spy* (q.v.).
[6] *Ibid.*
[7] *Thirty Years a Detective, supra.*
[8] See note 2.
[9] PNDA Detective Book No. 1, Toronto, and general order book, at Pinkerton Archives, Montreal; and Harold Pountney in conversation with the author, May 1993.
[10] GR429, box 17, Files 1 & 2, BCARS, Re: Dennis Golden, containing the correspondence and reports relating to this investigation. One of the expenses allowed the operative was the purchase of a bottle of liquor to be taken into camp for the logging crew he worked with.
[11] See note 2, *supra.*
[12] Siringo, *The Two Evil Isms*.
[13] Pinkerton Archives, Van Nuys, California. In a recently published book (1992 Dugan & Boessenecker, q.v.) about Bill Miner, the authors cite a reward poster circulated by Pinkerton's which goes beyond physical description to the psychological: "Is said to be a sodomist and may have a boy with him." Circulation of the poster was authorized by James Nevins, who was the superintendent of the Pinkerton office in Portland and who, during his tenure, had many dealings with the British Columbia Provincial Police Force. As will be described in a later chapter, the B.C. government engaged Pinkerton's to

recapture Miner, but the agency was unsuccessful. After escaping from a prison in Georgia, where he had been incarcerated, following yet another train robbery, Miner died of fever. There is, however, one inaccuracy in Pinkerton's dossier; Miner definitely was not a "Canadian."

[14] Talbot, Canada's Constables.

[15] British Columbia Police correspondence, BCARS, GR55, box 69, file PAR-PK.

[16] Porteous predicted Bertillonage would always be used. Bertillon himself died in 1914 and so did not live to see the almost universal use of fingerprints in preference to his own system. The date of first use in the United States, 1889, is that given by Porteous; others, including W.A. Pinkerton, have put the date earlier. The Detective, January 1911 and March 1914.

[17] Identification of Criminals Act, Statutes of Canada 1898 cap. 54. As of 1998 the legislation is still in the statute books. It may well be that the last occasion in Canada on which Bertillonage measurements were used was in 1906, when on their basis the British Columbia Provincial Police made positive identification of Bill Miner and his fellow thugs. B.C. Police correspondence, BCARS, GR55, Box 78, File WEA-WIL. Legally, there is nothing to prevent (apart perhaps from policy directives) an arresting officer from telling an accused suspect, "I wish to measure your cranium" or "Let me see your left foot."

[18] As to the historical background of fingerprint evidence, see The Detective, July 1916, reproducing a speech by William Pinkerton; the same magazine in its May 1922 issue noted the decision of the federal court. As to Foster's testimony, see Marquis, Policing Canada's Century, the Osgoode Society Toronto, 1993. Foster had learned his craft in 1904 from a Scotland Yard detective. A year later Foster was sent by Sherwood to the New York State Prison at Albany to study Bertillonage, a course of study which only reinforced the belief of both men in the superiority of fingerprint identification. Dominion Police Papers RG18E, vol. 3117 reel 013865, Sherwood to Collins September 13, 1905 (Item 133) N.A.C.

[19] As to Herchmer's influence, see Talbot. As to the Bureau of Identification, see the proceedings of the Chief Constables' Association of Canada held at Brantford, Ontario in 1912, as reported in The Detective, August 1912.

[20] Order-in-Council July 21, 1908. See Can. Stat. clxi (Orders-in-Council 50 Can. Gazette 3484). In 1995, Parliament authorized police to take DNA samples for testing from persons suspected of murder and other serious crimes when first authorized by a warrant issued by a High Court judge.

[21] The Detective, July 1918, July 1921.

CHAPTER 3

[1] Betke and Horrall, pp. 40 et seq. The authors state that McMicken consulted the "North American Detective Policy Agency" in New York but they must have meant the "National Police Agency" — the Pinkerton firm — since there was no other agency at the time bearing any resemblance to the name. For a good summary of McMicken's career, see the article by Carl Betke in Dictionary of Canadian Biography, Vol. 12, p. 675.

[2] There ensued a number of treason trials of captured Fenians, at least 18 of whom were convicted and sentenced to hang; virtually all of these bore Irish names: Quinn, O'Connor, Gallagher, etc. They had two principal defences, first, the lack of positive identification and the second, far more ingenious, that they were not levying war against the Queen, against whom they held no animosity, but they just did not like the people who were shooting at them, and fired back: The

Toronto Globe in its editions of January 12, 1867 *et seq.*, has full accounts of the court proceedings. No Fenian was hanged: all death sentences were commuted.

3 Macdonald Papers, Vol. 241, pp. 107639–107640, McMicken to Macdonald, December 15, 1868; Fallis to McMicken, December 19, 1868, Vol. 241, pp. 107641–107644.

4 Copies of official documents relating to the negotiations for and authorization of the extradition, and of correspondence are found in the Pinkerton Archive Binder 104. The request for assurances has an interesting parallel in Canada today, which has abolished the death penalty. Some states in the United States have restored it. In recent years two men have been extradited on murder charges to states having the death penalty, notwithstanding strenuous representations that Canada should not allow extradition if there is a possibility of execution; in at least one other instance, Canada sought for, and was given, such assurances; the issue remains controversial.

5 Accounts of the various stages of the extradition and court hearings, details of which follow, are found in the *Toronto Daily Leader* from August 15, 1868 to December 29, 1868. Horan, in his history of the Pinkerton agency, also refers to them but his account does not always accord with the contemporary newspaper accounts.

6 *Toronto Telegraph*, October 2, 1868.

7 Pinkerton Archives Binder 104.

8 *Toronto Daily Leader*, December 18, 1868.

9 *Toronto Telegraph*, October 16, 1868.

10 *Toronto Telegraph*, October 16 and 19, 1868.

11 *Toronto Daily Leader*, October 19, 1868.

12 Pinkerton archive, Encino, California, Binder 104.

13 *Toronto Daily Leader*, October 29, 1868; *Toronto Telegraph*, October 27, 1868.

14 *Toronto Daily Leader*, October 29, 1868.

15 Details of the lynchings and eyewitness accounts are found in the *Toronto Daily Leader* in its issues of December 18 and 28, 1868.

16 Thornton's letter dated December 21, 1868 acknowledged notice of the intended passage of the bill and is found in Pinkerton archive binder 104. The bill was Senate Bill 705 — 40th Congress, 3rd Session. Horan in his book also deals with the affair.

17 Macdonald papers, pp. 100774, 107653–107671.

18 Macdonald papers, pp. 100774; 107653–107671; 108096–108101.

19 The materials for this episode are found in Pinkerton Archive Binder 151.

20 Macdonald Papers, Reel 1668, McMicken to Campbell, May 28, 1867, page 105567.

21 *Thorold Post*, April 27, 1900–June 1, 1900.

22 Royal Canadian Mounted Police, (Dominion Police) Papers NAC RG18E, vol. 3105, reel CA13857, Sherwood to Pinkerton and vice versa, April 30, 1900–July 1900; Sherwood to Warden, July 4, 1900. Mount in his book says Dullman was an Irishman, Luke Dillon (p. 22).

23 The materials relating to this strange affair are in GR429, box 5, files 3, 4, and 5 BCARS; see also Mount pp. 14 *et seq.*

CHAPTER 4

1 The material containing nominal rolls of the force, its composition, and its work, is found in government record groups 55, 56, and 91 at BCARS from which the following discussion is mainly drawn.

2 GR55, Box 22, File A. Martin to Hussey, September 14, 1898. The attorney general

was the combative Joseph Martin Q.C. — "Fighting Joe." Some years later he gained distinction of another sort when defending a man accused of keeping a bawdy house. The man had kept records of his customers, which included a lot of prominent Vancouverites; the magistrate agreed with Martin that the affair should be hushed up for that reason, and dismissed the charge. *The Advocate*, vol. 45, p. V., September 1987, p. 677.

[3] GR429, box 13, file 1, Item 264/06 BCARS.

[4] GR 429, box 5, file 4, BCARS.

[5] Both the Grand Forks robbery and the arson case are found in GR 55, box 36, BCARS.

[6] GR55, box 37.

[7] GR56, vol. 4, Pinkerton's Agency File, Pinkerton-B.C. Police, July 26, 1911.

[8] They were, in addition to the *Industrial World*, the *Rossland Record*, and the *Rossland Miner*. Copies of these, which contain much of the material used in the preparation of this chapter, can be found at BCARS dating from May 1900 onward until October.

[9] What follows is drawn mainly from the official record of the inquest found in GR419, Vol. 83, File 1900/98 at BCARS.

[10] Details of the interrogations by Ahern are found in an account of the subsequent preliminary hearing by the *Rossland Miner* in its issue of July 25, 1900.

[11] The confession is found in GR419, Box 83, Item 1900/98 — transcript of the preliminary hearing.

[12] An account of the trial can be found in the *Nelson Tribune* in its issues of October 16 and October 24, 1900, and in the author's work, *With Malice Aforethought*.

[13] Dominion Police Papers, RG18E, Vol. 3118, Item 970; Vol. 3119, Items 83 and 85 N.A.C.

[14] The early activities of the Mafia and Pinkerton's involvement in combating them are discussed by Horan in his work. There are also documents relating to it in the Pinkerton Archive Binder 45.

[15] Details are found in the *Fernie Free Press* newspaper from July 3, 1908 et seq.

[16] GR429, Box 15, Files 4 and 5, BCARS.

[17] GR429, Box 16, File 4, BCARS.

[18] For the details of this case, see the *Revelstoke Mail-Herald*, June 19, 1909, et seq; for official correspondence relating to the case, see GR419, Box 139 and GR429, Box 17, BCARS.

[19] *Revelstoke Mail-Herald*, September 24, 1910, et seq.

[20] GR56, vol. 14, BCARS.

[21] GR56, vol. 3, BCARS.

[22] GR55, boxes 41 and 69, BCARS.

CHAPTER 5

[1] The materials for this episode are drawn from GR56, vol. 3, file 3 "1911 Pinkerton Reports," BCARS.

[2] The materials relating to the Bradshaw arson are in GR56, vol. 4, BCARS.

[3] GR429, box 13; GR55, box 67.

[4] The clerk pleaded guilty and was sentenced to 18 months. GR55, box 7 and 8; GR419, box 60.

[5] Most of the material relating to this affair is found in GR55, 56, and 429 *seriatim* BCARS.

[6] For the Pinkerton involvement see GR 56, vol. 3 and GR 56, vols. 18, 19, and 27.

Generally, see the *Victoria Daily Times*, April 20, 1911 et seq.; the *Times-Colonist*, March 31, 1991 and an unpublished thesis by P. Gale Paul for the Department of History, University of Victoria, February 22, 1988. The Admiralty Court report is in the Archer Martin papers G-81-50, vol. 187, BCARS.

[7] The materials relating to this affair are found in GR429, box 15, files 3, 4, and 5 BCARS.

[8] GR 429, box 16, file 1, Bowser to Minister of Justice, November 13, 1908.

[9] For a full discussion of this fascinating affair, see the author's article in *The Gazette*, Law Society of Upper Canada, "Judges at War" September-December issue, 1982.

[10] Minutes of the Judicial Committee of the Privy Council, Downing Street, London, July 27, 1908. The case was among the last attempts by Canadians to appeal to the Privy Council in criminal cases.

[11] All the material relating to the bootlegging investigation, including the Pinkerton reports, are found in GR429, box 15, file 5, BCARS.

[12] The materials relating to the Spinks theft are found in GR55, box 68, file PR-PK and box 73, file SP-SZ.

[13] *Vernon News*, November 12, 1908.

CHAPTER 6

[1] A great deal has been written about Miner and a film, *The Grey Fox*, was a popular success. It is impossible to refer to all the source material about Miner but some specific references will be found in the text. Among the principal sources are the first complete account of his life and career, *The Grey Fox* by Mark Dugan and John Boessenecker; the Pinkerton Archives Binder 130; government record groups 55, 56 and 429 BCARS; the Dominion Police papers RG 18E, vols. 3115 et seq., N.A.C.; the book by Frank W. Anderson *Bill Miner, Train Robber*; the book by Martin Robin, *The Bad and the Lonely*; and James E. Dye's scrapbook.

[2] Vancouver interview with Bill Abbott, *Vancouver Sun*, November 27, 1940; Sherwood to Chamberlin, January 31, 1905, DPP, vol. 3115.

[3] DPP vol. 3115 Sherwood to Chamberlin, February 9, 1905; Sherwood to Burns, May 22, 1905.

[4] DPP vol. 3115, Sherwood to Burns, July 15, 1905. Notice the easy tone of familiarity in which Sherwood refers to Pinkerton; the two were obviously good friends.

[5] Statement of "Edwards" GR55, box 45, file CAN-CK.

[6] See the Edwards' statement *supra*.

[7] Sherwood to Dawson, September 3, 1907 DPP vol. 3120.

[8] GR55, box 45.

[9] DPP vol. 3121 Sherwood to McLeod, December 7, 1907; January 3, 1908.

[10] GR 429, boxes 17, 18, and 69 BCARS.

[11] Interview with Bill Abbott, *Vancouver Sun*, November 27, 1940.

[12] Pinkerton Archives Binder 130.

[13] Hansard, House of Commons Debates, May 18, 1909.

[14] Hansard, House of Commons Debates, February 11, 1909 et seq.

[15] GR 56, vol. 3.

[16] Pinkerton Archives Binder 130.

[17] GR 56, vol. 4, Campbell to Ahern, July 10, 1912.

[18] The account in this chapter is based substantially on the copious Pinkerton reports running from May 1909 until February 1910 found in government record groups BCARS GR55, 56, 429 as well as in the British Columbia Police letterbook correspondence outward for the period. See also the author's biography of

Gunanoot, *Trapline Outlaw*, where in the bibliography can be found the principal secondary source material.

[19] Pinkerton report, July 24, 1909.

[20] For a full discussion of this issue see the author's biography of Gunanoot.

[21] B.C. Police letterbook outward 1897–1918 — Hussey to Ahern, September 24, 1909.

[22] The first message was in their report of January 11, 1910; the second January 15, 1910.

CHAPTER 7

[1] Quoted in Talbot.

[2] The activities of the Dominion Police force, Sherwood's role and Pinkerton's, are chiefly found in Royal Canadian Mounted Police (Dominion Police) papers RG18E, vols. 3091 *et seq.*, *seriatim* NAC.

[3] Sherwood to W.A. Pinkerton, August 15, 1896, vol. 3100.

[4] Sherwood to Robert Pinkerton, July 3, 9, 1901, vol. 3018.

[5] Sherwood to Ahern, March 9, 1903; Sherwood-PMG, March 11, 1903, vol. 3111.

[6] Sherwood to Pinkerton, March 3, 1888 *et seq.*, vol. 3092.

[7] Sherwood to Pinkerton, April 2, 1893, vol. 3095.

[8] Sherwood to Pinkerton, May 18, 1894, vol. 3124.

[9] Sherwood to Robert Pinkerton, December 15, 1897, vol. 3102.

[10] The Americans were to use the same argument 30 years later in the *I'm Alone* arbitration arising from the sinking by the American Coast Guard of a rum-runner flying the Canadian flag but in fact owned by Americans. See the author's work *Duff: A Life in the Law* for a full treatment of the subject. The account of the proceedings in this chapter is based on the standard work by Howay and Scholefield, *British Columbia from the Earliest Times to the Present*, The S.J. Clarke Publishing Company, Vancouver, 1914; *The Vagabond Fleet* by Peter Murray, Sono Nis Press, Victoria, 1988; and the Dominion Police Papers, NAC.

[11] Sherwood-Pinkerton, *seriatim*, April 9, 1897 *et seq.*; Sherwood-Peters, *seriatim*, April 14, 1897 *et seq.*, DPP Vol. 3101.

[12] Yukon Sun, Dawson, March 29, 1902.

[13] Sherwood-White, May 30, 1902, RG18, Vol. 229, File 149, NAC. The subsequent references to this source will simply be stated as "RG18".

[14] Snyder-White, December 7, 1901, RG18.

[15] Starnes' letters are September 20, 1901 and October 19, 1901, and are in RG18.

[16] Primrose-White, September 20, 1901, RG18.

[17] Snyder-White, January 6, 1902; Drake-Sherwood, May 2, 1902, RG18.

[18] White-Perry, January 29, 1902, RG18.

[19] *Canadian Almanac*, 1901–1915.

[20] Chamberlin-Sherwood, April 23, 1902, RG18.

[21] Quoted in *Ottawa Journal*, November 22, 1901.

[22] *Seattle Evening Times*, November 20, 1901.

[23] White to Laurier, November 19, 1901, December 9, 1901, RG18.

[24] Snyder to White, January 6, 1902 and White to Snyder, January 28, 1902, RG18.

[25] White to Sifton, May 22, 1902, RG18.

[26] Sherwood to White, May 12, 1902, RG18.

[27] Drake to White, May 13, 1902, RG18.

[28] White to Constantine, February 11, 1902; White to Wood, March 15, 1902, RG18, vol. 232, File 195.

[29] Constantine to White, April 4, 1902; White to Maude, (undated); Constantine to

Sayers, April 11, 1902; Sayers to Constantine, April 24, 1902, RG18.
[30] White to Sifton memo, December 9, 1901, RG18.
[31] White to Laurier, April 22, 1902; White to Constantine, April 22, 1902, RG18.
[32] White to Sherwood, March 15, 1902, RG18.
[33] Memo, Whiteto Sherwood, April 23, 1902; Chamberlin to Sherwood, April 27, 1902, RG18.
[34] Pinkerton Reports, May 2, 3, 4, 5, 6, 10, 11, 12, 1902; Constantine to White, April 17, 1902, RG18.
[35] White to Sifton, May 22, 1902, RG18.

CHAPTER 8

[1] For a particularly vitriolic attack upon Pinkerton's role in labour disputes, see the book written by a former employee of the agency, Morris Friedman.
[2] Quoted in Morn p. 103.
[3] *Victoria Times*, May 28, 1977; *Vancouver Sun*, May 31, 1977.
[4] Interviews with Lloyd Greene of Nanoose Bay, B.C. and Dr. Kenneth Williams. Greene after being fired went into commercial fishing. Williams went on to study medicine becoming a hospital administrator both in Canada and in the United States before retiring to Victoria; the delegate's remark was reported in *Vancouver Sun* on April 5, 1944.
[5] Howay and Scholefield have a full description of the growth of the Kootenay mines; they and also Margaret Ormsby in her history of British Columbia have a limited discussion of the politics involved.
[6] Nevins to Henderson, November 3, 1899, GR 429, box 5, file 3.
[7] Pinkerton report November 17, 1899, GR 429, box 5, file 3.
[8] Pinkerton report November 18, 1899, *supra.*
[9] Pinkerton report November 19, 1899, *supra.*
[10] Pinkerton report November 21, 1899.
[11] Pinkerton reports, November 24, 1899 and December 2, 1899, *supra.*
[12] Pinkerton report, November 27, 1899, *supra.*
[13] Hussey to Attorney General, January 6, 1900, *supra.*
[14] Bell-Irving to Attorney General, GR 429, box 6, file 1, item 2524/00; see also the reports by W.H. Bullock-Webster, who had been brought down to the Fraser River because of his competent and resolute behaviour in the Kootenay mine disputes, in the same file.
[15] GR 441, box 15, file 3.
[16] *Vancouver Province*, July 24, 1901.
[17] Pinkerton report, July 26, 1901, GR 429, box 7, file 3.
[18] Japanese Consulate to F.S. Hussey, September 25, October 7, 1901, GR 55, box 71, file SHA-SP.
[19] *Vancouver News Advertiser*, July 12, 1901.
[20] Hussey to Eberts, July 12, 1901, GR 429, box 8, file 1; Bowser to Eberts, October 11, 1901, GR 429, box 7, file 5; *New Westminster Daily Columbian*, July 12, 1901 *et seq.*
[21] *Hamilton Spectator*, November 5, 1906.
[22] *Hamilton Spectator*, November 6 and 7, 1906.
[23] It also did undercover work in 1911 for the B.C. Police in the serious labour disturbances in the construction camps of the Canadian Northern Railway in which the International Workers of the World — the Wobblies — were attempting to organize the workers; the Thiel Agency was also involved, perhaps

hired by the railway company. Again, it is difficult to tell from the surviving documents what exactly it was that Pinkerton's was hired to do, but their work was not extensive. An interesting side light of the affair is that one of the B.C. Police constables very much involved in the business was J.W. Burr, father of Raymond Burr, the late renowned actor and "Perry Mason." GR 56, vol. 4; GR 56, vol. 31, file 18 and GR 56, vol. 30, files 5, 6.

[24] Pinkerton's to B.C. Police, October 31, 1906, GR 55, box 67, file PF-PQ.

[25] Pinkerton Reports, March 29, April 1, 1912, GR 56, vol. 4.

[26] The operative also interviewed Tom Uphill, the Secretary of the Local Miners Union. He later became the redoubtable Socialist member of the British Columbia legislature, notable for his strong views irreverently expressed.

[27] GR 56, vol. 4.

[28] The reports, totaling 220 closely typed pages, have been collected and are found in GR 429, box 19, BCARS.

[29] See Boss Whistle by Lynne Bowen, Oolichan Books, Lantzville, 1982 at p. 157; for an account less sympathetic to the union cause — but still valuable — see the paper presented by John Mackenzie Norris to the B.C. Studies Conference at Victoria in 1979. The principal contemporary source for the events of the 1912-14 strike is the Nanaimo Free Press, from September 16, 1912 et seq; and the Pinkerton reports of August 14, 1913 until January 31, 1914.

[30] The question of cost-sharing was a lively one. Who should pay the soldiers in those circumstances, the provincial or the federal government? Presumably, the federal government paid the costs of the calling up in 1913 but fifteen years later when an identical situation arose in Cape Breton there was litigation; the Supreme Court of Canada ruled that the federal government had to pay: Re Cape Breton (1930), SCR 554.

[31] Interview, March 19, 1992.

[32] "Memoirs" by Walter Bapty, M.D. 1959, unpublished manuscript in possession of his daughter, L.E. Williams.

[33] Report August 29, 1913.

[34] Report December 19, 1913.

[35] Report September 12, 1913.

[36] Report, September 9, 1913.

[37] Reports, September 6 , 1913, January 28, 1914.

[38] Report, November 30, 1913.

[39] Reports, August 25, September 12, October 15, 1913.

[40] Reports, September 13, 1913, January 1, 1914.

[41] For the compilation of the figures, see Bowen, p. 188.

[42] Report, November 17, 1913.

[43] Report, December 12, 1913.

[44] Norris, pp. 12–13.

[45] Reports, October 27 and November 5, 1913; January 14 and 22, 1914.

[46] Report, October 24, 1913.

CHAPTER 9

[1] Sherwood to Eaton, December 13, 1907, RG 18E, vol. 312 on reel C13869, item 80.

[2] For a full account of his sentiments, see Horan, p. 495-6.

[3] Spring-Rice to Sherwood, June 7, 1915; Pinkerton to Sherwood, June 10, 1915, RG 24, vol. 3986, file 1055-3-1; Spring-Rice had not shown the same confidence in the agency as in the year previous when he passed on to the Canadian authorities

a recommendation by President Wilson's secretary that in security matters the Canadian government hire Pinkerton's: Hadley and Sarty, p. 109.

4 RG 18, B-1, file 722, Royal Canadian Mounted Police papers, NAC.

5 See Horrall and Betke, p. 348 et seq.

6 RG 24, vol. 3986, file 1055-3-4.

7 Hadley and Sarty, p. 110; the material on which this episode is based is in RG 24 vol. 3986, file 1055-3-2.

8 February 22, 1915.

9 Pinkerton to Sherwood, February 23, 1915.

10 Pinkerton Report, March 15, 1915.

11 Report, April 3, 1915.

12 Sherwood to Stephens, April 9, 1915, April 24, 1915.

13 Pinkerton Reports March 11–17, 1915, RG 24, vol. 3986, file 1055-3-3.

14 All the material about this automobile episode is found in Dominion Police papers, RG 24, vol. 3986, file 1055-7-2.

15 Stephens to Sherwood, June 8, 1915.

16 Sherwood to Stephens, June 10, 1915.

17 Pinkerton to Sherwood, June 16, 1915.

18 The material relating to this episode is in RCMP papers, RG24, vol. 3986, file 1055-7-3.

19 The proceedings at the trial are found in the *Portland Oregonian* in its issues of December 9, 1916 to January 11, 1917.

20 *Windsor Evening Record*, January 21, 1916.

21 Dimaio left an account of the circumstances of the Windsor affair and the arrests of Lefler and Respa on which the author has relied in the preparation of this section of the chapter. It is dated June 24, 1942 and is in Pinkerton Archive Binder B122. As well, the issues of the *Windsor Evening Record* from June 21, 1915 until March of 1916 have been relied upon.

22 *Evening Record*, March 7, 1916.

23 *Evening Record*, March 8, 1916.

24 Pinkerton Reports, September 5–17, 1915. Ontario Archives RG4-32, file 1915, #1194.

25 Ontario Archives RG23, appendix A, series E-66, box 1, 2, 1915-16.

26 Pinkerton Report, March 6, 1916, RG23 *ibid.*

27 *Evening Record*, March 7, 1916.

28 Pinkerton Report, October 12, 1916, Ontario Archives RG23, Appendix A, series E-66, box 1, 2, 1915–16.

29 Dimaio recollections, *ibid.*, *Detroit Free Press*, December 18, 1917, July 7, 1927.

30 They are found in the Pinkerton Arvhives at Montreal, PNDA Detective Book No. 1, Toronto, pp. 40-43; the *Toronto Globe* in its issues of Nov. 23 and 24, 1915, has brief accounts of the explosion.

31 See the book, *Fire on Parliament Hill* by Varkaris and Finsten.

32 The materials relating to this affair are in RG24, vol. 3986, file NSC 1055-3-5.

33 In a fiery speech at Toronto in November 1915 Billy Sunday gave his typical anti-liquor pitch: "If all the devils in hell wracked their brains to bring forth the deadliest foe, they could not discover a worse one than liquor." *Toronto Globe*, November 22, 1915.

34 Pinkerton Report, April 14, 1917.

35 Reports, February 8, February 25, 1917.

36 Reports, February 15, March 28, April 2, April 5 and April 13, 1917.

[37] Report, March 3, 1917.
[38] Pinkerton Report April 8, 1917.

CHAPTER 10

[1] Most of the materials relating to this episode are found in Hansard, Debates of the House of Commons, March 30, 1899 et seq.; and the Journals of the House of Commons (which are subsequently referred to simply as "the Journals") vol. XXXVIII, May 10, 1898 et seq., reprinting the proceedings of the Public Accounts Committee; vol. XXXIV, May 3, 1899 et seq. and vol. XXXIV (Appendix Vol.) for 1899, pages 26, 29; the letter from Sifton to Laurier, July 17, 1896 and the letter Laurier to Sifton, July 24, 1896 are found in the Journals for June 1, 1898, pages 104-5.

[2] Journals, June 3, 1898, pages 116, 118.

[3] Journals, 1898, pages 34, 38, 50.

[4] Journals, June 1, 1898, page 113.

[5] Journals, May 27, page 59; May 30, page 100.

[6] Journals, June 3, 1898, page 151.

[7] Sessional papers 1898, vol. 32, no. 1; Auditor-General report, June 30, 1897.

[8] Journals, vol. XXXIV, 1899, pages v.i, v.ii.

[9] Hansard, March 30, 1899, pp. 738-9 et seq.

[10] The materials for this episode come mainly from the unpublished Master's thesis by B.R.D. Smith, Queen's University, 1959, and Ormsby in her history of British Columbia.

[11] Smith to author, January 7, 1990.

[12] It is found in Attorney General's correspondence GR 429, box 18, file 1, item 2518/10, BCARS.

[13] Notes of the meeting are found in RG 10, vol. 3820, file 59335, part 3A, reel B at 316, BCARS.

[14] GR 1323 Attorney General's correspondence reel B at 2062, item 1412/09, BCARS.

[15] GR 1323, B2067, item 2599/10, Lafleur to Attorney General, June 9, 1910.

[16] GR 441, BCARS, vol. 183, file 1.

[17] It is found in BCARS, N.W.p. 970.5/A784

[18] (1991), 79 Dominion Law Reports (DLR) (4th) 185.

[19] GR 441, vol. 391, p. 325 BCARS.

[20] Reports dated March 16-20, 1911 are found in GR 56, vol. 3, file 3. "1911, Pink Reports," BCARS.

[21] The Pinkerton reports on this curious episode are found in GR56, vol. 3, file 3 "1911 Pink Reports," BCARS; the case is Leckie et al. vs. Watt et al. (1906), 12 British Columbia Reports 129..

[22] For articles about him see NWP./921/A474L for one by Ingrid Laue and ADD.MS 2555 for one by Mary Louise Stacey, both at BCARS.

[23] Kitchen, page 257.

[24] See McBride-Piper, Sept. 2, 1914, Premier's correspondence inward file, 1914-1915 BCARS, GR441, vol. 167, file 1; the GR441 series is simply referred to hereafter as Premier's papers.

[25] Premier's papers, vol. 396, page 91.

[26] Premier's papers, Ahern to McBride, Nov. 7, 1914; the Seattle Daily Star, Nov. 7, 1914.

[27] Phillipps-Wooley to McBride, Dec. 10, 1914, Premier's papers, vol. 125, file 3; McBride's letter to Technical Press and Ahern are Dec. 16, 1914 and are in McBride letterbook, 1912-1915, ADD.MSS, vol. 1, file 2, BCARS.

[28] Ahern to McBride, December 19, 1914; McBride-Ahern, December 22, Premier's papers, vol. 125, file 3.

[29] Premier's papers, vol. 125, file 3.

[30] The materials for this episode are found in RG4, C-3, 1909, #1639, 4-32, in the Ontario Archives; see also the article by McLaren, "Recalculating the Wages of Sin..."

[31] The Pinkerton reports are dated January 11–20, 1910.

[32] Report February 4, 1918; it, and other reports, together with the correspondence referred to, are found in the Ontario Archives, RG 23, E-83, 1.1 (RIOTS).

[33] Report January 26, 1918.

[34] Reports January 27, 1918, February 5, 1918.

[35] Rogers-Storie, February 12, 1918.

[36] The Pinkerton reports and a few official letters are found in the Ontario Archives, RG6-93 Box 2. For a full account of the affair see Oliver, *Public and Private Persons*; for a shorter account see *Just Lawyers* by the author, in the chapter on "W.N. Tilley."

[37] Report, April 8, 1924.

EPILOGUE

[1] As to Pinkerton's Protective Patrol, see *The Detective*, August 1910. And as to the Exposition, see the issues of March and May 1915 and January 1916.

[2] The United States Senate report of proceedings ... Res. 266, September 25, 1936, Washington, D.C. Transcript at Pinkerton Archives, Montreal.

[3] For the background of the 1988 merger and the corporate restructuring see *Fortune* magazine, July 31, 1989; the Third Quarter Report of Pinkerton's of October 1992; the Proxy Statement of Pinkerton's, Inc. of March 31, 1993 issued in respect of the corporation's annual general meeting, and *Forbes* magazine of September 17, 1990.

[4] Annual Reports, Pinkerton's, Inc., 1992 (*et. seq.*)

[5] Pinkerton Prospectus, April 30, 1991.

[6] For the correspondence, see Ontario Archives RG4-32, File 1920 #3125, interim box 18; for the newspaper coverage see the *Toronto World*, October 11, 12, 13, 1920. There is some piquancy in the situation. The attorney general, W.E. Raney, was known to be hotly opposed to race tracks and betting and would have despised Orpen and it is quite possible that the complaint was a put-up job designed to embarrass Orpen. Raney was one of the beneficiaries of Charles Millar's eccentric "Stork Derby" will, receiving as an unwelcome legacy shares in a race track, which he promptly sold, giving the proceeds to charity. Orpen was a close friend of Millar, and claimed to be aware of the provisions of the will; indeed, he may have prompted Millar to leave the shares to Raney in the hope the gift would embarrass him, which it certainly did.

[7] The discussion of Pinkerton's current activities and position is drawn from the Securities and Exchange Commission filing of December 28, 1990, the Annual Reports (*supra*) and the author's interviews with Thomas Wathen, and Harold Pountney.

Index